# PERSONALITY
# DECORATING

# PERSONALITY
# DECORATING

by Lynda Graham-Barber and
Elizabeth V. Warren

Illustrated by Ray C. Barber
Room Photography by James Levin
Montage photography by Don Banks

Fawcett Columbine ■ New York

In loving memory of Augustine.
To Irwin, for his love and support.

The authors of *Personality Decorating*, Lynda Graham-Barber and Elizabeth V. Warren, do not endorse the suitability or safety of any of the merchandise featured in this book, nor have any fees been paid to the authors by manufacturers or retailers in exchange for having their products mentioned.

A Fawcett Columbine Book
Published by Ballantine Books

Copyright © 1985 by Lynda Graham-Barber and Elizabeth V. Warren

All rights reserved under International and Pan-American Copyright Conventions. Published in the United States by Ballantine Books, a division of Random House, Inc., New York, and simultaneously in Canada by Random House of Canada Limited, Toronto.

Library of Congress Catalog Card Number: 85-90596
ISBN 0-449-90111-4

Cover design by James R. Harris
Cover photo by Don Banks
Interior design by Michaelis/Carpelis
Montage photos:
Design and art direction by James R. Harris
Photographs by Don Banks
Photo styling by Lynda Graham-Barber

Manufactured in the United States of America
First Edition: January 1986

10 9 8 7 6 5 4 3 2 1

## Acknowledgments

The authors wish to extend their warmest thanks to the following people, whose contributions are immeasurable:

To Ray, for his graphics sublime and the thread of sanity he weaves so lovingly;

To Irwin, for his superlative suggestions on the manuscript;

To Mrs. Frances Vogel, the English major, who also checked the manuscript;

To Don Banks and James Harris, who, together with a stellar crew, produced inspired color photography;

To James Levin, for his splendid photographs, his abiding patience, his unfailing good humor, and his educated eye;

To Cynthia Hill and Bill Wylie for their assistance with the photography;

To Susan Collins, for her energetic and cheerful enthusiasm in helping to obtain photographs and products;

To Susan Herold, who went shopping and made telephone calls at a point where we needed help most;

To Richard Horn, for his helpful suggestions of who and where;

To the eight interior designers—James Bloor, Michael Braverman, Beverly Ellsley, Georgina Fairholme, Stanley Hura, Sybil Levin, Nicholas Pentecost, Lyn Peterson —and their talented assistants, who created the eight personality rooms;

To the homeowners who welcomed us into their homes and allowed us to photograph;

To all the designers, especially Kevin Walz and Mario Buatta, who responded to our questionnaires and granted us interviews;

To all our friends, relatives, coworkers, and neighbors who took the personality quizzes—and helped us make them work!

To Allison Kyle Leopold, who brought two collaborators together;

To Edite Kroll, our literary agent, for her steadfast support;

To Lisa Boalt of Schumacher, for her kind cooperation;

To Louise T. Brennan of American Olean Tile, who always found time to lend a hand;

To Joelle Delbourgo and Michelle Russell, our editors, for their guidance, encouraging words, and faith;

To all the homeowners we interviewed for the personality profiles;

To all the manufacturers and their public relations representatives, who helped us to obtain photographs, merchandise, and information;

To Barbara Morgan of Springs Mills and Rose Gerace of J. P. Stevens, who believed in us enough to help us decorate two of the personality rooms with sheets;

To the Wallcovering Information Bureau and especially David S. Lewandowski, vice president, Sumner Rider & Associates, Inc.;

To all the retail sources who loaned us merchandise for photography in the personality rooms (see credits);

To all our friends for their interest and unflagging support;

To Alan Wood, for his generous gift of space;

To Lynda, for making this collaboration so pleasant and successful;

To Liz, who made it all work—and became a good friend in the process.

# Contents

**Part One** Discovering Your Personal Stamp
Introduction 2
The Personality Decorating Quizzes 14

    General Quiz 16
    General Quiz Analysis 18
    Period Quiz 22
    Period Quiz Analysis 25
    Contemporary Quiz 28
    Contemporary Quiz Analysis 30

**Part Two** Personality Ingredients—Putting Them All Together
Coloring Your Personality 34
    Your Personality Color Scheme Chart 40
Lighting Up Your Personality 42
    Your Personality Lighting Chart 44
Windows—Their Many Personal Faces 46
    Your Personality Window Treatment Chart 48
Making Space Work for You 50

**Your Personality Decorating Montage and Color Chart**

**Part Three** Your Personality Profile Sourcebook
How to Shop for Your Personality Home Furnishings 58
*The Naturalist* Sourcebook 61
*The Romanticist* Sourcebook 81
*The Traditionalist* Sourcebook 101
*The Classicist* Sourcebook 121
*The Individualist* Sourcebook 141
*The Young Professional* Sourcebook 159
*The Modernist* Sourcebook 179
*The Futurist* Sourcebook 199

**Glossary of Decorating Terms** 219

**Personality Montage Product Information** 223

**Personality Room Product Information** 231

**Personality Room Interior Designers** 233

**Buyer's Guide** 234

**Index** 242

## PART ONE

# Discovering Your Personal Stamp

# Introduction

As writers in the home furnishings field, we continue to be intrigued when we encounter interiors that tell us something about who lives there. It is our firm belief that the most successfully designed living environments are those in which the owners' personalities are reflected in their decorating choices.

We also believe that this is what everyone who cares about his or her home wants—not to simply mimic the hottest look or a popular designer's style, but to express the "me" in their rooms.

Discovering your personal decorating style and then implementing it in your interiors is what this book is all about. In *Personality Decorating*, we show you how to achieve an overall decorating focus by identifying with a recognized interior style and, then, how to tailor that style to your specific personality.

To give you an example of how personal characteristics bring a room to life, consider Alexis Colby's (Joan Collins) *Dynasty* penthouse. Doesn't the glamorous, chichi decor of this home form the perfect frame for Alexis's high-powered, stainless-steel personality? Then, picture Mary Richards' (Mary Tyler Moore) studio apartment in a charming Victorian house. It is as homey, warm, and—face it, cute—as Mary Richards herself. Both Alexis and Mary fit naturally into their television settings. Their surroundings mirror their on-air personalities to the point that one certainly can't imagine them trading sets. Can you, for example, envision satin-clad Alexis struggling to open Mary's sleep sofa or, on the other hand, Mary in her tweed pantsuit sipping champagne at Alexis's ultrasleek bar?

Of course, neither Alexis nor Mary actually decorated her television "home." But it's evident that professional designers put a lot of time and effort into fashioning spaces with these characters in mind. Unfortunately, few of us can afford the luxury of hiring interior designers and psychologists to personalize our spaces for us. And even a professional designer needs a great amount of input if he or she is to capture the true "you" in your home. What we do in this book is to help you make that often formidable leap involved in taking your attitudes and interests from a vague notion or abstraction to a room full of furnishings.

*Personality Decorating* presents that elusive but critical focus, without which buying something as trivial as a candleholder can be an overwhelming task. With your decorating personality firmly in mind, you'll be able to enter any home furnishings department with assurance instead of trepidation. From the bewildering blur of wallpaper patterns to the floor full of sofa styles, you'll be able to zero in on which designs best suit you and your home. And, just as importantly, you'll save time and money by eliminating costly mistakes.

## An Idea, A Collaboration, A Book

In assembling this book, we approached the subject of personality decorating from two different angles. The original idea came to Lynda while vacationing in the Florida Keys. "I recalled how frequently friends visiting my apartment and writing studio had commented on how much the rooms reflected my interests and personality. They asked how I did it. And I began to wonder, too.

"I then began to think of the various looks my friends' homes conveyed and to what extent, if any, their spaces reflected the owners. I realized that my favorite interiors were those that had that 'something extra,' and, upon examination, that nebulous 'something' turned out to be a *personal point of view*."

With the germ of a book beginning to take shape, Lynda began to explore what part life-styles and pastimes play in decorating and, particularly, how to put them to use in interiors. After compiling a list of individuals along with their traits (i.e., a purist antique lover, a trendy art freelancer), she narrowed her choices to a representative grouping. Then, Lynda consulted an expert in the field of home furnishings: Elizabeth Warren, editor of *House Beautiful's Home Decorating*.

In her role as home furnishings writer and editor, Liz has been a guest in hundreds of homes. In the process, she has talked to owners and helped them address a wide range of decorating concerns. She also found that a commonly asked question was, "Where do I begin?"

After meeting with Lynda, Liz thought about the scores of interiors she'd been exposed to during her twelve years with home furnishings magazines, both in person and through photographs. She took note of the dominant decorating styles, sifting through the many variations, and selected those she felt to be the key ones.

Then, armed with our respective research, lists, and opinions, we met again and found that the major decorating styles Liz had come up with corresponded to the distinct personality types Lynda had singled out.

It was clear that we had a valid premise: that there is a definite correlation between interior styles and personal attributes.

After a period of further defining, during which we consulted many designers, consultants, and manufacturers in the home furnishings marketplace, the eight decorating personalities emerged.

## The Eight Personality Decorating Styles

We'd now like to introduce you to these eight personality decorating styles and give you some idea of the underlying psychological and decorating characteristics that distinguish each.

### THE NATURALIST

Over the last five years this style has really come into its own. Into this grouping fall all of today's popular country looks—including American, French, Scandinavian, and Japanese. This is a look that can be realized equally well with antiques or good reproductions, and is usually accessorized with folk arts and handmade crafts. All of the rooms pictured in magazines where quilts, decoys, and baskets are used to accent pine and maple furnishings are in the Naturalist style. At home, Naturalist decorating personalities tend to be no-fuss, easygoing people who would probably regard a new scratch on an old blanket chest as yet another badge of antiquity.

### THE ROMANTICIST

We feel there's a little of this personality in all of us. But if you're totally captivated by the rich, sensuous moods of the velvets and brocades associated with the late nineteenth century, or the lighter, wicker-airiness of ruffles and lace as typified by Laura Ashley, than you're a Romanticist with a capital *R*. Romanticists take special joy and pride in creating an evocative mood that casts its spell over all who enter. Romanticist tendencies usually extend to clothing choices as well—dressing up in lace and frills to match the setting that they've worked so hard to create.

## THE TRADITIONALIST

Think of the way your mother and grandmother decorated—they probably incorporated many elements typical of a Traditionalist decorating personality. Furniture sales prove that more people still embrace this style than any other, in almost every part of the country. To a large part, this is because it's a highly adaptable style that incorporates our warmest feelings about the past. Not bound to any one decorating period, the Traditionalist is free to draw from many different looks. This decorating style is characterized by plump upholstery, textured fabrics, and plush floorcoverings. Traditionalists, like their homes, can be either formal or informal personalities, and often blend elements of both. Generally conservative decorators, Traditionalists avoid embracing change for its own sake and are not likely to fall prey to the latest passing fancy.

## THE CLASSICIST

This is our most formal decorating personality. Classicists have an unfailing sense of purity, an attribute that frequently takes them on exhaustive searches for just the right chair to accompany an antique federal-style secretary, for example, or a fabric copied from a historic document to frame the windows in the living room. Many Classicists prefer to decorate with antiques or with fine reproductions—such as those sanctioned by Williamsburg and Winterthur Museums—in settings that re-create the past as authentically as possible. Frequently they are inspired by the architectural style or period details of their homes, as in the case of our Classicist family in the profile on page 125. However, the authenticity inherent in this decorating personality does not mean Classicists strive to create rooms that cannot be comfortably used. Classicists care more than most about details and immerse themselves in projects (home or business related) until they are rendered to perfection.

**THE INDIVIDUALIST**

Can't decide whether you like old or new interiors? Perhaps you live in an old house, but find yourself drawn to contemporary furnishings, or perhaps you like the idea of taking pieces with modern lines and upholstering them in classic fabrics. There's nothing wrong with wanting the best of both worlds; you probably do in the rest of your life as well. The trick is to make it all work, to assemble harmoniously what may seem like disparate elements. Individualists see no reason why their many interests in life should not extend into their decorating. They may enjoy browsing through antiques shows as much as visiting the studio of a contemporary artist. And, as in the case of our profiled couple on page 145, you'll most likely find objects from both displayed in their home.

**THE YOUNG PROFESSIONAL**

Perhaps you've just come out of school and are on your own for the first time. Or, for one reason or another, you're living in smaller quarters than before. You'll probably find yourself shopping for good-looking, multipurpose furnishings at reasonable prices. Young Professionals are on their way up —they're assertive, purposeful, sociable, physically active, open to new ideas, and need a living space that—even if it's only one room—is as adaptable as their attitudes and personalities. For example, Young Professionals can easily cope with an overnight guest or a last-minute dinner, with a futon that's a chair or a bed, and a desk that opens out to accommodate a buffet crowd. Given more experience and income, we feel the Young Professional may one day evolve into a Modernist.

**THE MODERNIST**

Picture, if you will, the interior of a luxurious penthouse. Chances are a Modernist decorating personality lives here. Chic. Elegant. Comfortable. All of these, and up-to-date in a way that will never go out of style. The Modernist style, besides including such classic contemporary elements as armless sofas, modular seating, neutral color schemes, and contemporary artwork, also incorporates today's popular looks, such as Art Deco and postmodern. This is our most secure, established contemporary decorating personality.

Often urban, of some means and sophistication, Modernists usually enjoy using their elegant surroundings to entertain stylishly.

## THE FUTURIST

No idea is too way out for our Futurists to at least consider. They are fun, funky, faddish, and usually young, urban, and creative. Many of today's experimental Futurists steep themselves in a range of twentieth-century styles, including fifties revival, ultramodern Italian, and high-tech. A Futurist's home is usually an ever-changing scene stimulated by street finds, visits to secondhand shops, artists' studios and commercial suppliers, or furniture and artwork of their own design. In the hands of the creative Futurist, cast-off objects are turned into unique furnishings that make a highly personal statement.

**Personality Style Decorators**

To help you visualize these eight looks, we asked eight interior designers to create, or help us find, representative rooms that illustrate the key elements of these styles. In some cases, these prototype spaces are actually in the designer's own home —Georgina Fairholme's Traditionalist living room, Michael Braverman's Futurist studio apartment, and Sybil Levin's Modernist living-dining area. These rooms best reflect the designer's own personal style. In the other five interiors, the designers helped their clients discover and evolve their own personalities —Nicholas Pentecost in the Classicist dining room, Stanley Hura's Romanticist bedroom, Lyn Peterson in the Individualist bedroom, Beverly Ellsley's Naturalist living room, and James Bloor's Young Professional studio.

We offer these eight prototype rooms, not for you to slavishly copy, but as guidelines and inspiration, as a means of helping you lay claim to an individual style. Look at the rooms as stepping stones, which will, in turn, give you the confidence to apply your own distinctive stamp in your interiors.

## The Authors' Personality Decorating Styles

We compiled this book to assist you in identifying and embellishing your personality decorating style. But perhaps, first, you would like to know a little about ours.

Several years ago, an event occurred in Lynda's life that gave her the opportunity to develop her ongoing interest in personal style into a professional career.

After eight years of working as an editor in the book publishing industry, she decided to try her hand at free-lance writing. At about the same time, she and her husband moved from a tiny apartment into a larger one and, in the process, discarded their eclectic accumulation of street finds and college holdovers. "We wanted antiques, but we simply couldn't afford them. So we bought antique reproductions in unassembled, unfinished (kit) form. Drawing on my husband's woodworking expertise, we fashioned good-looking, quality furniture at affordable prices. As a bonus, I learned a lot about what goes into a good piece of furniture.

"I queried the 'Home' section of the *New York Times* to see if they were interested in our experience with kit furniture. They were. The result was a two-page lead article for the 'Home' section, which, in turn, led to *The Kit Furniture Book*. Not only did we end up with a nicely furnished apartment, but I was launched on a new free-lance career writing about interior design."

To bolster her knowledge in the field, Lynda enrolled in courses at the New York School of Interior Design and attended numerous lectures and seminars in the decorative arts at The Cooper-Hewitt Museum and the Metropolitan Museum of Art. She wrote articles on interiors and style for magazines like *Travel & Leisure, Ms, Mademoiselle*, and *Redbook*. Her apartment and writing studio have twice appeared in the "Home" section of the *Times* and have been featured in *McCall's, Family Circle, Country Living, Newsday*, and *House Beautiful's Home Decorating*.

In terms of both personality and decorating, Lynda is primarily a Romanticist with strong streaks of both the Traditionalist and the Naturalist mixed in—a bona fide pastiche!

She loves traveling and reading about England and Scotland (which explains her preference for the furnishings and decorative styles of eighteenth-century England), and enjoys portaging a canoe or climbing a mountain to paint wildflowers just as much as getting decked out for a night at the opera or

Royal Ascot, or curling up with her three dogs at home.

Lynda's more casual side (cross-country skiing and roughing it) is manifested in her country kitchen, with its pine and maple cabinetry and rural collectibles (especially folk art rabbits), as well as in the one-room (no conveniences!) Vermont cabin, which both she and her husband built themselves, with its Shaker-style furnishings and muslin and stenciled accessories.

As a Romanticist she describes herself as "a hopeful one—they're worse off than the hopeless romantics!" (Her favorite movie is the original *Wuthering Heights*; favorite color, mauve.) These romantic tendencies unfold especially in the bedroom, with its four-poster bed, all bowed and frilled, botanical watercolors, and collections of garden-party straw hats, silver dressing-table accessories, and music boxes. Her husband? He loves it!

The period blend of eighteenth- and nineteenth-century furnishings in the living room point up the Traditionalist side. Here, the opera-loving (evening black is her *second* favorite color) sit-down dinner personality comes to life. The room is furnished with Persian rugs, a French armoire, Chippendale love seats, and Queen Anne chairs, all accented with English porcelain boxes and oil paintings—including portraits of Lynda by her husband's art students and colleagues.

"Home is very important to me. I'm a born nester. Even before we raised the walls on the cabin in Vermont I was planning what kind of curtains and accessories would work best."

A Romanticist bedroom, Traditionalist living room, Naturalist kitchen—a hodgepodge, you might be tempted to say. Yet the transition from room to room works because two basic concepts were kept in mind: consistency of tonal palette (wall paints and floorcoverings) and subtle intermingling of different styles. For example, the formality of the living room is undercut by ecru, heart-shaped pillows and long, ruffled draperies, which both soften the formality and introduce the more Romanticist style of the bedroom.

**The Coauthor's Personal Decorating Claim**

"When I think back on it," says Liz, "I guess I've always been interested (even if unconsciously) in decorating my surroundings. When I was a little girl, my mother would let me choose fabrics that she would then sew into curtains and bedspreads—I was the designer, she ran the workroom! Later, when I went to college, I made my decision about where to go partly on the basis of what dorm I liked best. (It was a hundred years old and the rooms had window seats and fireplaces.) I then, again, chose fabrics, pillows, colors, etc., my mother did the sewing, and both my parents paid a visit to do the installing. I was the only one I knew with a totally coordinated dorm room!"

It was not surprising, then, that after college, Liz found herself on staff at the *House Beautiful* family of magazines, starting as an editorial assistant and winding up as editor of *Home Decorating*. During that time she worked with some of the most talented home furnishings designers, manufacturers, and editors in the business. She even met Lynda when scouting her writing studio for the magazine! (Liz did photograph it as part of a very popular *Home Decorating* feature on how to personalize your decorating.)

"I've been exposed to practically every new decorating product and trend in the last decade. And after looking at the multitude of styles available, my own preferences became clear. Especially after researching and writing the text for *American Country*, I knew I was a country girl—a Naturalist."

Eventually Liz and her husband became so involved in pursuing country antiques that they started spending spare weekends and vacations visiting antiques shows and shops. "It's really an addictive habit!" Liz got so interested in what she saw on these excursions that she began taking as many courses on antiques and folk art as she could. Last year, her studies culminated in earning a master's degree in American Folk Art, and this, in turn, led to a new career as curator at the Museum of American Folk Art.

"We have pared down our desire for country things to a preference for only the best antique case pieces (cupboards, blanket chests, secretaries, etc.) and folk art, especially quilts. But I have decided I like them best when combined with contemporary sofas and minimal backgrounds—you can't beat the look of a boldly-colored, geometric Amish quilt against white walls. And my kitchen is basically sleek and white, with stoneware and spongeware accessories. I guess this shows that there's some Individualist in me, too."

In the bedroom, Liz, like Lynda, tends more toward the Romanticist decorating personality. As we say, there's a little bit of this personality in all of us. Liz planned their bedroom

## How to Use the Book to Discover Your Decorating Personality

around an engagement present from her parents—an antique blue-and-white, floral-patterned pitcher and bowl set. After a few false starts, she decided that this was the piece in the room she loved best, so why not let it set the mood for the space? The pitcher and bowl are combined with an antique bed of white wrought iron and brass, a marble-topped Victorian dresser, and Laura Ashley miniprints, all in a soft blue color scheme.

In fact, all the rooms in Liz's home have a lot of blue in them. "It's our favorite color, and you see it, too, in our favorite clothes—blue jeans. We're basically homey, easy-going people. When we go out, it's usually to a sporting event (we're basketball and baseball fanatics), and I think our home reflects this casual approach to life."

If you, like Lynda and Liz, are two or more different decorating personalities, why not have your living space reflect them all in special ways? You're not a one-dimensional person, so why try to be a one-dimensional decorator? And blending a little of each can tie it all together and make a distinctly personal statement as well.

### THE QUIZ

Perhaps by studying the eight sample room photographs and reading our previous description of each personality decorating style, you'll spot yourself right away. But just to be sure, we've put together a Personality Decorating Quiz, an entertaining, enlightening series of questions on a wide variety of subjects geared to ferret out your decorating personality.

By taking the quiz, you will first discover whether your tastes lean toward the contemporary or the traditional. Then, we further help you to refine your individual tastes by offering a second quiz that will indicate your *primary* decorating style.

We are not suggesting that you follow this style to the letter. But once you've identified with at least one of our eight personalities, the next step is to build on this look, applying your preferences. Anyone can copy a room detail by detail from studying a photograph; it's adjusting that picture to suit your individual interests that makes for good—and exciting—decorating.

It may turn out that you fall mainly under the Modernist decorating umbrella, with a sprinkling of Futurist answers. This means that you could build a Modernist background with major furnishings, but be more daring in a less public room. You may, for example, want to really let go in the bathroom by painting the walls an intense shade and hanging a shower curtain in an offbeat design.

Pay attention to all your answers. They'll give you the decorating clues you've been searching for. Once you're in tune with the many diverse facets of your life and feel confident enough to translate them into decorating decisions, you'll begin to feel truly "at home" in your surroundings.

## BACK TO BASICS—WITH PERSONALITY

Everyone needs help with the basics of decorating, whether or not a personal style has been determined. With this in mind, we've assembled a section dealing with many of the fundamentals of color, lighting, window treatments, and coping with space problems. These discussions are further tailored to the eight personalities in the form of charts that highlight the eight style characteristics along with personality specifics for color, lighting, and window treatments. A chapter on spatial considerations outlines tips on how to visually alter dimensions and add personality at the same time.

## THE PERSONALITY DECORATING SOURCEBOOKS

Next comes the heart of the book: the personality profile sourcebooks. For each of the eight personalities we present a room illustrated with characteristic personality furnishings; an interview with the interior designer who created the prototype room that embodies the style; a profile-interview with people whose homes and life-styles exemplify the particular decorating personality; and eight individual personality shopping directories, which feature a representative sampler of principal furnishings, lighting fixtures and accessories, and illustrations of window treatments. *All items in the directories are readily available at retail, either at furniture and department stores, through local dealer representatives, or by mail order.* We've also included the manufacturer's name, model number, materials, dimensions, and price range for every product, to help facilitate selection.

But again, don't feel restricted to any one personality directory. Feel free to browse one for your main purchases and another one or two directories for smaller items or even for other rooms, *depending on your quiz responses*.

What will really bring your decorating personality to fruition is the array of colors and patterns you choose to dress your interiors. Colors convey their own personal moods, and a subtle change in tone can go far in injecting personality in a setting. With this in mind, we have assembled personality montages, which include color palettes compatible with the eight personalities, coordinated with selected fabrics, wallcoverings, and floorcoverings—all of which are, like the furnishings in the directories, available at retail.

Choose the color or schemes you like and select fabrics for furnishings and window treatments to harmonize. Again, do not feel bound to any one personality in the color charts. Depending on your quiz answers, you may want to choose an Individualist palette for the bedroom and a complementary Traditionalist color scheme for the living room. Be adventuresome, yes, but remember to work for an overall uniformity. We don't recommend, for example, that you employ a Futurist color in the living room and a Romanticist shade in an adjacent bedroom. You'll tire of it long before your eyebrow-raising visitors!

## Our Hope — Your Goal

*Personality Decorating* is a synthesis of many of the ingredients necessary to shape your personal decorating style vocabulary. Bringing all the elements together is a process that slowly evolves, takes new directions, and matures, just as we do in our lives. But this is what makes it so challenging and rewarding.

Neither of us formed our decorating focus overnight. And we certainly cannot predict that even after you've discovered yours, you will enjoy eternal happiness or a better life. But we can say that your home, decorated to reflect what pleases and expresses *you*, will be a more enjoyable and comfortable place for you, your family, and your friends. Your guests may not even realize why they feel so at ease in your newly designed living room, but you'll know.

Standing in the center, looking around at the carefully chosen pieces, you'll smile to yourself and say, "It's ME!"

## The Personality Decorating Quizzes

**Introduction**

We've designed the three Personality Decorating Quizzes as tools to help you, by taking stock of your tastes, habits, and life-style, build a foundation for your decorating.

The quiz results will give you the overall decorating picture. The frame you place around it—by accenting with your unique touches—will give your interiors the unmistakeable sense of *you*.

We feel that the quizzes will prove especially meaningful to those of you who've not yet laid claim to a particular style of decorating, a category that includes both young people dealing with housekeeping for the first time and those now on their own who had previously left decorating decisions up to their partners. But it will also prove useful to those of you who may feel the need for a "housecleaning" of style, whether you want a slight modification of your existing look or a total overhaul. For those whose quiz responses indicate they should carry on in their already-established style, the book offers fresh ideas and new perspectives.

For reasons of simplicity and clarity, we've divided the quiz into two parts. The first—the General Quiz—will determine your general group: period or contemporary. Then, depending on your responses, take either the Period Quiz or the Contemporary Quiz, which will indicate the personality (or personalities) that best describes you.

Some of you may be saying, "I'll just skip the General Quiz and go on to the more specific one since I already know whether I favor period or contemporary furnishings." We urge you to put aside whatever preconceived decorating thoughts you may have and take the General Quiz. It just may hold a few surprises for you, and even if it merely upholds what you've known all along, you'll enjoy taking the quiz and having your style confirmed.

Our reason for asking this is not an arbitrary one. During the time we researched material for the book, we administered the quiz to a great many people. Their answers ran the gamut from predictable to unexpected; always, though, they proved illuminating. Some of these first respondents, who had always thought of themselves as firmly entrenched in either the period or contemporary camp, were amazed to find they had a fair smattering of answers in the opposite style, indicating either: that they were in a transition period in their lives, that they were in the process of changing their opinions about how their home should look, or that these feelings have always existed but had simply never been heeded.

So, just because up until now you've filled your rooms with sleek, lacquered furniture does not mean there's not a soft spot in your decorating heart for floral chintz!

The research period also taught us that quiz takers should bear in mind the following advice while answering the questions, in order to achieve the most accurate profile possible.

■ Read the questions carefully and answer thoughtfully *and* honestly. This is not an IQ test—there are no right or wrong answers. Don't reply to impress your friends. Unless you share your responses with anyone, no one but you will know. The quiz is for measuring *your* tastes, not those of your spouse or your best friend. So, consider only your own feelings when answering the questions.

■ Choose only one answer, even though it's difficult to decide. If you find you're continually torn between two answers, make note of both. This could indicate a dual decorating personality (see part 2). Whatever you do, do not make up your own answers. There's no way you can get an accurate interpretation of your results by adding outside elements that cannot be evaluated.

■ When there are two choices offered, keep in mind that you don't have to like *both* choices to choose that response letter. "Or" means just that—*either* one.

■ We've tried to take a broad range of tastes into account, but you may still find on occasion that none of the choices pinpoints your preference precisely. In this case, select the answer that most closely identifies you. For example, if your idea of a perfect pet is an English sheepdog (not a choice offered), then the answer to question seventeen on the General Quiz that includes collie and Labrador would be the one to check.

■ And remember, in addition to being revealing and instructive, the quiz was meant to be entertaining as well. So loosen up, pour a glass of your favorite brew (just for a warm-up, your *favorite* brew is: *a.* a root beer float; *b.* tea with lemon; *c.* a white wine spritzer; *d.* a frosty mug of Coors), and enjoy!

**General Quiz**

1. When a spouse or friend offers you one of the following, you choose
    *a.* a three-month health club membership
    *b.* a one-year membership in the Flower-of-the-Month Club
    *c.* a generous gift certificate at a high-style designer boutique
    *d.* a long weekend at a restored inn

2. You read or are most likely to read
    *a.* cooking, fitness, decorating books
    *b.* romance and historical novels
    *c.* spy, adventure, science fiction books
    *d.* period fiction, biographies, natural history books

3. In your opinion, the place you'd most like to see materials such as glass and metal would be
    *a.* in your living room furnishings
    *b.* on your car
    *c.* in your art collection (sculptures, collages)
    *d.* in a flashy disco

4. You would most like to celebrate a *momentous* event in your life at
    *a.* a four-star hotel or restaurant
    *b.* a place that holds special memories for you
    *c.* a lively late-night spot
    *d.* your favorite neighborhood restaurant

5. When Aunt Edith leaves you an unexpected bequest of $150,000, you
    *a.* buy a vacation condominium
    *b.* invest in tax-free bonds or blue-chip stocks
    *c.* buy a new wardrobe and do what it takes to upgrade your life-style
    *d.* sail to Europe on the QE II and take the grand tour

6. You are most likely to take an evening course in
   a. short- or long-term investments
   b. cooking, calligraphy, pottery
   c. filmmaking or photography
   d. how to identify antiques

7. Your favorite kind of party to throw is
   a. theme party (costume or specific holiday)
   b. sit-down dinner
   c. cocktail buffet
   d. brunch or outdoor barbecue

8. You would put a favorite photograph for display in a frame of
   a. Plexiglas
   b. wood
   c. chrome
   d. ornate brass or antiqued silver

9. You would most like to spend a vacation
   a. skiing in Colorado
   b. exploring the Scottish Highlands
   c. beaching it in the Caribbean
   d. antiquing through New England

10. Hollywood calls! You have an opportunity to star in the remake of one of these classics, so you pick
    a. *Some Like It Hot*
    b. *Gone With the Wind*
    c. *Star Wars*
    d. *Wuthering Heights*

11. Eyelet and chintz are fabrics you
    a. have little or no use for in your rooms
    b. like only in the bedroom
    c. can appreciate in period rooms in museums
    d. would use freely throughout your rooms

12. Your ideal home would be
    a. a penthouse with city-sweeping views
    b. a restored eighteenth-century farmhouse
    c. an architect-designed solar house
    d. a white clapboard house with lots of gingerbread

13. You would be most likely to attend a museum exhibit of
    a. twentieth-century photographs
    b. old master paintings
    c. abstract expressionist or minimalist art
    d. American folk art

14. Which of these color schemes most appeals to you for use in your interiors?
    a. bold primaries
    b. blue and white
    c. black, white, gray or all white
    d. rose and cream or green

15. You would prefer a friend bring you
    a. a potted green plant
    b. mixed wildflowers in a basket
    c. exotic tropical blooms
    d. long-stemmed roses in your favorite color

16. When it comes to accessorizing your home, you feel that
    a. less is more
    b. more is always best
    c. a few unfussy accessories are okay
    d. your favorite antiques or heirlooms are fine

17. Your idea of the perfect pet is a
    a. Siamese cat or an exotic bird
    b. dog like a collie, Labrador, or setter
    c. pooch resembling an Akita, Lhasa apso, or Samoyed
    d. mixed-breed dog or cat

18. In your *favorite* movies, the hero and heroine
    a. have a meaningful relationship with no strings
    b. are usually based on figures (real or imaginary) from the past
    c. encounter lots of adventure or intrigue, usually eclipsing personal relations
    d. pledge undying vows of love at the end

## General Quiz Analysis

The Personality Decorating Quiz was structured to analyze the decorating style to which you aspire, which may not be the one you are currently pursuing. Therefore, keep in mind that if your test results do not jibe with your current preference, it may be that your tastes are in flux, or for reasons of economics or circumstance you have not explored your bona fide decorating personality.

A friend took a quiz in a popular women's magazine a few years ago to determine which color best expressed her disposition. The profile indicated she was a "blue" person who yearned to be "purple." She admitted the results were accurate: she outfitted both herself and her rooms with blue—but she had a yen to try purple. She was attracted to the splash of energy that purple conveyed to a conservative "true blue" individual.

It's our hope that if the quiz does point you on a new course (even if an unpredicted one), you will consider dropping the fetters of "blue" and plunging into "purple," either in a trickle of accessories, or as a full-blown expression in totally new surroundings.

If you answered at least eleven of the questions with the letter *b* or *d* (combined), you are more comfortable with period styles. In this event, you should go on to take the Period Quiz to determine which of the four period personalities—Naturalist, Romanticist, Classicist, or Traditionalist—best typifies you.

If you answered *a* or *c* (combined) to a minimum of eleven questions, your basic decorating style leans more to the contemporary. You should now complete the Contemporary Quiz to see if you are a Young Professional, a Modernist, or a Futurist.

If, however, your answers are divided equally or almost equally between the *b-d* and *a-c* groups (i.e., 10–8, 9–9, 8–10) and you don't feel totally at ease with any of these seven personality styles, you fall into a decorating personality we call the Individualist.

The Individualist's decorating style might be contemporary in focus (upholstered seating in sleek, angular forms) backed with primitive country case goods, or the reverse: a period emphasis (formal mahogany furnishings) placed sparingly against white walls, track lighting, and bare floors. It is the interaction of past and present, of period and contemporary, that inspires Individualists, rather than one particular style. Individualists probably have wide-ranging interests in life that defy any effort to pin a label on them. To find out about two Individualists who gracefully marry the old and the new in a contemporary setting, turn to page 145. An Individualist room designed by Lyn Peterson especially for the book is shown following page 24.

Should you fit into this Individualist category, take either the Period Quiz or the Contemporary Quiz, depending on which category the majority of your answers fall into. Thus, eight *b-d* and ten *a-c* respondents should take the Contemporary Quiz, and ten *b-d* and eight *a-c* respondents should take the Period Quiz. The answers to the quiz will help you find decorating alternatives to those shown in the Individualist sourcebook. Also take into regard which of the prototype personality color photographs most appeals to you.

If you're surprised by your results and feel your determined personality may not be accurate, you may want to retake the quiz—perhaps you rushed through it. It might also prove useful to examine the roots of your decorating rationale and your background. Have you, for example, been decorating with *your* preferences in mind, or have you been influenced by the environment in which you were reared (or furnishings you've inherited), or have you been bridled by the opinions of spouses, close friends, or colleagues at work?

Because many of us do not live alone, there are problems that may naturally arise when two people, each with his or her own decorating style, try to feather the same nest. Opposites may attract, but do opposite decorators have a chance at design happiness? Perhaps your contemporary furnishings were put into storage when you married in favor of your partner's less worn traditional pieces? And, in the process, did your decorating personality go into storage with them?

If this is the case, now is the time for the two of you to find a personality that suits both of you or a way to "marry" your decorating styles so that you are *both* satisfied.

**PERIOD MEETS CONTEMPORARY . . .
AND THE WINNER IS . . .**

Very often it's the interaction of two styles that makes the difference between a ho-hum decor and an exciting one. Decorating doyenne Elsie de Wolfe's advice from *The Leisure Class in America*, published over seventy years ago, still has relevance. "Don't go about the furnishings of your house with the idea that you must select the furniture of some one period and stick to that." But she goes on to suggest that this eclecticism be tempered by suitability. "Do," she cautions, "use your graceful French sofa and New England rushed chairs in *different* rooms."

But what happens if your test results point to contemporary and your partner's a period person? And, to further complicate matters, what if you both contribute an apartment-full of furniture from your solo days?

Before you start impulse buying and come to verbal blows in showrooms and shops, you might first take stock of exactly what you have and what condition it's in: What needs reupholstering, what accessories should be weeded out, which pieces may be ready for the Goodwill or the church bazaar? If your more comfortable sectional sofa wins out over his faded overstuffed Tuxedo, consider upholstering the sectional in a more classic fabric to placate his decorating tastes. If, on the other hand, you end up sacrificing your platform bed, insist on vertical blinds instead of his more traditional draperies in the bedroom.

If you plan well, you can turn what might seem like a design liability into an asset. "If there is a complexity in the relationship between two people, this can work to enrich the space being designed," replies interior designer Kevin Walz. "If one person favors clean, cool, and spare lines and the other warm and soft, they can both be pleased with, for example, chairs that have angular, modern lines but are covered in an overstuffed fashion in soft, classic fabrics. The plump softness minimizes the sleekness, and the opposite is true: the lines of the chair diminish the more traditional qualities."

You might also eliminate or disperse some of the more traditional pieces, using only a few in given rooms to create a more open, contemporary look. Remember, too, your own personality style can extend to walls and furniture. Crisp, all-white walls will play down period fussiness, and Windsor or other "old-fashioned" chairs painted a light shade or upholstered in a bold pattern will undercut their period lines.

If you're still having trouble deciding whose style will take precedence, ask yourself who spends the most time at home. If one of you free-lances at home and the other works outside in an office, the needs of the free-lancer should be taken into strong account. But perhaps the person who works outside the home is a gourmet cook and frequently invites friends over for dinner. In this case the kitchen and dining room style should bear his or her decorating stamp.

Ask yourself, too, about the architectural style of your house or apartment. Are there built-in details that lend themselves to one style over another? If so, you might choose to take your design inspiration from the century-old façade, the interior French doors, or the neoclassic fireplace motifs.

If, after much thought and trial and error, your compromise ends up in an unresolved decorating quagmire, then perhaps it's time to consult a professional. Since all interior designers face such problems when hired to decorate spaces, they will have a large visual library for you to consult for possible ideas. When you initiate the contact, be certain to precisely define your requirements, as fees are commensurate with the scope of services rendered.

With careful planning, the winner is... both of you!

**Period Quiz**

1. If you were to collect quality antique prints, they would probably be
   a. primitive scenes or barnyard animals
   b. English watercolors
   c. sailing ships and maps
   d. formal animal portraits

2. You would redeem a bed-linen gift certificate for sheets of
   a. white or solid pastel
   b. a soft floral or striped pattern
   c. oxford-cloth cotton or mattress ticking
   d. eyelet or a miniprint

3. If you had your choice of one of these authentically furnished houses, you would choose
   a. a century-old stone house or log cabin
   b. a gardener's estate cottage or carriage house
   c. a colonial or federal-style house
   d. an English Tudor-style house or city town house

4. When a rich relative offers to back you at an estate auction, you go all out and buy
   a. an early-nineteenth-century dining table and chairs
   b. a collection of antique Oriental blue-and-white porcelain
   c. a Pennsylvania German painted chest

d. antique silver and crystal accessories

5. Your very favorite clothes are mostly made of
   a. denim, corduroy, cotton
   b. velvet, taffeta, silk
   c. linen, cashmere, wool
   d. tweed, gabardine, wool blends

6. Which of these statements comes closest to describing your present feelings?
   a. I want to re-create my favorite period with authentic pieces.
   b. I like to blend different looks in a comfortable setting.
   c. I feel most at ease with informal, rustic furnishings.
   d. I want my home to reflect my idealized sentiments about the past.

7. Which of these magazines would you most likely read regularly?
   a. *Early American Life*
   b. *Victorian Homes*
   c. *Antiques*
   d. *House & Garden*

8. The bed of your dreams would be a:
   a. carved pencil post
   b. four poster with draped canopy
   c. curly maple bed with turned post headboard
   d. painted wrought iron or antique brass bed

9. Which of these statements comes closest to describing you outside of your job?
   a. I'm a casual person.
   b. I'm something of a dreamer and idealist.
   c. I'm a bit of a perfectionist.
   d. I'm a practical-minded realist.

10. You'd love to fill an empty display case with a prized collection of
    a. antique engraved silver or Chinese export porcelain
    b. fine china collectibles (willowware, Nanking)
    c. handcrafted ceramics (spongeware, stoneware, redware)
    d. antique gloves, band boxes, miniatures

11. You are most likely to spend an afternoon free of work and/or family responsibilities
    a. at some outside activity—gardening, walking
    b. pampering yourself at a beauty salon
    c. planning a gourmet dinner or browsing at a museum
    d. doing personal shopping for you or the family

12. Your idea of a splendid fall getaway is
    a. an inn in a historic village
    b. a big-city weekend splurge
    c. a cabin in the mountains
    d. an off-the-beaten-track island

13. On your way home alone from a trip, you're stranded in a lovely village. To make the best of it, you
    a. take an exploratory walk
    b. find out what's playing at the local movie theater
    c. check the library or residents for historical highlights and visit them, if possible
    d. photograph or sketch local scenes

14. If you had been offered front-row seats for the taping of one of the following series, you'd have selected
    a. *The Adams Chronicles*
    b. *Upstairs/Downstairs*
    c. *Shogun*
    d. *Brideshead Revisited*

15. You would volunteer to work during your free time at the
    a. zoo or nature center
    b. local community garden or botanical gardens
    c. performing arts center
    d. public library

16. The fence surrounding your preferred style of house would be
    a. brick
    b. shrubbery
    c. split rail
    d. white pickets

## The Naturalist

Room photographs by James Levin. Naturalist living room/den designed by Beverly Ellsley for *Personality Decorating*.

## The Romanticist

Room photographs by James Levin. Romanticist bedroom designed by Stanley Hura for *Personality Decorating*.

## The Traditionalist

Room photographs by James Levin. Traditionalist living room designed by Georgina Fairholme.

## The Classicist

Room photographs by James Levin. Classicist dining room designed by Nicholas Pentacost for Parish-Hadley Associates, Inc.

## The Individualist

Room photographs by James Levin. Individualist bedroom designed by Lyn Peterson of Motif Designs for *Personality Decorating*.

## The Young Professional

Room photographs by James Levin. Young Professional bedroom/eating area designed by James Bloor for *Personality Decorating*.

## The Modernist

Room photographs by James Levin. Modernist living room/dining room designed by Sybil Levin.

## The Futurist

Room photographs by James Levin. Futurist living room/kitchen designed by Michael Braverman, Juan Montoya Design Corp.

## Period Quiz Analysis

In order to make scoring the quiz easier for you to tabulate, we have included a scorecard. Simply enter the letter you chose opposite each question number. Then, beginning with the odd-numbered questions, tally up the responses and indicate the number under the respective letters. For example, next to the letter *A* you might have ~~HH~~ , which would equal five. Do the same with the even-numbered questions.

PERIOD QUIZ SCORECARD

| | |
|---|---|
| 1. b | 9. b |
| 2. c | 10. c |
| 3. b | 11. d |
| 4. c | 12. c |
| 5. a | 13. a |
| 6. b | 14. b |
| 7. a | 15. b |
| 8. b | 16. b |

| ODD | EVEN |
|---|---|
| *a.* III | *a.* |
| *b.* IIII | *b.* III |
| *c.* | *c.* III |
| *d.* I | *d.* |

If the majority of your answers to the odd-numbered questions was the letter *d* and the even-numbered questions letter *b*, this confirms that you are a Traditionalist. You probably have very strong, deep-rooted feelings about home and family, and this comes through in the warm style you have chosen for your decorating. As a Traditionalist, you appreciate the look of the past. However, rather than re-create any one period, you prefer to combine favorite pieces from various times and places in order to achieve a cozy, yet often elegant, look. You love the friendly feeling that draperies, skirted tables, and comfortably upholstered seating—perhaps in coordinated floral or geometric prints—can bring to a room. And while you admire antiques, and may include some cherished heirlooms among your possessions, chances are that many of your furnishings are reproductions or adaptations, usually in woods such as mahogany or cherry, which are durable and good-looking. To discover more about a Traditionalist family, turn to page 105. A photograph of a Traditionalist living room, designed by its occupant, Georgina Fairholme, appears following page 24.

If you answered the majority of the odd-numbered questions with the letter *a*, and letter *c* to the even questions, you are a Naturalist. You favor rustic "farmhouse" pieces with scrubbed, weathered, or painted finishes as opposed to high-style, "townhouse" furnishings—and this holds true whether your look is best defined by the furnishings of rural America, England, or France.

Whether you choose antiques or reproductions depends largely on your budget and the availability of country pieces in your area, but a Naturalist personality expresses itself equally well with either. You're most likely to select folk art and functional objects reminiscent of the rural past—quilts, decoys, baskets, handcrafted ceramics and calico, homespun and stenciled fabrics—to complement your furnishings. If you're drawn to this relaxed look for your decorating, you probably prefer an informal life-style as well, opting for casual ways of entertaining, comfortable clothes, and a free-form garden. For an interview with a Naturalist couple, turn to page 65. A Naturalist room, designed by Beverly Ellsley for *Personality Decorating*, can be seen following page 24.

If, when you tally your responses, you have a majority of *b* replies for the odd questions and a majority of *d* answers for the even ones, you most likely didn't need to take the test to find out that you are a Romanticist at heart. The Romanticist decorating personality ranges from those who favor the deep, rich colors and carved, ornamental dark woods of the Victorian period to those who prefer a less formal, lighter pastel look. Lace and ruffles, complex floral prints, rich satins, silks, and brocades all appeal to the Romanticist, as do wicker and brass furnishings and upholstery with skirts, tassels, and fringe. But the Romanticist probably gives freest decorative rein in the bedroom, which may include a brass or wrought-iron bed (or perhaps a canopied four-poster), dressed in appliquéd or lacy sheets, a skirted vanity (with pretty toiletry accessories), and balloon window shades or ruffled curtains. As a Romanticist you may also exhibit this fondness for lace and silks and velvets in clothing, especially evening wear. You would gladly choose a turn-of-the-century "gingerbread" house or a clapboard cottage with a wrap-around porch as your dream house. To read about a couple who express their Romanticist personalities in an urban setting, turn to page 85. A Romanticist bedroom, designed by Stanley Hura especially for *Personality Decorating*, can be found following page 24.

If over half of your odd-question answers were letter *c* and your even-question answers letter *a*, you are a Classicist. Whether your favorite period of the past is eighteenth- or nineteenth-century American, English, or French, you choose to duplicate this look as authentically as possible in your rooms. But a Classicist does not just decorate in this period—it is also important that you be knowledgeable about your favorite time in history and its furnishings. You like to visit museums, restoration villages, and antiques shows and shops, and to read relevant books and magazines. You may even plan to visit noteworthy historical sites and famous collections during your holidays. Given a choice, you would rather buy antiques, but you also understand the value of quality reproductions when originals are unaffordable, impractical, or just not available. Naturally, your ideal home would be one that was actually built during or in the style of your period—a colonial-revival or a federal-style house, for example—but your decorating personality is so strong that you can infuse your given style into any room. To learn more about Classicists, turn to page 125. A Classicist dining room, designed by Nicholas Pentecost for Parish-Hadley Associates, Inc., appears following page 24.

After taking the Period Quiz, did your answers fail to point definitively to any *one* personality? Perhaps you found yourself on the fence between a Naturalist and a Romanticist. If this is the case, don't despair—rise to the challenge!

If you chose the Naturalist as your primary style and the Romanticist as a secondary one, you might set a primitive harvest table with lacy mats under stoneware plates. Or choose principal upholstered pieces in country styles, and casegoods—a secretary or an armoire—in a formal, more ornamental style. If you are still torn, consider dividing your home by rooms. While the Naturalist holds forth in the living room, the Romanticist part of you could manifest itself in the bedroom with a canopied bed and chaise, or in the often-neglected bathroom. There you could hang a pale pastel shower curtain with a ruffled valance and introduce painted porcelain and glass objects.

Individualists who take the Period Quiz and determine they are Traditionalist might choose to set overstuffed chairs and long draperies in a room with sleek accent pieces and highly polished bare wood floors.

**Contemporary Quiz**

1. You feel that hiring a caterer for a special event is
    a. a splendid idea—you do it as often as you can afford
    b. usually beyond your budget
    c. probably not creative enough for the kind of parties you throw

2. You'd be most likely to subscribe to
    a. *Cosmopolitan* or *Self*
    b. *Rolling Stone* or *Interview*
    c. *Metropolitan Home* or *Architectural Digest*

3. Your idea of getting physical is
    a. playing tennis or swimming
    b. a minimarathon or a long walk
    c. working out in the gym

4. Old, dear friends spring a surprise visit and space is tight, so you
    a. offer them your bed and you take the sofa
    b. insist they stay and round up some sleeping bags
    c. make some hotel suggestions and offer to call for reservations

5. When your mother offers you her 1950s dinette set, you
    a. know she's kidding and have a good laugh with her
    b. tell her you've already got a kitchen set and graciously decline
    c. snap it up at once and probably use it as is

6. You consider unfinished pine furniture
    a. a good way to save money
    b. too boring for your tastes
    c. incompatible with your furnishings

7. When you buy makeup, it's
    a. a name brand you've come to count on
    b. because you're low and there's a special

    *c.* you're excited by the latest shade or new line

8. The idea of using a stainless-steel surgical table somewhere in your space
    *a.* mildly interests you—but you might cover the top, at least partially
    *b.* intrigues you, perhaps to use as a bar or a buffet
    *c.* offends you

9. When you go clothes shopping it's usually at
    *a.* better department stores
    *b.* stores that discount well-known brands
    *c.* whatever boutiques carry the styles you like

10. Which of these statements best describes your feelings about where you now live?
    *a.* I don't know where I'll be in a few years, so I buy adaptable furnishings I can probably use later on.
    *b.* I may or may not be living here much longer, but it's very important that my furnishings reflect me *today*.
    *c.* I have no plans to move, so I buy what furniture I need now.

11. Open storage in the kitchen is
    *a.* too messy for you
    *b.* okay as a temporary measure
    *c.* a great look

12. Furniture assembled from found objects (wood skids, cable spools) is
    *a.* fine for now
    *b.* a good way to add unique decorative touches
    *c.* not for your interiors

13. You consider deep-pile, wall-to-wall carpeting
    *a.* beautiful—a decorating plus
    *b.* a nice look, but too expensive for your budget
    *c.* too staid for your tastes

14. The decorating book you'd most likely buy from the following list would be
    *a.* *Upscale Decorating at Lower-Level Prices*
    *b.* *Industrial Design for Interiors*

  c. *The Best of Architectural Interiors*

15. When you invest in the audio system you've always wanted, you
    a. spend what it takes to have all the components built in
    b. buy a suitable cabinet and try to place the speakers unobtrusively
    c. incorporate the various parts into your decor—why hide them?

16. You can have ringside seats to one of these events, so you pick
    a. Frank Sinatra's farewell concert
    b. Burt Reynolds' wedding
    c. Tina Turner's next video taping

**Contemporary Quiz Analysis**

Use the scorecard below to tabulate your responses. Enter the letter you chose opposite each corresponding question number. Then tally up the totals for each letter for both odd- and even-numbered questions and enter that figure next to the letter under the appropriate heading.

CONTEMPORARY QUIZ SCORECARD

| | |
|---|---|
| 1. | 9. |
| 2. | 10. |
| 3. | 11. |
| 4. | 12. |
| 5. | 13. |
| 6. | 14. |
| 7. | 15. |
| 8. | 16. |
| ODD | EVEN |
| a. | a. |
| b. | b. |
| c. | c. |

If a majority of your answers to the odd-numbered questions was the letter *a* and the even-numbered *c*, you fall into the category we call the Modernist. While your basic look is marked by spareness and clean lines, you also want comfort in your home, in the form of soft upholstered seating, deep-pile carpeting or fine rugs, platform beds, and built-in cabinetry to house such necessities as books, television, and the stereo equipment. You regard your furnishings as an investment, so you're willing to pay for quality items in luxury materials—such as marble, imported tile, and rare woods, like ebony and rosewood—that you know will last a lifetime. A sophisticated consumer, you shop the better department stores and designer showrooms and peruse high-style design magazines and books for your decorating inspiration. Given a choice, you would no doubt opt for an architect-designed contemporary house or an apartment with a spectacular view as your ideal residence. To read more about how a Modernist lives, turn to page 183. A photograph of a Modernist living-dining room, designed by Sybil Levin, appears following page 24.

If you chose a majority of *b* answers for the odd-numbered questions and *a* for the even-numbered ones, our test indicates that you are a Young Professional. To be a Young Professional, you don't have to be necessarily young *or* professional. We selected this name for this casual, easygoing style because so many young career-oriented people find it to their liking. However, the look is just as appropriate for older people who may have given up a large house for a less formal space, or for divorced or separated individuals, who are starting over again with a clean decorating slate. Characteristic of this style are easy-maintenance pieces that can usually be bought off-the-floor at such stores as Conran's and Workbench in the East, Crate & Barrel in the Midwest, or Barker Bros. in the West. A Young Professional will choose light-colored woods such as pine and oak, often in assemble-it-yourself (knockdown) furniture, and wood laminates, and will be certain to provide for ample storage space for books and a stereo system. Many people in this category feel that their current residence —usually an apartment—is only temporary. But it is vital that their belongings, such as butcher-block tables, Breuer and director's chairs, and sleep sofas be of good enough quality to find a spot (perhaps in a spare room) when they move to larger quarters. To read a more in-depth profile of an upwardly mobile Young Professional, turn to page 163. A Young Professional room, designed by James Bloor especially for *Personality Decorating*, is featured on page 24.

If more than half of your responses for the odd-numbered questions was the letter *c* and *b* for the even ones, you fall under the personality umbrella we call the Futurist. So forward-looking are you, in fact, that you are often among the first to see the decorative possibilities in objects others would overlook. The Futurist, for example, would be delighted to accept Mother's butterfly chairs, a vinyl sofa, or dinette set and use them as part of a "Fabulous Fifties" decor. Unfettered by traditional home furnishings, Futurists comb sources like restaurant and other commercial supply houses, thrift shops and flea markets, artists' studios, and craft shops. Even serendipitous finds—on the street, demolition sites, or factory castoffs—will prove more inspiring than department or furniture store merchandise. Futurist rooms may be minimal (few furnishings, monochromatic color schemes), playful, cluttered, and funky (plastic seating, vinyl-checked floors, hot colors, offbeat collectibles), or marked by the practical simplicity of high-tech (metal folding chairs, restaurant kitchen equipment, industrial lighting, metal shelving). For an interview with a highly original Futurist, turn to page 203. His apartment, which he designed himself, is pictured following page 24.

If you found your responses fairly equally divided between two styles—say, Futurist and Young Professional—this indicates there's a strong trend-setting, unorthodox streak in you. Take advantage of it by choosing fun fabrics (like a leopard print) for your sling or director's chairs. Or consider a factory lamp, or a warehouse wood pallet as a coffee table.

Individualists who took the Contemporary Quiz have rich and varied options in accordance with their main personality grouping. If you turn out to be a Modernist, you might enjoy decorating with modern Italian furnishings and recessed lighting, accented with more traditional collectibles such as Blue Canton porcelain or pewter—or perhaps by throwing a colorful quilt over a white contemporary sofa.

Whether you're a dyed-in-the-lace Romanticist, or a fast-forward Futurist, you can probably—like all of us—benefit from a review of the rudiments of decorating. Part II explores these basics, and ushers in the eight individual personality sourcebooks in Part III.

## PART TWO

# Personality Ingredients — Putting Them All Together

## Coloring Your Personality

We are an increasingly color-conscious society. We color-coordinate our kitchen appliances, our eye shadow and our clothing, even our bathroom tissue with our shower curtains.

Yet committing oneself to an interior color scheme can, in some cases, be just as forbidding and intimidating as shopping for furniture. Virginia Jackson, Home Fashions Coordinator for Celanese Fibers, who lectures widely on color, advises, "Learn to love color; learn it as a language."

Yet, if you've ever read any books that discuss color psychology, you know there is little agreement about the effects of individual shades and the language they "speak." Joan Kron in her book *Home-Psych: The Social Psychology of Home Decorating* warns, "Beware of sweeping claims about the power of color. No aspect of psychology is as susceptible to review."

Despite this reigning disaccord, there are a few insights about the correlation between color and personality upon which the experts agree. One is that regardless of age, people will more often choose lighter shades over darker ones. Also, research shows that people change their color preferences as they mature. An infant's unfailing predilection for yellow and white evolves to blue and red in later years; even the colors you chose when you first moved into your home may no longer suit your personality.

Studies also confirm that exposure to the ever-popular red accelerates heart rate, breathing, and blood pressure. Elsie de Wolfe, who designed many fashionable interiors, including those of the Duchess of Windsor, advised, "If you are inclined to a hasty temper . . . you should not live in a room in which the prevailing note is red. On the other hand, a timid, delicate nature could often gain courage (from this color). . . ."

Statistics also confirm that even with the ever-expanding palette of colors offered the public each year, there is still a tendency among people to choose a few colors. Color allegiance is undeniably strong, and over the years blue has proved to be universally the most favored shade.

Well, perhaps blue is not one of *your* true interior colors —but what are they and, just as important, how do you establish them?

## Flying Your Interior Colors

To assist you in the search for your compatible personality colors, we have included a montage for each of the eight personalities (beginning after page 57), which features a color palette, along with an arrangement of wallpapers, fabrics, and floorcoverings, all coordinated to the decorating personalities. In this section we also present a Color Scheme Chart, with suggestions on primary colors, accents, and combinations. Look upon these charts, though, merely as guides to help you narrow your choices when you go shopping for these elements.

Selecting color schemes flattering to your interiors is not unlike shopping for your wardrobe. When you buy clothes, you pick shades and styles that compliment your skin tone, hair color, age, and environment. Chances are a pale, blue-haired grandmother living in Florida would not be drawn to the same colors and styles chosen by a raven-haired, olive-skinned teenager in Oregon. In general, people with fair complexions have different responses to color than those with darker skin tones; blondes tend to prefer warm colors, brunettes cooler ones.

When you color your interior, you make similar considerations: the age of your residence, building materials, its location, exposure to light. Thus, the hues that complement the interior of a newly built glass beach house in Malibu would not be harmonious in a maple-shaded stone farmhouse in New Hampshire. Research shows that people who live in areas that get abundant sun tend to prefer strong, brilliant shades like reds and golds, while those who live in low-sun spots lean toward softer, more muted shades, especially in the blue and green spectrum.

After taking stock of the details of your home, you might then peek into your closets. If you find a predominance of beiges and browns and you feel comfortable in those colors, then you'll probably be most comfortable if your interiors wear them, too. Similarly, if there's a noticeable absence of bold shades like red, perhaps you should steer clear of that color when making *major* decorating color decisions.

Other hues and combinations to avoid are those that are currently the fad. "I don't want my clients to worry that in six months they'll pick up a magazine only to find that their new living room color scheme has been judged passé," proclaims Kevin Walz, a modern designer who always shuns the hottest trend.

If you just can't resist whatever is in fashion at the moment, indulge your passion in a way that won't destroy your decorating budget. Buy items like pillows, bath towels, posters, and everyday dinnerware rather than sofas, wallcoverings, and carpeting. A few accessory items can give your home an instant update, and can easily be replaced should you grow tired of the color scheme.

How can you tell whether a paint shade will be out of vogue before it dries on your walls? Most colors have a four- to five-year life span, so if stores and magazines have been heavily promoting a particular hue for the past couple of years, the tide is undoubtedly about to ebb. Take cues as to which colors may become popular in tomorrow's home furnishings market by watching the fashion scene. If purple makes a big splash in clothing for a season or two, expect to see it follow in the interior design industry in paint, bed linens, dinnerware, upholstery fabric, etc. (which happened in the early 1980s).

Whatever you do when making major color decisions, don't be hasty, especially if you've just relocated. Perhaps the freshly painted pale green walls did not appeal to you when you toured the rooms before you moved in. But rather than investing in gallons of paint and yards of material that might prove disappointing, first let your furnishings settle into their new color surroundings. Green may just turn out to be the most flattering shade, whereas the mauve you had your heart set on might not have worked at all!

And, when in doubt, stick to a few colors rather than a bewildering rainbow. Use the lightest hues in the main areas, slightly brighter ones in the secondary spots, and save the most intense shades for accessories or in smaller areas.

## A Color Focus

If you're completely at sea about choosing a color plan and your closets offer no hint, look to other objects for guidance. Perhaps you just inherited or bought a lovely painting or a Chinese rug you plan to display prominently in the living room. Let that object direct your color decisions.

If you have interesting architectural details in a room, you can bring them to life by painting them a contrasting shade and then tying in an upholstery fabric or rug with this color. Consider, too, your curtains and draperies, an artwork collection, or perhaps an antique chest. Is there a particular color that would bring out their beauty more than another?

Whether you're repainting one room, the entire house, or your apartment, design your living space as a unit. If you've been painting with bold primaries you might think twice before introducing a muted eighteenth-century-inspired color in another room. Changing moods from room to room is fine, but the visual effect should not be a jarring one. Noted interior designer Mario Buatta works out an overall color scheme, beginning with the entryway. "I like the idea of using blue there, particularly in a somber urban apartment—it adds a sense of sky-openness. Once I've established an inviting shade there, I then orchestrate a color plan that will flow from it and, at the same time, infuse the individual rooms with different moods."

As part of your interior color research, buy a large blank notebook that opens flat (at least nine by twelve inches), with fairly stiff paper—index card weight is perfect. As you collect samples of paints, wallcoverings, floorcoverings, fabrics, and tiles, mount them on the paper (one room per page), making note of specifics (shade or pattern, manufacturer, date ordered, etc.). If it's impractical to mount an actual sample, ask the dealer to provide you with a color reproduction of it or sketch it on the page with colored pencils or magic markers.

In this way, you'll get a visual sense of whether your choices work together in pleasing and exciting combinations. As you reject samples, remove them from the page and look for better ones. Take the workbook with you when you shop—it will save you time and disappointment.

If you're decorating an entire house or apartment or simply more than one room at a time, you may want to take your research a step further. Buy a large (twenty-by-thirty-inch) piece of poster board (or an inexpensive sheet of "showcard") from any art supply store. Divide the board into as many rooms as you are decorating. As you accumulate paint chips and swatches, lay them out in the proper room and use masking tape to attach the backs to the board. Prop the board up on a chair and move back to study it. Concentrate on the individual rooms first and see if you've struck a good balance of color and pattern. You might see a color in one of your major fabrics that you can play up in an accessory or tie into a window treatment. Then look at the chart as a unit and ask yourself if you've achieved a good balance in tone of color among all the rooms. Perhaps the pink in the bedroom is too intense in comparison with your other wall colors.

Your notebook or poster board will also make a ready reference should you decide to reorder fabric or paint later on. And when you decorate other rooms, keep adding to your notebook. You'll then have a permanent record and history of your decorating choices and a basis from which to work should you decide to repaint or buy a new carpet later on.

## Sunlight and Color

Depending on the direction of the light source, colors take on different personalities. You can, however, compensate for the effects of the sun's rays on hues by selecting warmer or cooler shades.

For example, if your windows face east, the morning sun will be strong but gentle for the remainder of the day. So, if it's a bedroom, you may want to choose cooler tones that the strong morning sun will warm up naturally. North light is the coolest of all and the most constant (which is why painters like to paint in this light). This means that walls facing a northern exposure that are painted a cool green will appear even cooler, and walls painted a warm yellow will appear less warm. On the contrary, the hot sunlight from the west and south (the hottest exposure) tends to warm colors considerably. Cool tones appear warmer and warm ones hotter yet. To "cool" a room under these exposures, choose colors in the blue-green-violet spectrum.

Remember, too, that daylight will tend to fade pale neutrals, so you may want to go a tone or two darker to get the effect you want.

Interior designer Kevin Walz does not even broach the subject of color with his clients until he first turns his attention to space and light. "My primary consideration is light—how much or how little do the rooms receive? Then I discuss with the client a palette of colors that I feel is compatible with those factors."

## Color and Dimension

Also bear in mind the size of the room and its dimensions. Color will go far to visually correct a room's layout. (For more information on this, see "Making Space Work For You," on page 50.) In small, dark areas, use light colors to make the space appear brighter and larger. To create a warm, cozy atmosphere in a large space, consider using strong colors such as dark blues, browns, and bottle greens.

Dark colors will also seem to lower ceilings and vice versa—light shades will visually add height to a low-ceilinged room.

To make a thin, narrow room seem wider, paint the shorter walls a darker shade (to bring them forward) and the longer ones a paler color (to move them out).

**Shopping for Paint**

Paint chip display racks are all too often tucked away in the backs of stores, under fluorescent lights, and usually several feet from a window. Be sure to take the chips you've selected outside and examine them under natural light as well as under the store lighting.

Then take the samples home and place the strips on the wall, masking out with black any shades you're not considering. If possible, take the samples to a well-stocked art supply store (those that serve colleges and universities are best) and buy large sheets of paper that most closely approximate your paint samples. You can often find papers (Pantone makes a line) in both matte and glossy surfaces. Or buy a piece of fabric to match your selections. Then hang the paper or the fabric on the wall and live with the color for a few days, observing it at different times during the day (and at night with artificial light) and in conjunction with your present furnishings and draperies or samples of the new ones you may be choosing.

Remember that once applied to walls, paint will be far more intense than it appears on the small swatch. So if you're set on using a fairly intense shade, you may want to choose a tone or two lighter.

Once you've made a final decision, buy the smallest quantity of paint possible and brush out several two-by-two-foot strips on the wall. Then allow the paint to set for a couple of days (light paint darkens as it dries and dark paint dries lighter). Consider then whether the shade shows off your furniture and accessories to best advantage. If so, buy all the paint you need at one time so you'll be sure to get the same lot number. A little extra paint is fine for touching up any surface imperfections later on.

## Your Personality Decorating Color Scheme Chart

### The Naturalist

Rustic comfort for no-fuss, easygoing life-styles. Painted-and-stripped-pine pieces like cupboards, benches, chests, ladder-back chairs, trestle tables. Decorative grain-painted and stenciled finishes. Folk art (decoys, weather vanes, samplers) and handcrafted quilts, baskets, stoneware, old tools and implements as accessories. Homespun, calico, checked, and print fabrics. Stenciled walls or painted in buttermilk shades, small-print wallcoverings. Braided, rag, and hooked rugs; painted floorcloths, and wide planked flooring.

**Major colors:** Nutmeg, Navy, Barn red, Cinnamon, Stone blue, Bottle green.

**Accent colors:** Eggshell white, Black, Wild rose, Yarrow.

**Color schemes:** Navy, Stone blue, Yarrow. Nutmeg, Bottle green, Cinnamon. Stone blue, Barn red, Nutmeg. Navy, Nutmeg, Wild rose.

### The Romanticist

Evocative opulence for the heartfelt nostalgic. Light, airy furnishings such as wicker, as well as ornate Victorian styles, including brass beds and dark, carved woods. Porcelain, silver, glass, and other delicate accessories such as fans, frames, miniatures, and dressing table items. English floral chintzes, luxurious silks, and velvet fabrics; intricate laces and linens. Wallcoverings in fresh garden prints (both large and small scale) and richly colored stripes. Needlepoint rugs; plush wall-to-wall carpeting; hand-painted tiles.

**Major colors:** Wood violet, Antique white, Tea rose, Hunter green, Sheer pink.

**Accent colors:** Misty blue, Plum, Cornsilk, Celadon.

**Color schemes:** Tea rose, Celadon, Antique white, Hunter green, Sheer pink. Misty blue, Sheer pink, Cornsilk. Antique white, Plum, Wood violet, Misty blue, Tea rose, Wood violet, Hunter green, Antique white. Wood violet, Sheer pink, Celadon, Antique white.

### The Traditionalist

Inviting elegance for graceful family living. Furniture includes overstuffed chairs, sofas, skirted tables, wing chairs, period-style case pieces in dark woods. Accessories include brass, pewter, silver, needlepoint pillows, and china figurines. Large floral and understated geometric print fabrics; woven cotton, linen, or rayon (damask) and wools; twill; leather. Subdued botanical and figural motif wallcoverings; glazed and stippled wall finishes; woven and textured papers. Wall-to-wall carpeting; dhurrie rugs, Oriental-style rugs; ceramic tiles; heavy-gauge vinyl.

**Major colors:** Garnet, Spruce green, Regimental blue, Cocoa brown, Apricot.

**Accent colors:** Terra-cotta, Seafoam, Jonquil.

**Color schemes:** Cocoa, Seafoam, Spruce green, Apricot. Terra-cotta, Seafoam, Cocoa. Regimental blue, Garnet, Spruce green, Cocoa brown. Seafoam, Apricot, White. Garnet, Spruce green, White, Cocoa (pale).

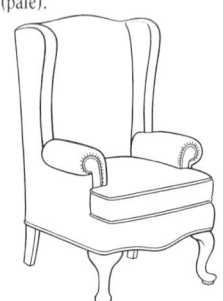

### The Classicist

Authentic atmospheres for discriminating perfectionists. Period antiques and quality reproductions, in eighteenth- and nineteenth-century styles. Intricately carved pieces such as sideboards, breakfronts, library bookcases, and highboys in polished woods. Chinese porcelains, delft, fine silver accessories. Moiré, silk, satin, brocade, documentary fabrics (cotton sateen and rayons), and leather. Documented-reproduction wallcoverings, including neoclassic and Oriental murals; historic paint colors. Oriental rugs, bare wood floors.

**Major colors:** Parchment, Regal blue, Oxblood, Viridian green, Marigold.

**Accent colors:** Delft blue, Chestnut, Off-white, Copper, Burnt orange.

**Color schemes:** Parchment, Delft blue, Regal blue. Oxblood, Delft blue, Viridian green, Copper. Burnt orange, Regal blue, Parchment. Regal blue, Delft blue, Viridian green, Parchment. Marigold, Copper, Regal blue.

## The Individualist

Creative intermingling of past and present for the diversified. Period-style furniture updated with fashionable fabrics; contemporary pieces softened by classic coverings; or a composite of both old and new styles (e.g., modern seating with rustic case goods). Old-fashioned accessories in an *au courant* setting, or contemporary accents in traditional rooms, or a tasteful melding of both. Fabrics and wallcoverings in lively, crisp patterns, both abstract and figural, and solids in muted and bold shades. Dhurrie rugs; woven-fiber matting; low-pile, wall-to-wall carpeting; wood flooring.

**Major colors:** Candy pink, Old pewter, White, Taupe, Toast, Nantucket blue, Warm red.

**Accent colors:** Black, Peach, Mauve, Navy.

**Color schemes:** Taupe, White, Nantucket blue. Brick, White, Navy. Nantucket blue, Toast, Taupe. Candy pink, Ecru, Brick, Taupe, Nantucket blue. Warm red, White, Black. Old pewter, Slate blue, Toast.

## The Young Professional

Adaptable environments for adaptable people. Informal, multipurpose furniture, such as stackable storage units, convertible sofas, and desk/dining tables in neutral and colorful laminates and paint-it-yourself unfinished woods. Dual-purpose accessories, including decanters, glassware, dinnerware that are both smart and serviceable; posters and photographs. Canvas, corduroy; textured cotton fabrics in solids, pin dots, stripes, and impressionistic designs. Sheet-covered walls; striped, pin dot, and geometric wallcoverings. Natural rag rugs; Indian wool geometric rugs; woven fiber matting; parquet wood squares; vinyl flooring.

**Major colors:** Sand, Slate blue, Poppy red, Black, White, Gray flannel.

**Accent colors:** Midnight blue, Daffodil yellow, Spring green.

**Color schemes:** Poppy red, Daffodil yellow, Spring green, White. Slate blue, Sand, White. Midnight blue, Poppy, Red, Sand. Poppy, Slate blue, Daffodil yellow.

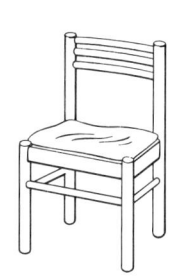

## The Modernist

Timeless looks for the style-conscious cosmopolitan. Luxurious, clean-lined seating; built-in storage units; glass, brass, and lacquer finishes in sleek designs. Glass and ceramic accessories; Oriental collectibles; contemporary artwork. Soft wool fabrics such as camel hair and flannel; simple geometric woven cotton prints; leather; suede. Fabric-upholstered walls; subdued geometric, striped, and abstract-patterned wallcoverings; glazed, painted wall finishes. Sculpted-pile and flat wool wall-to-wall carpeting; dhurrie rugs; ceramic tile; marble and terrazzo tiles.

**Major colors:** Champagne, Pale mauve, Peach, White, Dove gray.

**Accent colors:** Chinese red, Bronze, Black, Azure, Aquamarine.

**Color schemes:** Champagne, Black, Chinese red. Azure, Champagne, White. Camel, Dove gray, Peach, Pale mauve. Pale mauve, Dove gray, Peach, Azure. Aquamarine, Pale mauve. White.

## The Futurist

Up-to-the-minute interiors for adventurous, spontaneous personalities. Homemade furniture assembled from discovered objects (e.g., a coffee table made from a concrete slab with a glass top); one-of-a-kind, handpainted furnishings; pieces from restaurant, medical, and office supply houses; the latest avant-garde designs. Funky souvenirs; contemporary art and crafts; high-tech commercial items as accessories. Hand-designed fabrics; jungle prints; playful abstract designs. Monochromatic walls for creative furnishings/artwork display. Flooring in industrial carpeting; glossy graphic vinyls.

**Major colors:** Black, Fire-engine red, White, Bubble-gum pink, Chartreuse, Steel gray.

**Accent colors:** Wild canary, Cobalt, Jungle green, Burnished gold.

**Color schemes:** Black, Steel gray, Burnished gold. Fire-engine red, Black, Wild canary. White, Steel gray, Black, Fire-engine red. Bubble-gum pink, Cobalt, Black. Chartreuse, Black, Wild canary.

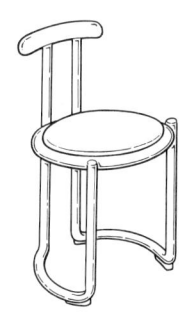

## Lighting Up Your Personality

Nothing could be more elementary than flipping a light switch. But what kind of light and in what style of fixture? Choosing from the many lighting options available to "light up" your decor—track lighting, portable uplights, can lights, downlights, recessed lighting, not to mention the rich variety of table and standing lamps—is not such an easy task.

Basically, a room needs three different light sources: indirect light that shows off the room's architecture; lights to work and read by; and light that illuminates specific objects, such as a painting or plants.

In the same way that painting a room is a relatively inexpensive way to convey a fresh look, experimenting with different kinds of lighting can give new perspective by accenting a collection or highlighting colors and textures.

This section is not intended to take the place of an informative, detailed book on the general subject of lighting. What we offer here are a few tips to guide you in making practical lighting decisions. Also remember to refer to the lighting directory under each of the eight decorating personality sourcebooks in part three to help you shop for all your rooms.

**Lighting Tips**

- Before you invest in a floor lamp or an uplight, buy a reflector lamp in a socket attached to an extension cord. Walk around your rooms with the light, holding it in different places to see where the light looks best with your furnishings.
- The bottom of a table lamp shade should be at eye level when you're seated. So the higher the table, the shorter the lamp should be.
- Floor lamps should measure approximately forty-five inches from the bottom of the shade to the floor.
- If your space affords no possibilities for installing recessed lights, buy portable uplights and experiment with bouncing reflected light off ceilings to get the mood you want.
- Before focusing light onto ceilings and walls, make certain they are not marred by cracks, peeling paint, or unevenness. Imperfections do not need *extra* attention.
- Use an extender lamp over a dining area that can be

adjusted up and down to prevent glare. Put the lamp on dimmers so you can adjust the mood, too.
- To provide both task and mood lighting in the kitchen, mount two fixtures to the ceiling: a fluorescent tube and, next to it, a track light equipped with porcelain sockets on a dimmer. Use both lights when working, but only the track light when you want atmosphere.
- Dresser lamps should be placed with the center of the shade about twenty-two inches above the top of the dresser.
- For best light diffusion, buy soft-white bulbs.
- Buy shades that measure a minimum of sixteen inches across the bottom to allow light to escape.
- To make your furnishings and objects appear warmer and more inviting (for example, a sofa or a sculpture), place atmospheric lighting behind them. You'll find your guests naturally move toward the backlit objects.
- In a traditional setting, illuminate artwork with recessed ceiling fixtures rather than track lighting, which is too contemporary in appearance. Or, choose individual picture lights that actually attach to the frame.
- Wall lamps should be placed approximately twenty inches to one side of your reading position and about forty-eight inches above the floor.
- Locate desk lamps to the left if you are right-handed, and to the right if you are left-handed, with the bottom of the shade fifteen inches above the work area.
- A bathroom should have a minimum of two light sources —over the sink for grooming and a general light source for the rest of the room.
- As an alternative to chandeliers (which are often unflattering to human and architectural features), consider using low-voltage narrow-beam fixtures (Lightolier makes one) over the dining area; small floor can lights; or several sconces, positioned about fifty-six inches from the floor.
- Remember, the higher the wattage, the cooler, hence harsher, the light. You might be better off using four twenty-five-watt bulbs rather than a single hundred-watt one.
- For an alternative to an adjustable hanging fixture over the kitchen table, consider connecting an eight-foot track to the ceiling outlet and mounting four seventy-five-watt bulbs on it. You can then direct the lighting however you wish.
- To reduce eye strain while watching television, place low-level, indirect lighting next to the set.

## Your Personality Lighting Chart

### The Naturalist

Naturalists illuminate their space with soft, diffused light that embodies the characteristics of daylight without dramatic harshness.
**General lighting:** table lamps (stoneware and redware crocks); black, wrought-iron standing lamps; tin chandeliers; turned wood and metal chandeliers.
**Accent lighting:** tin sconces; pierced-tin lanterns; firelight; candleholders (e.g., metal "hog scrapers").
**Shades:** pierced or cut paper; checked, miniprint, and solid fabric; stenciled fabric or paper; heavy parchment.

### The Romanticist

This decorating personality works to create moods, whether it's an inviting corner niche for curl-up reading or skin tone–flattering light to dine by.
**General lighting:** Tiffany lamps; standing and table lamps and chandeliers with frosted glass globes; metal lamps and chandeliers in floral shapes; Art Nouveau table lamps with glass, porcelain, and metal bases; candles (can't have enough!); crystal chandeliers.
**Accent lighting:** petite dressing table lamps; lacy handkerchief-draped table lamps; tiny Christmas tree lights; porcelain and cut-glass candleholders.
**Shades:** frosted, etched, and stained glass; wicker; crystal; lacy and floral printed fabrics.

### The Traditionalist

Despite the prevailing period look, Traditionalists may choose to incorporate modern technology in their lighting choices—perhaps inconspicuous recessed lighting in the living room, in addition to the more traditional table and floor lamps.
**General lighting:** porcelain, glass, and metal-based table lamps; adjustable metal standing lamps; pewter, porcelain (delft), and brass chandeliers; recessed ceiling wall washers.
**Accent lighting:** hurricane shades and candles; brass candlesticks and candelabras; brass pharmacy lamps; wall-mounted, swing-arm lamps.
**Shades:** parchment; linen; fabrics (often coordinated with walls, windows, and upholstery); glass.

### The Classicist

In duplicating the authentic mood of a particular room's period, a Classicist might choose to light a dining room solely by candles and wall sconces or, in other rooms, use lamps made from reproductions of antique porcelain urns.
**General lighting:** crystal and metal chandeliers; metal (e.g. painted tole and brass) and porcelain table lamps; historic iron/brass candlestands.
**Accent lighting:** fine glass hurricane lamps; cabinet undershelf lighting (for collectibles); picture lights; brass antique or reproduction candlesticks, candelabras, and lanterns.
**Shades:** painted metal (tole); linen; heavy glazed paper; leather; silk; hand-blown glass.

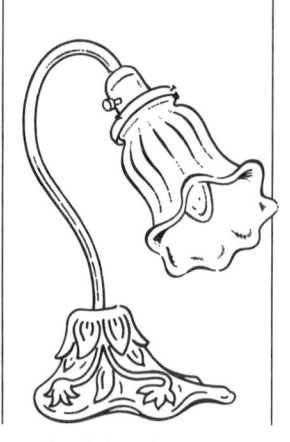

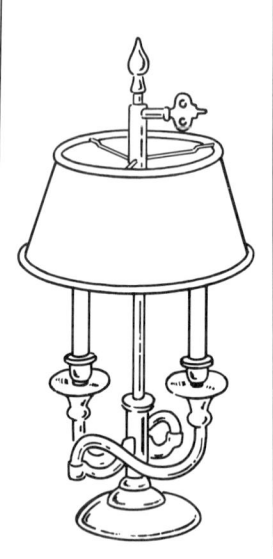

*See individual directories for photographs of lighting fixtures featured here.*

## The Individualist

Lighting choices are based on the major mood the Individualist wants to set. If, for example, the prevailing mood is contemporary with period accents, the lighting would be primarily modern, and vice versa.
**General lighting:** solid-color ginger jar lamps; recessed ceiling wall washers; track lighting; brass table and standing lamps with frosted glass and metal shades.
**Accent lighting:** pendant downlights; pharmacy lamps; wall-mounted, swing-arm lamps.
**Shades:** lacquered paper; linen; wicker; rattan; brass.

## The Young Professional

Portable is the key word for Young Professional lighting, which combines different kinds of task lighting to meet multiple needs.
**General lighting:** ceramic and metal-based table lamps; clamp-on adjustable metal desk lamps; metal and ceramic geometric sconces; metal pendant suspended lamps; metal and glass torchère standing lamps.
**Accent lighting:** tensor lamps; votive candles; floor and ceiling cans.
**Shades:** lacquered paper; fabric; glass; metal.

## The Modernist

Lighting is a major part of the overall room design of our Modernist—subtle, but highly effective. Usually built-in, other lamps such as floor and table lamps are used as decorative objects.
**General lighting:** track; recessed wall washers; floor and ceiling cans; metal and glass torchère standing lamps.
**Accent lighting:** Lucite and metal base floor and table lamps; table lamps with sculpted bases; pharmacy lamps; Art Deco–style sconces and table lamps; metal, glass, and Lucite chandeliers.
**Shades:** glass; parchment; linen; metal.

## The Futurist

Lighting ranges from heavy-duty industrial fixtures from factories, streets, and shipyards, to one-of-a-kind works of art. Art-inspired Futurists use lighting to highlight a favorite collection or piece.
**General lighting:** glass, metal and porcelain suspended pendants; porcelain-on-steel industrial hanging fixtures (RLMs); track with theatrical spots; standing halogen lamps; mercury vapor lights; "Noguchi" Japanese paper shade lamps; photography studio lighting.
**Accent lighting:** bulkhead ship lights; geometrically-shaped metal sconces, fluorescent strip lighting; floor and ceiling cans; neon.
**Shades:** metal, glass, porcelain.

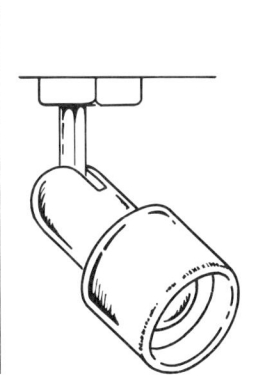

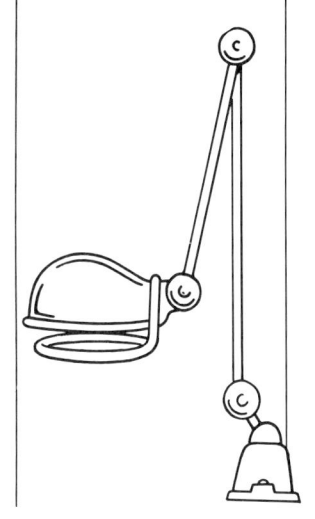

## Windows—Their Many Personal Faces

If you've expended considerable time and money injecting personality into your rooms, you owe it to yourself not to overlook your home's "eyes on the world"—your windows.

Few rooms ever look finished if the windows are bare. (Windows with wonderful views, privacy, and/or strong architectural details are the exception.) But merely covering them is not the point. At this stage, you should realize that your window treatments can reflect your personality as much as any other furnishing element, and we've made the job of selecting the right style for you much simpler.

In the eight individual personality sourcebooks, we've illustrated window treatments compatible with these personal styles. If your quiz responses were divided between two or more different personalities, feel free to glance through more than one directory for suggested ways to dress up your windows.

The ideal time to choose your window dressing is not when everything is in place, but while the room is still taking shape. This way, you can decide on such matters as whether you want drapery fabric that matches the upholstery. If so, it should be ordered at the same time. Do you need valances or woodwork specially ordered? These things take time. Are you going to want to paint or paper the trim or mullions? If so, you won't want to wait until the carpeting or upholstery has been installed.

In general, give the same degree of care and thought to choosing and installing your window treatments as you would to any other decorating element. Just as you would not enclose a valuable painting in a five-and-dime-store frame, so, too, you would do a great disservice to your room by framing it with makeshift window dressings.

Here are a few things to bear in mind when designing your windows:
- Your decorating personality
- Your budget
- Aesthetics of treatment
- Privacy requirements
- Window size and scale
- Noise factors

- Energy efficiency
- Amount of light admitted (how much should be blocked out)

After weighing all these factors, choose then from a wide assortment of treatments in your personality and price range. Basically, they fall into four major categories:

- Shades (roller, Roman, balloon, pleated)
- Blinds (horizontal and vertical; fabric, wood, metal)
- Draperies and curtains
- Shutters

While you're making up your mind, don't forget to consider where you live and how it could affect the maintenance of your window dressing. For example, those tiers of white-eyelet café curtains may admit the light you want and give the room a crisp, airy feeling. However, if you live in a large city, near major industry or highways, white and crisp will all too quickly turn to gray and limp. In addition to keeping curtains and draperies looking fresh, taking them on and off the rods can be cumbersome (especially if they're heavy, full-length, albeit energy-efficient, draperies), unwieldy to launder, or expensive to dry-clean. A more practical choice would be shutters painted a pale glossy (easy to clean) shade.

The window treatment illustrations that accompany each of the eight personality directories in part three will be a good source of ideas. If you're interested in making your own personality window treatments, we recommend two fine books: *Curtains and Window Treatments* by Angela Fishburn, published by Van Nostrand Reinhold, New York, and *Sewing to Decorate Your Home* by Joanne Schreiber, published by Doubleday & Co., New York.

If you don't sew, and you want to invest in custom-made draperies, check with a local interior designer or the home furnishings department of better department stores.

## Your Personality Window Treatment Chart

### The Naturalist

Simple window treatments in keeping with the unpretentious furnishings. When window architecture is interesting and privacy no problem, windows may be left uncovered.
**Basic treatments:** tab curtains, café curtains, shutters, bare windows, wood blinds.
**Fabrics:** homespun, calico, checked and miniprint cotton and linen.
**Accents:** stenciled fabric, grain-painted shutters, contrasting painted window trim, stenciled window frame, simple swag with folk-art style finial.

### The Romanticist

Fussy, opulent window treatments often ruffled and sometimes in multiple layers; for example, a sheer panel topped by a tieback curtain in a heavier fabric. Windows are dressed to match mood-evocative room settings.
**Basic treatments:** balloon shades, Austrian shades, sheer panels, ruffled tieback curtains, gathered and tied in multiple tiers, lacy or frilly café curtains.
**Fabrics:** lace, cotton plissé, velvet, floral printed glazed cottons, eyelet, gauze, shirred fabrics, tissue taffeta, organdy, dotted swiss, point d'esprit.
**Accents:** ribbons and bows, shirred painted valance, or fabric-covered poles, ornamental porcelain tiebacks, fabric (braided, ribbon) borders on draperies.

### The Traditionalist

Soft window treatments, frequently in fabrics coordinated with wallcovering and upholstery. Short or long draperies, depending on architecture and degree of room's formality.
**Basic treatments:** tieback and café curtains, full-length draperies, painted or stained shutters, Roman shades, miniblinds.
**Fabrics:** chintz, woven cotton and linen damasks, geometric and figural prints, cotton plissé, sheers (especially for underlayer).
**Accents:** Fabric-coordinated valances, decoratively shaped cornices, metal ornamental rod "finials", painted and fabric-covered poles, fabric borders on edges of draperies, fabric panel shutters, fabric folded screens paired with coordinated Roman shade, heavy brass rods, oversized rings.

### The Classicist

Historic treatments in keeping with room's period. Styles range from ornate to simple, depending on the window detail and view.
**Basic treatments:** draperies with decorative valance treatments, i.e., swags and jabots, wood venetian blinds, floor-to-ceiling tieback curtains.
**Fabrics:** moiré, taffeta, brocade, jacquard, silk damask, documented reproductions in cotton sateen, silk, linen, wool, especially in figural and fauna motifs.
**Accents:** wood or metal ornamental rod "finials" in carved shapes, decorative tiebacks (tasseled cord, sashes, metal or wood hooks, knobs, bars, or rosettes), painted or fabric-covered poles, cotton or silk fringe.

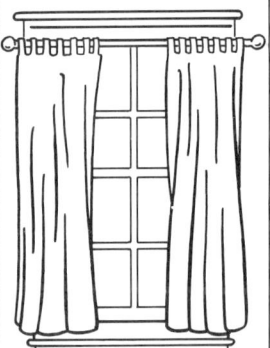

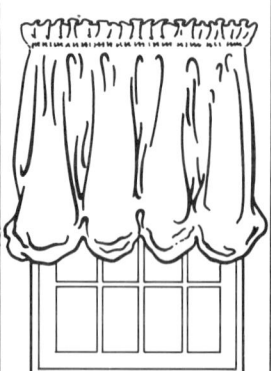

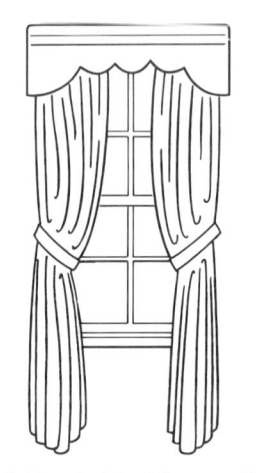

*For more information, refer to the window treatment illustrations included in each of the eight personality decorating sourcebooks.*

### The Individualist

Individualists may choose window treatments that complement both period and contemporary styles; for example, white shutters or simple curtains. Or, they may want to add warmth to a contemporary space with a more ornate period window treatment or "modernize" an old home with a contemporary window dressing.
**Basic treatments:** shutters (often painted), fabric panels, vertical blinds, Roman shades, horizontal miniblinds.
**Fabrics:** bright polished cottons, lace, sailcloth, heavy printed cottons.
**Accents:** fabric roll-up shades, painted window frames, contrasting drapery fabric linings, pinned back.

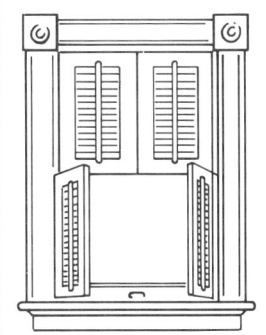

### The Young Professional

Casual, easy-to-install, clean-lined window treatments, often space-expanding and used to camouflage an unsightly view.
**Basic treatments:** pleated paper shades, horizontal miniblinds (metal or bamboo), fabric or canvas flat shades.
**Materials:** paper, metal, wood, printed cotton, woven fabric and fibers, sheeting.
**Accents:** painted shades and blinds, knotted or pulled-back draped panels, treatments that extend beyond windows (see page 000, Young Professional prototype room).

### The Modernist

Simple and classic monochromatic treatments, often in vertical blinds that can be adjusted to admit light and alter the mood.
**Basic treatments:** vertical blinds, horizontal mini-blinds, simple, monochromatic floor-to-ceiling draperies, woven straw shades.
**Materials:** metal, woven fabrics, straw woven and smooth cottons, linen, silk.
**Accents:** trompe l'oeil painted frames, brass hardware, bleached rods.

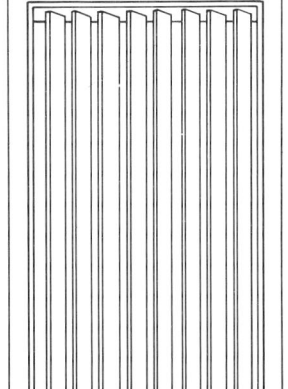

### The Futurist

Window treatments as unique as their individual styles, ranging from fifties-style venetian blinds and fabric shower curtains on a ceiling track to non-glare, amber-cellophane shades (the kind used in department store windows).
**Basic treatments:** wide metal venetian blinds, pleated paper shades, floor-to-ceiling mosquito netting, wrapped and knotted contrasting cotton fabrics, small shoji screens, pull-up window shades, cloth on removable rollers.
**Materials:** metal, opaque and corrugated papers, coated canvas, sheers (e.g., cheesecloth) solid cottons.
**Accents:** commercial hardware for tiebacks (grommets), painted blinds and shades, painted window frames, offbeat objects used for tiebacks (e.g., jump ropes).

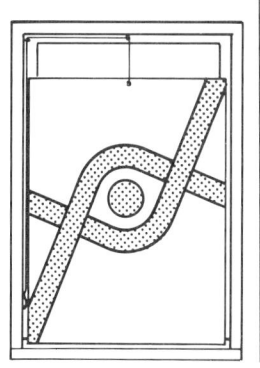

## Making Space Work for You

We all have to deal with space, whether we live in a ten-room house in the suburbs or a one-room studio apartment in the city. Too small, too boxy, too long — whatever particular challenges your space presents, there are ways to visually alter spatial proportions without undergoing expensive major renovation.

*Visually* is the key word. If you have painted your room in such a way that it *looks* larger than it actually is, then you have created the feeling of space without expanding your square footage.

You can visually expand, diminish, camouflage, and/or add depth and dimension to your space by thoughtfully selecting appropriate colors, textures, patterns, and lighting. Three-dimensional surfaces, such as mirrors, and well-planned furniture arrangements can also help you alter your space.

The advice given here sums up some of the most economical and accessible ways of dealing with the space problems that confront all of us, irrespective of personality. When possible, we're given information on how to further add a dash of your personality decorating style while working to modify your room's proportions.

**With Color**

One of the simplest and least expensive ways of cosmetically modifying space is with color. In general, you can visually shrink space by using dark, strong shades both for walls and furnishings. The reverse is also true: pale, light colors will tend to open up space and make it appear larger.

■ To diminish the narrowness of a long hall or room, paint a darker intense color on the shorter (end) walls. This will visually cause the shorter walls to move in toward the middle of the room, thus de-emphasizing the narrowness.

■ High ceilings can be visually lowered by choosing a strong, dark color in a matte (non-glossy) paint. Use a lighter shade for the walls.

■ You can give the appearance of raising a low ceiling by

painting it with high-gloss paint a shade or two lighter than the walls.

■ To make a spacious room seem more unified and cozy, paint the floor a dark color or use dark floor coverings. Paint or stencil (or use a paper border) a continuous design around the entire room, either near the ceiling or at chair-rail height. The horizontal design at the same height tends to bring the walls closer. Also, if you don't have one, consider adding a chair rail, a horizontal molding on the wall at chair height.

■ To stretch a small space, bleach or paint the floor a light color, then paint a bold design across the floor and continue it onto the baseboard and wall. The eye will follow the design, which gives the impression of pushing the walls outward.

■ Narrow rooms can appear to be virtually doubled by painting the floor in a pattern of diagonal stripes in contrasting colors (e.g., black-and-white chevron stripes in a Futuristic studio).

**With Pattern and Texture**

Using pattern and texture correctly is a subtle but highly effective way of both visually altering space and adding an individual touch. If pattern and texture are juxtaposed carefully, you can camouflage or draw attention from awkward spatial proportions.

A glossy wallpaper in a loose lattice weave creates an entirely different spatial look than a fussy, small print—the first will tend to enlarge a room, the second contract it. When buying furnishings, think in terms of the kinds of prints and fabrics that will work best for your space and your decorating personality.

■ By decorating with contrasting textures (e.g., rough vs. smooth), you can add spatial interest to a room and create a good visual balance as well. To cite an instance, an Individualist might place a love seat covered in a textural nubby weave (rough) under a window hung with long, sheer curtains or a paper roll-up shade (smooth). A Naturalist may mingle a woven check (rough) with a calico print (smooth).

■ Large, sprawling patterns on light-colored backgrounds (in both fabrics and wallcoverings) will tend to exaggerate space and make it appear more open. A Young Professional faced with a "closet" kitchen might select all-white fixtures and plastic accessories along with a white, glossy wallcovering with large squares outlined in bright red or yellow. Sisal matting on the floor will further "enlarge" the kitchen.

■ Small, detailed patterns close together (especially in dark shades) will tend to give a spacious room a more intimate feeling.

■ Texturally interesting wallcoverings will take attention away from a room's shape. A Modernist might diminish unappealing proportions in a living room by hanging a textured fabric or a vinyl wallcovering that simulates suede or leather.

■ Texture can be created with living things, too. Consider the different looks various plants can give—a cactus as opposed to a lacy fern or a smooth rubber plant. A bank of plants will also add to a room's coziness and take away the coldness of a cavernous space.

■ Remember that paint, depending on how it's applied, has texture, too. At least six coats of a glossy paint with steel wool rubbings between coats will produce a shiny high-gloss finish that will visually expand space. Depending on the color used, you'll create a beautiful background for a Classicist, a Romanticist, or even a Futurist.

### With Furniture and Furniture Arrangements

To take maximum advantage of your space and to show off your possessions to their best advantage, take time to work out room layouts. But don't feel wedded to any given arrangement; the least expensive way to give a room a lift is to reposition the elements.

■ Vary the height of the furniture you use in a room. Break up the low lines of seating, for example, with taller pieces—a secretary, an armoire, or an étagère.

■ To make a large room appear less spacious, use oversized

pieces of furniture, and vice versa—small-scale furnishings will give a more open look to a studio space.

■ Shapes of furniture can distract the eye from unflattering room dimensions. *Oval*-shaped pieces will minimize the look of a dull, *boxy*-shaped room.

■ *Never*, no matter what the size of your room, line up all the furniture against the walls. This makes for boring decorating, and emphasizes any space problems you may have.

WHEN SPACE IS TIGHT

■ Use furniture made of light or transparent materials, such as wicker, Plexiglass, chrome, and glass—they look lighter and so seem to take up less space.

■ Always place larger furnishings against the long walls. With more breathing space, they'll make the room look less crowded.

■ When possible, hang furniture from the walls or buy built-in units, both of which will free precious floor and closet space and give a less cluttered look to small rooms. A Naturalist may want to store chairs Shaker-style, by hanging them from pegs on the wall. Futurists and Modernists might consider clear acrylic folding chairs that can be stowed away when not in use.

■ Remember that two smaller pieces of furniture are often preferable to one larger, bulkier piece in a small room. Two Traditionalist love seats would be a better seating solution than one large Tuxedo sofa.

**With Three-Dimensional Effects**

There are several ways to add depth and dimension to a room creatively and inexpensively. These include using folding screens, plants, platforms, and reflective surfaces. By reflective surfaces we mean glossy paints, highly polished or varnished wood floors, glass, chrome, brass, and, of course, mirrors.

■ Before you mount costly mirrors on a large expanse, make certain the mirror will reflect an interesting object (a beautiful painting, for example), not your closet door or a mundane storage area.

■ Changing levels (e.g., platforming a sleeping area) is one of the best ways to create spatial depth and interest, especially in a one-room studio. Strip lights placed under the platform will add a special mood—a great idea for any of the contemporary decorating personalities.

■ Creating a physical divider in a small room is an effective way of defining separate areas. Young Professionals might consider hanging an attractive piece of fabric or rice paper from the ceiling (but *not* flush with the wall edge—let the eye travel around the divider to continue the illusion of space).

■ A hinged screen placed in a corner, behind a sofa, or at the end of a narrow room will add to a room's depth. Romanticists may cover their screen in a soft floral fabric or wallcovering. Futurists would feel more at home with one painted in a lively, bold abstract pattern.

■ A collection of live plants, perhaps between the eating and seating areas of a living/dining room, is also a good spatial divider.

■ In a Modernist setting, mirror the bases of bed platforms or sofas. The reflective quality will give a feeling of spatial airiness and add a dramatic touch as well.

■ Those who want the benefits of mirrors without the high reflectiveness should consider frosted, smoked, etched or painted mirrors. (Try painting an attractive border design yourself.) These mirrors would work especially well for Traditionalist, Classicist, or Romanticist decorating personalities.

■ For a less costly mirrored effect, buy mirrored tiles (some even come with patterns), aluminum tiles, or one or more large mirrors, attractively framed.

## With Lighting

Lighting, used correctly, can work miracles in changing room dimensions and colors, and can also make a dramatic decorating statement.

- To add life to an architecturally dull space, place an upturned canister light on the floor behind a large plant or sculpture. It will cast moody shadows of objects onto walls and ceiling.

- If space is at a premium, mount light fixtures on walls and ceiling. Romanticists could wall-mount swing arm lamps with pretty fabric shades at either end of a love seat or skirted sofa.

- The right lighting can set apart discrete areas within a room. Light can, for example, separate a seating from a dining area. Dimension is added by breaking up the space. Place spotlights on a track so they cast pools of light onto a cozy grouping of furnishings (a sofa and chairs), a plant, or an art object.

- Picture lights—mounted on the picture frame or above, on the wall—will lend an interesting vertical brightness to a room.

- A pendant downlight (or a series) hung low over a planter will act as a pleasing room divider.

- Use dimmer switches to control the brightness of your lighting. The varying intensities of illumination will contribute depth.

(For more information see "Lighting Up Your Personality," page 42 and the lighting chart on pages 44–45.)

## With Art and Collectibles

When displaying artwork, consider how the piece relates to the space around it, the viewer, and the surrounding objects.

- Vertically placed art or collections will take the eye up to the ceiling, thereby making the room appear higher than it actually is.

■ To diminish the effect of a high ceiling in a room, concentrate on placing objects in horizontal arrangements, restricting the eye from moving up.

■ Keep scale in mind. Always balance a large painting or other work of art on a wall with neighboring furnishings that are large enough to "carry" it.

■ A cluster of objects placed close together on a wall (e.g. botanical prints and watercolors, heart-shaped wreaths, ballet shoes in a Romanticist setting; or samplers, old tools, stenciled mirrors in a Naturalist room) will lend warmth to a large space. Conversely, just a few items on a wall with lots of surrounding white space (e.g. a large framed montage in a Futurist living room) will not only add a feeling of spaciousness, but will give the pieces importance.

# Your Personality Decorating Montage and Color Chart

The solid color samples on the following charts will convey the distinctive moods associated with the eight decorating personalities. Use these shades as a guide when shopping for paint (either for walls or trim), solid fabrics, wall-to-wall carpeting, even vinyl and ceramic tiles.

Keep in mind also that many of the wallcoverings and fabrics shown have coordinating patterns and border trims (and that fabrics may have matching wallcoverings, and vice versa). This minimizes the guesswork involved in harmonizing your decorating choices. In addition, many fabric and wallcovering manufacturers produce their designs in several colorways. So, if you find a paper or fabric you like and it's not shown in the shade you want, consult the pattern book or the manufacturer.

We've endeavored to bring variety to the color chart and montage selections, in the scale and type of design, fabric weight, and price. Featured are fabrics and wallcoverings that cost anywhere from seven to sixty dollars a yard, and ten to seventy dollars a roll. Of course, we couldn't show the entire range available for each personality, but we think we've given you a start—an idea of the kinds of patterns compatible with the look you're trying to achieve.

And last of all, don't forget white as a color choice, either major or accent, for all personalities. Frequently, it's all you need to make a room look fresher, or to set a background for dramatic furnishings and artwork.

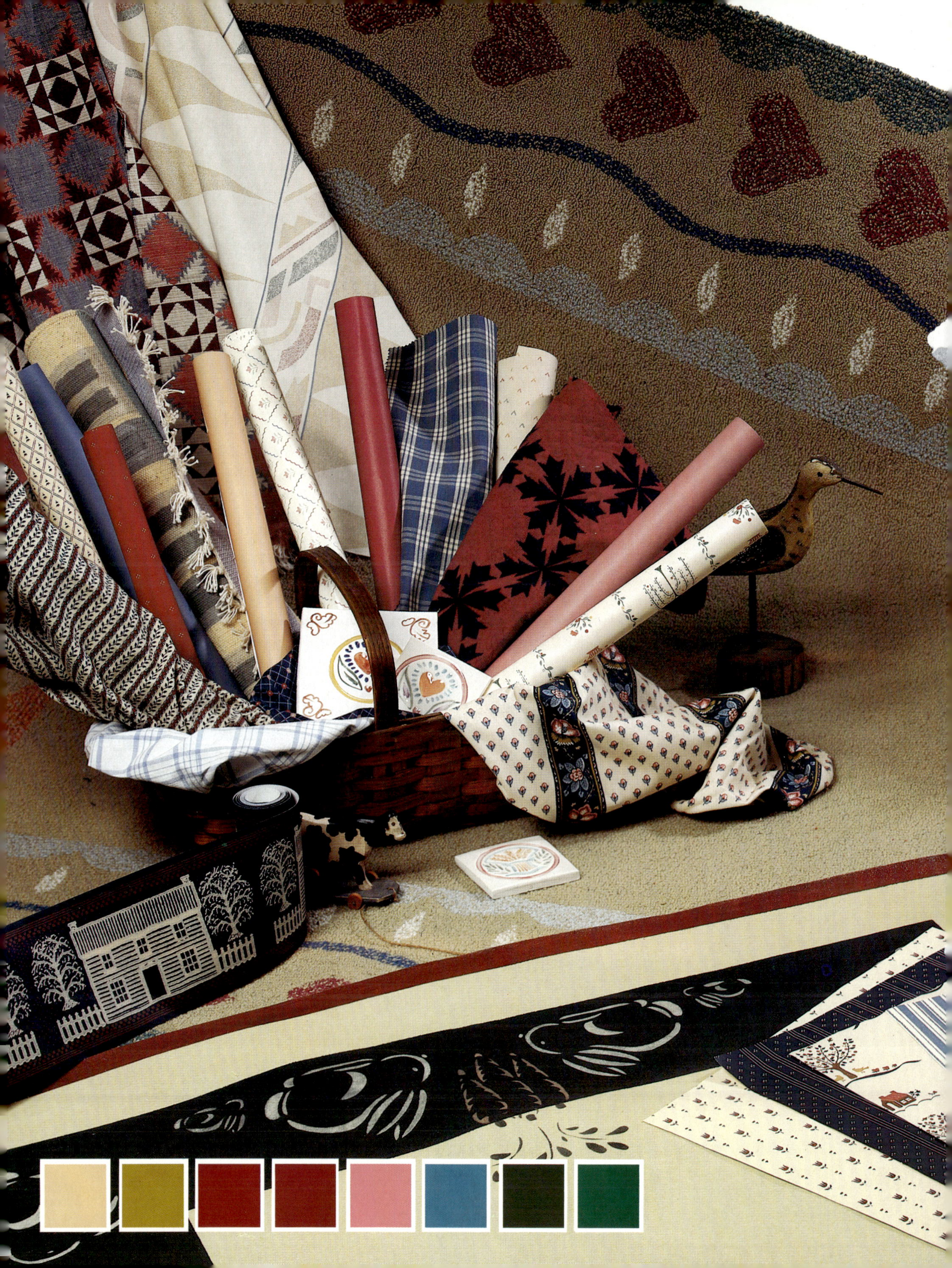

*Naturalist*

# Romanticist

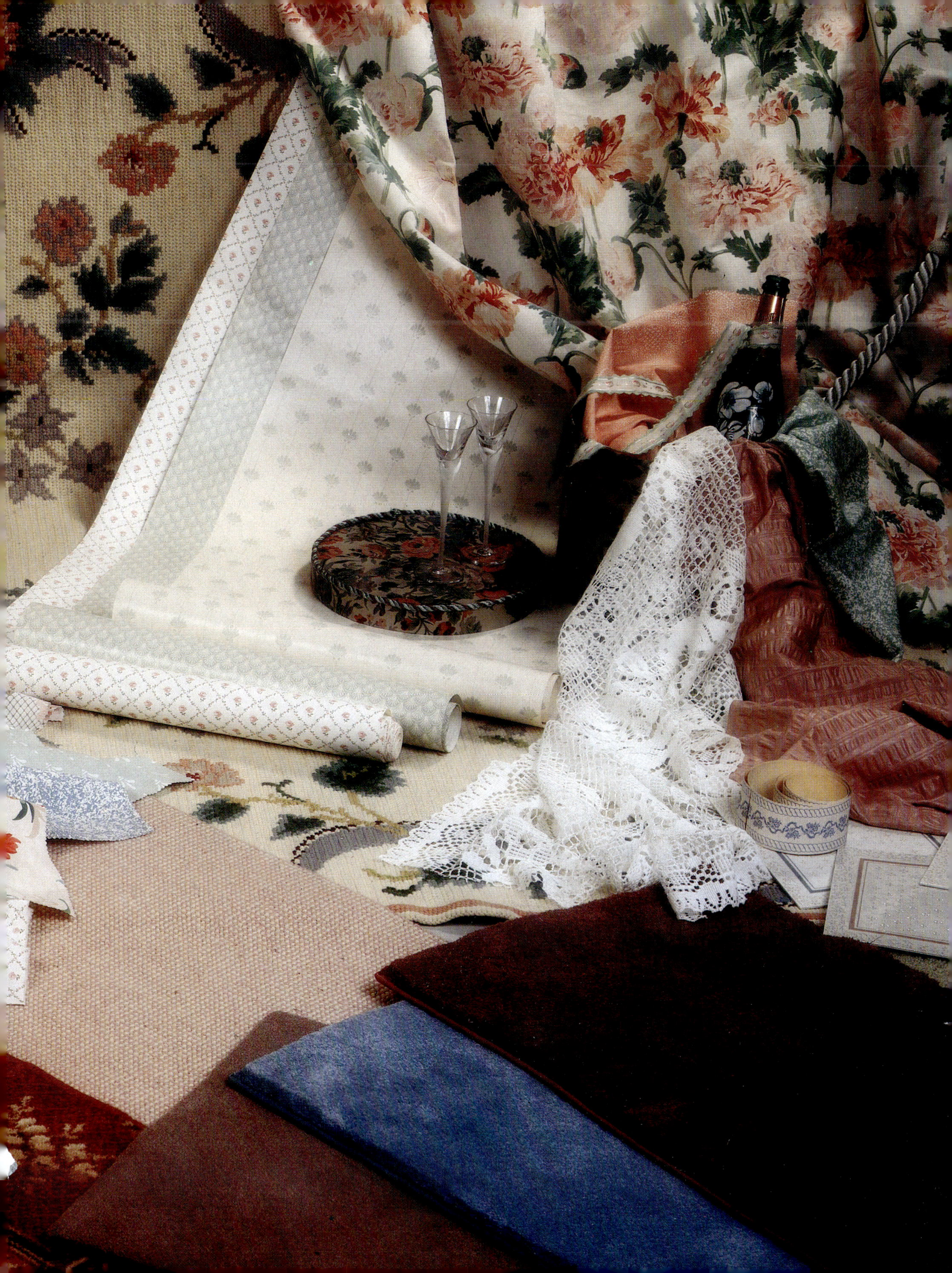

*Traditionalist*

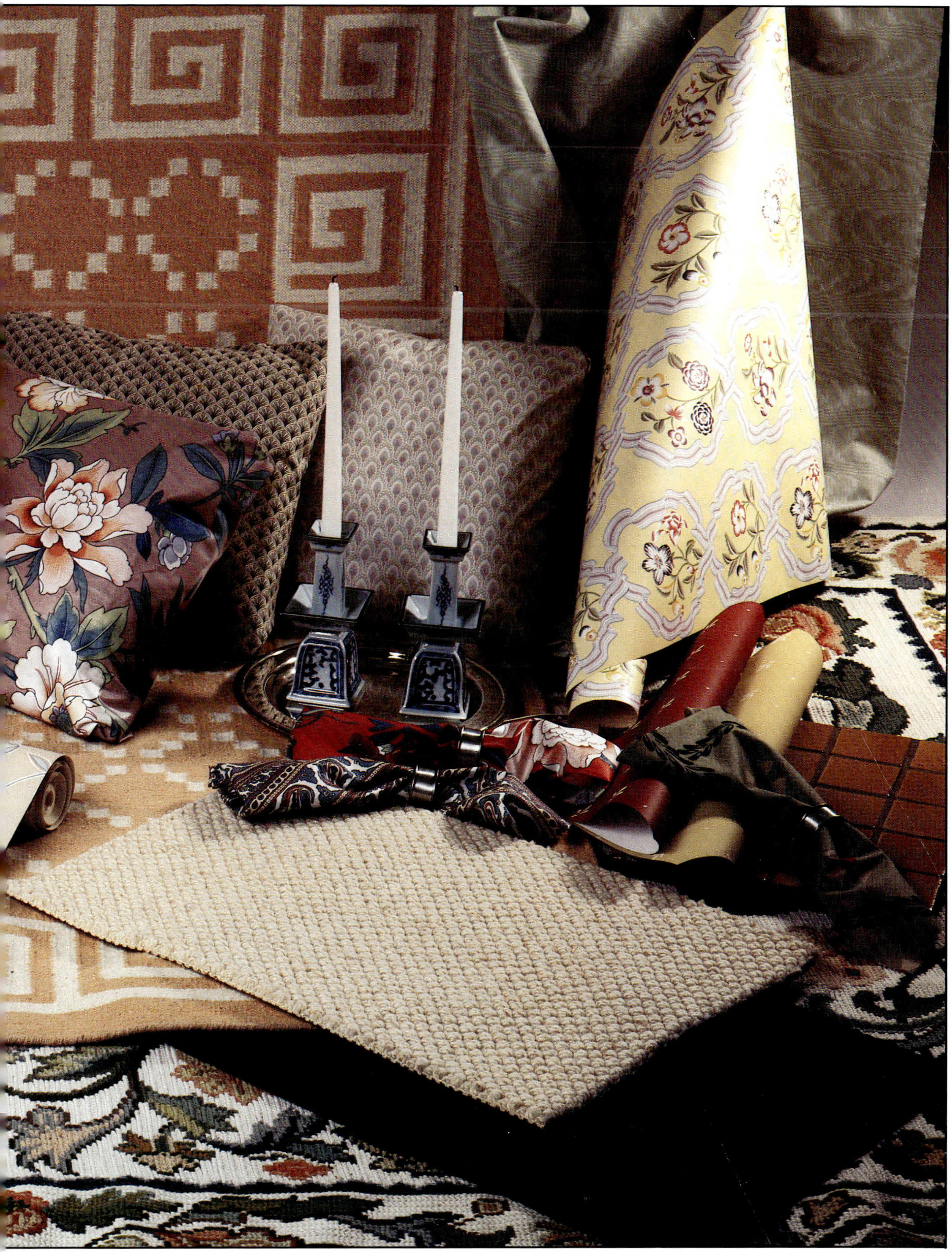

*Classicist*

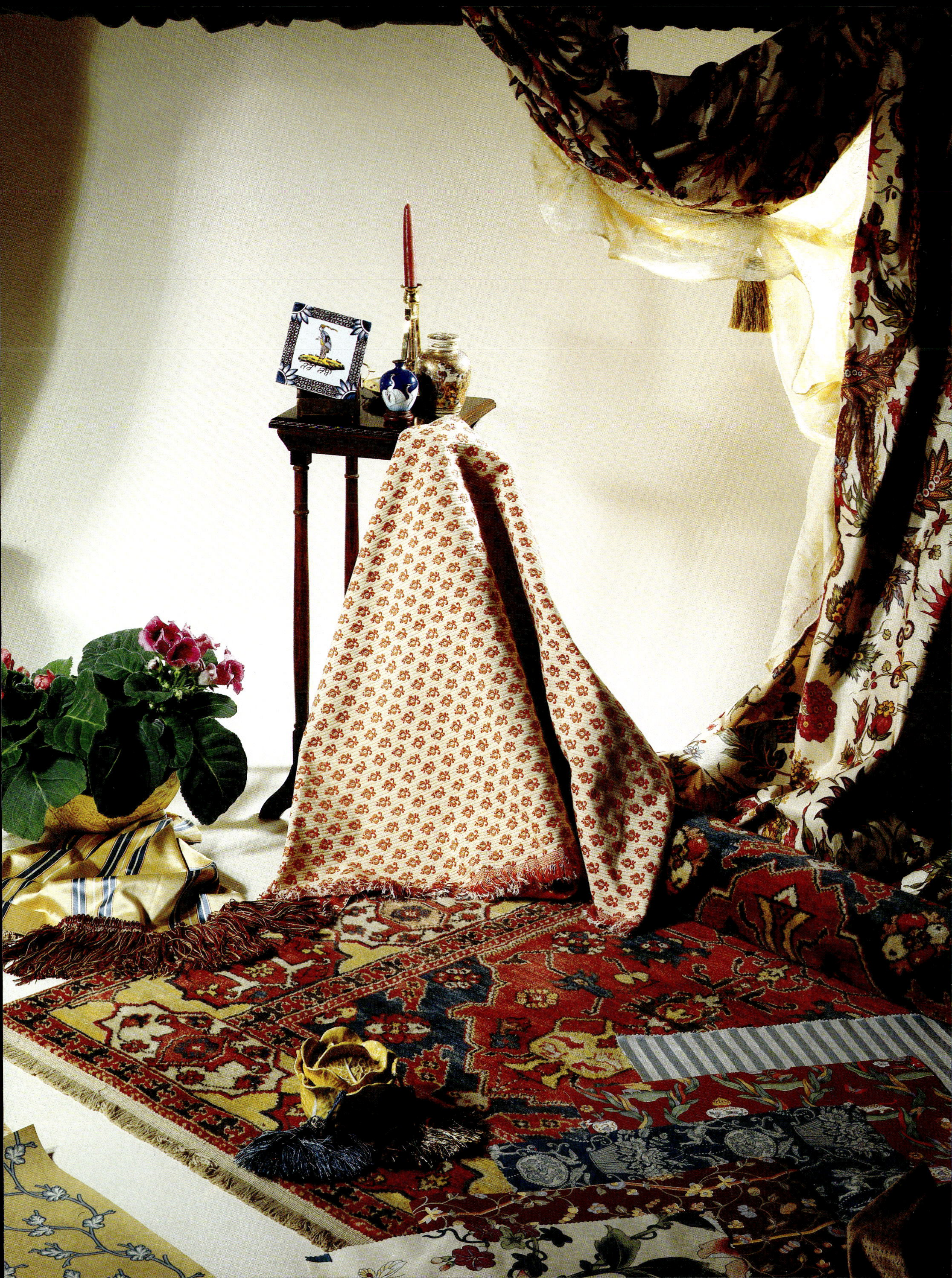

*Individualist*

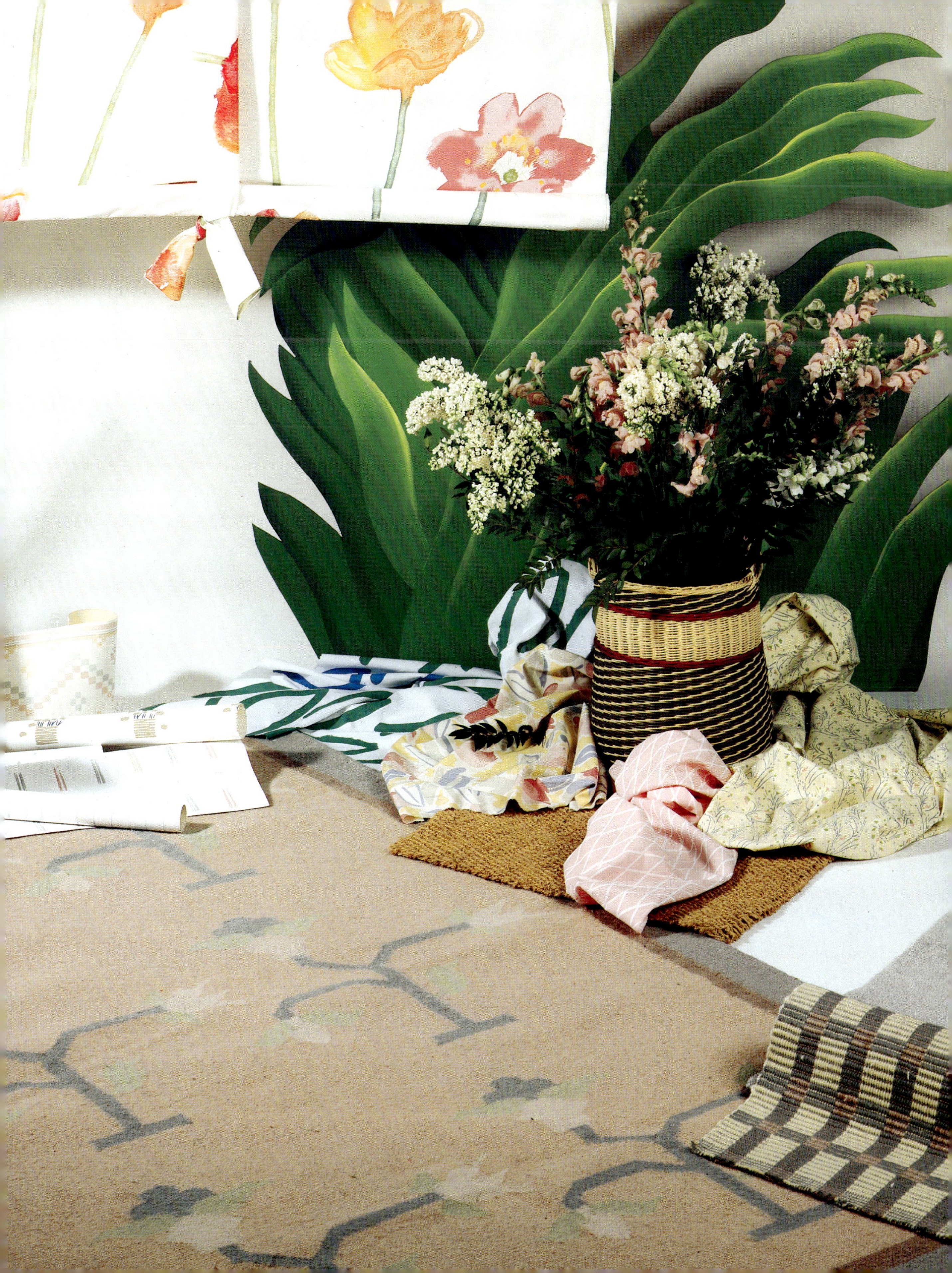

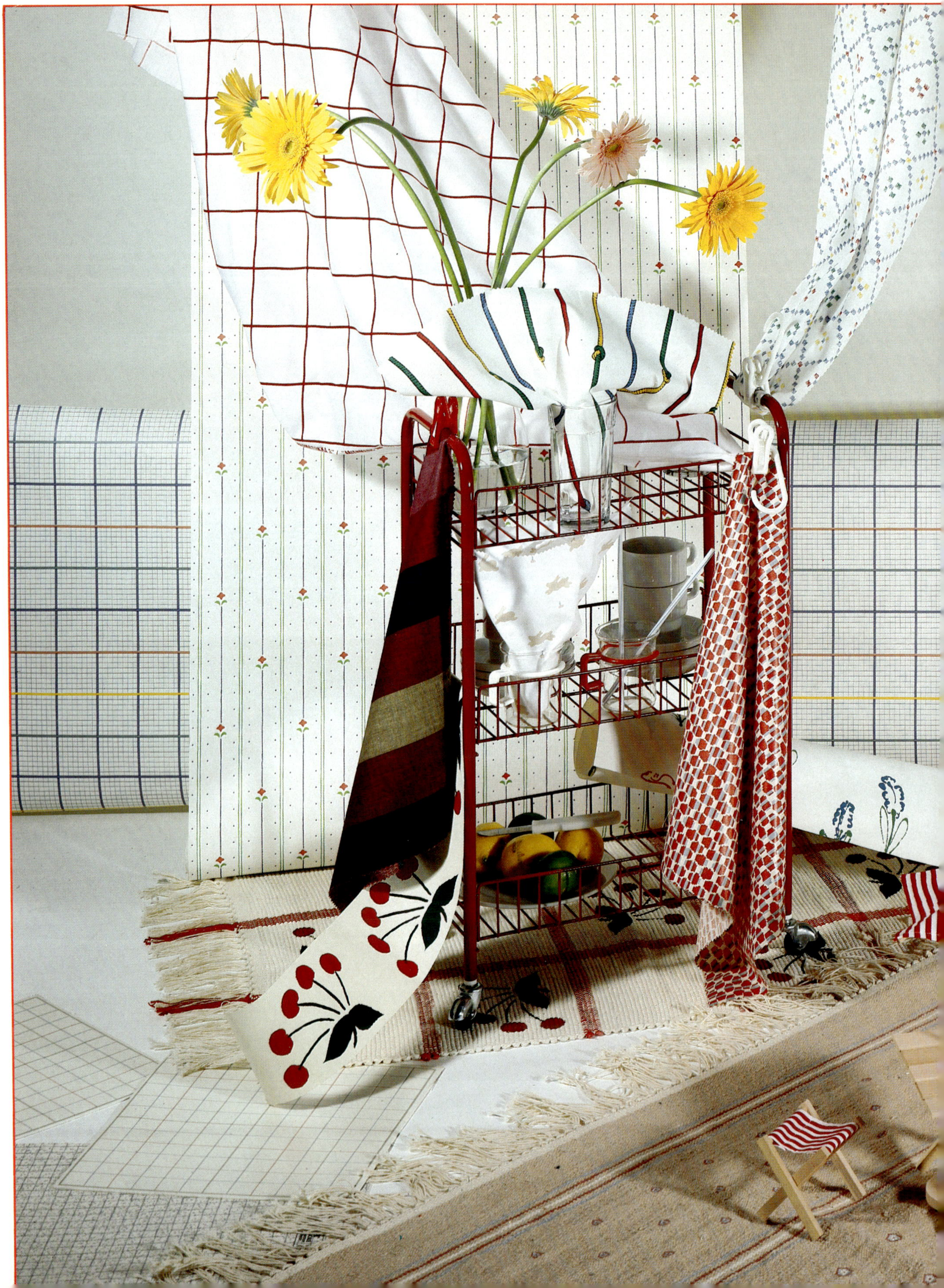

*Young Professional*

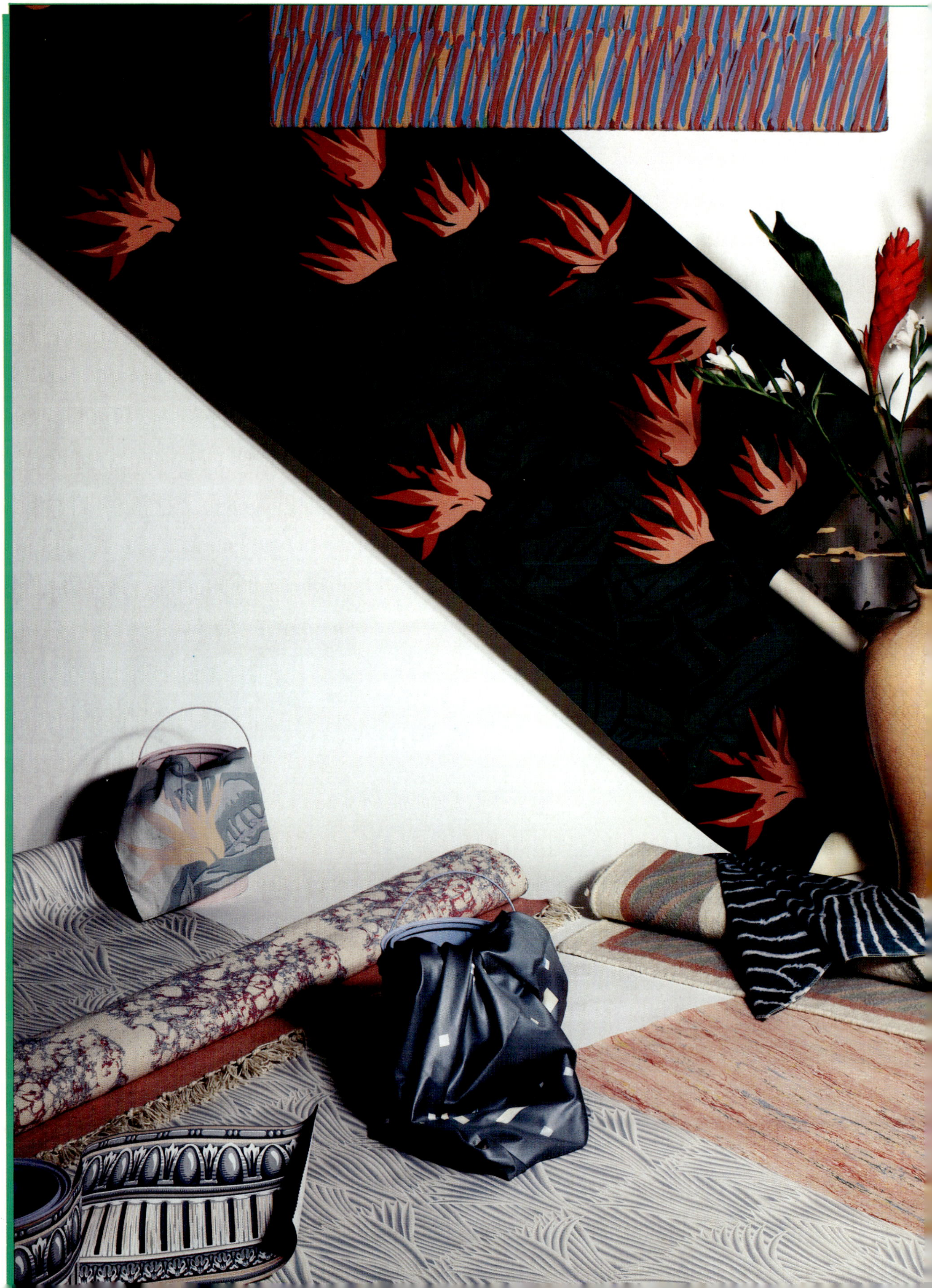

*Modernist*

# Futurist

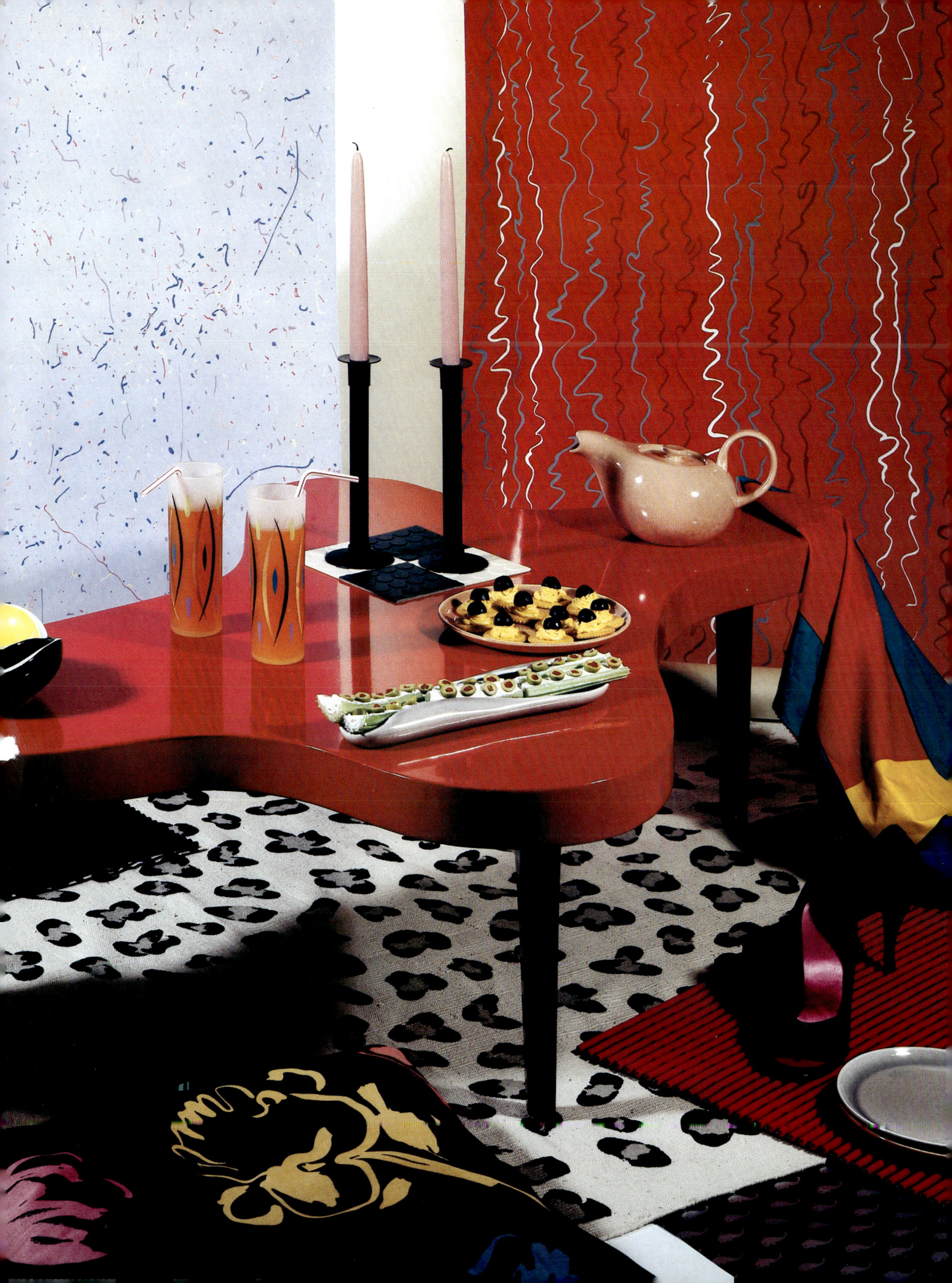

# PART THREE

# Your Personality Profile Sourcebook

### How to Shop for Your Personality Home Furnishings

How much you pay for the furniture you buy has little to do with whether your space is ultimately personal, well-designed, or even attractive. It's how the various elements mingle and relate to one another—and what they say about you—that determine how successful your decorating is.

Choosing essential furnishings such as dining room tables, seating, and beds, as well as items like lamps, clocks, carpeting, and paint, is all too often a fatiguing fifteen-round event. Shopping expeditions, coping with high-pressure salesclerks, agonizing over choices, and waiting for back-ordered merchandise can all add up to high anxiety.

**Using the Directories and Charts**

The individual furniture directories together with the full-color wallcovering and floorcovering charts will make your shopping more pleasant and productive. We encourage you to take the book along with you when you visit stores. Being able to point to specific pieces and patterns will save everyone involved considerable time and energy.

Although space does not permit us to include an exhaustive collection of interior furnishings for each personality, we culled countless examples during our research and have gathered here a sampler of today's prevailing modes. All products pictured are widely available at retail outlets or by mail. Items sold through mail order are indicated with this symbol: *

Because, in general, the period decorating personalities are more popular than the contemporary ones, there is, naturally, more furniture designed and produced in these styles. We found this to be true when conducting our review of companies and retailers in requesting product information and photographs. For this reason, you will find a greater selection of Traditionalist items than Futurist ones. Bear in mind, too, that two of the personalities, the Futurist and the Individualist, would be more likely to improvise and adapt furnishings or discovered finds in an inventive way that is characteristic of their decorating personalities. And these items cannot, of course, be pictured.

The directories are a means of narrowing—but not restricting—your furniture and accessory choices within the boundaries of the given personality style or styles you lay claim to. They will also expedite decisionmaking for those of you who are a synthesis of two or more personalities. Thus, if you are predominately a Traditionalist with shades of a Romanticist you can select more significant pieces by turning to the Traditionalist Directory, and add little Romanticist touches with accessories from the Romanticist Directory.

When you locate a product that interests you in one of the directories or charts, we suggest that you first check the manufacturer or retailer. If it's a name you've seen advertised in national magazines or newspapers—such as Henredon, Ethan Allen, or Marimekko—first visit or call the better department or furniture stores in your area, giving the manufacturer, along with any style number or name.

If you do not have access to these outlets, contact the company directly by consulting the alphabetical listing in the back of the book.

In agreeing to supply photographs of their products for inclusion here, manufacturers acknowledged their willingness to offer this consumer-referral service. When communicating with companies, consider posing these questions:

■ Where (store, address, telephone number) can I purchase the item in my locale? Describe in detail the product in question featured in this book. (If you live in a small town, refer to the closest major city where you shop.)

■ If there is no retail outlet within close proximity of my home, could you, if possible, please send details on how I can order this merchandise, either from you directly or from another source?

■ If this item is no longer available, do you manufacture a similar model or pattern? If so, please advise me of the style name and number. (The more specific your queries, the more helpful your response will most likely be.)

We have made every effort to check availability with individual manufacturers and retailers. In some cases, however, disappointment will be unavoidable. Furniture styles and wallpaper patterns are subject to change, although certainly not with the same frequency as in industries such as fashion or beauty.

You'll probably observe the most significant movement in contemporary furnishings, reflecting the latest trends and colors. In compiling the eight individual directories and color charts, we have included products that both we and our designer consultants felt would be available for some time after publication.

But if the chair or rug you had chosen is no longer being made, do not despair. In addition to writing the manufacturer to see if they make a comparable product, take the book with you when you shop and ask salesclerks to help you. Often, when styles are modified or upgraded, they are improved upon or the line expanded to include a wider range.

There will also be fluctuations in price, over which we have no control. So, rather than list here suggested retail prices, we have instead used the terms "Budget," "Moderate," and "Top of the Line" to give you a general guide to pricing. As a rule, major furnishings such as sofas and beds that retail for under one thousand dollars are considered "Budget." Those that sell from one thousand to twenty-five hundred dollars are "Moderate." And if you see a piece marked "Top of the Line," expect to pay more than twenty-five hundred dollars. Accessories and lighting fixtures priced under one hundred dollars will be marked "Budget," and those from one hundred to three hundred dollars, "Moderate," while anything that retails for over three hundred dollars is considered "Top of the Line." All accessory pieces are so marked.

# *The Naturalist* Sourcebook

**The Naturalist Bathroom**

## THE NATURALIST

No matter what the rest of their lives are like, when they come home, Naturalists want to find a cozy, comfortable, put-your-feet-up environment, which requires little upkeep and exudes informality.

Rooms in Naturalist homes tend to feel like small, warm farmhouse spaces, even if they're in big new houses. This is because Naturalists instinctively place furniture in intimate groupings. And since Naturalists are almost always inveterate collectors, walls, floors, and tabletops are usually filled with all the accessories—quilts, baskets, decoys, pottery, etc.—that give this style its distinctive flavor. This also makes space feel cozier.

If this is your personality, you can see the beauty and practicality an sell-worn furnishings of the past and are ingenious in finding new uses for them: a painted jam cupboard is recycled as a stereo cupboard; an old buggy seat, mounted on legs, is the perfect size for a love seat; a weather-beaten child's wagon now carries a nineteen-inch color television set in true country style.

Naturalists may buy fine country-style antiques, pieces with only some age but great appeal, or reproductions, depending on their tastes and pocketbook. If you peruse the many magazines and books now devoted exclusively to the "country" look, you'll see that Naturalist homes range from those furnished exclusively with the best examples of eighteenth- and early nineteenth-century pieces (we actually consider this a Naturalist-Classicist personality) to those that chummily blend the old and new to create a pleasing look, rather than an accurate recreation of the past.

Think of the colors you'd find around an old farmhouse in New England—barn red, stone blue, spruce green. These are the shades the Naturalist most favors in decorating. They tend to be subdued, but definitely not dull hues, and you usually feel nostalgic just looking at them!

In the past, few country homes had window treatments except where absolutely necessary for privacy. Today, too, Naturalists who are lucky enough to have a secluded home and good-looking windows (such as colonial-style six-over-six or twelve-over-twelve panes) will usually eschew any coverings.

Pictured Opposite: *Electrified pierced-tin ceiling lantern. Tape-back Shaker-style ladderback chair. Glass hurricane lamp with cut-out paper shade. Stenciled apothecary chest. Collections of fraktur paintings, redware plates, decoys, baskets, salt-glazed stoneware. Converted antique dry sink. Rag rug. Tin sconces with old pine mirror. Railed oak shelf/towel holder. Stenciled wall border.*

After bare windows, the most popular Naturalist treatments are tab curtains, usually in a homespun check or a stenciled or plain cotton, shutters, and café curtains. But never anything fancy or fussy.

Lighting also tends to be simple, and helps to create that warm glow one finds in Naturalist homes. Candles—in metal "hog scraper" and pottery candlesticks and old wooden spools made into candleholders—abound, but these, of course, are used mainly for atmosphere. On tabletops, most prefer lamps made from utilitarian objects (crocks, canning jars, antique bottles) and oil lamps. Wrought iron and/or wood chandeliers provide illumination from above.

Comfort and informality, then, are key words in the Naturalist decorating vocabulary, and probably in many other phases of their lives as sell. If you're a true Naturalist, chances are you cherish the days when you don't have to get dressed up, and you wouldn't hesitate to serve a buffet dinner to a crowd with a few of your guests sitting on floor cushions.

Since it's pointless to show antiques that would not be readily available across the country, the Naturalist decorating directory only presents the reproductions, adaptations, and new furnishings that we feel are compatible with this personality. We think you'll be pleased with the many choices you'll find here, and the many more available in the stores.

## Beverly Ellsley Talks About the Naturalist

"The family that lives in this house is, I feel, very representative of the Naturalist decorating personality. They are a suburban, two)career Family with active teenagers and a large dog.

"This style lends itself especially well to dogs and kids. It's casual but also very warm and inviting. People who choose this look generally want a living area they can walk into with feet muddy from the garden and not have to tiptoe around, worrying about where they'll step.

"The furnishings were purchased at area shops and at auctions; they're old, but they're not so precious they have to be kept under glass. One more nick or stain will just become part of the history of the piece. Tle fabrics aren't silk damasks but homespun and linen, which hold up well under wear and tear.

"There are, in general, certain colors that are favored by Naturalists, including barn red, mustard yellow, and a faded teal-turquoise blue. These shades are based on historical references, although in reality the original colors were much more intense. Today's Naturalists prefer more muted shades, but I've noticed Williamsburg is restoring in the original brighter tones, so we'll probably see this trend trickling down into residential use in the next few years.

"Naturalists respond to strong textural looks—fabrics that have weaves and furnishings with various wood grain surfaces. In colonial times, fabric and textiles were expensive and used sparingly. So our authentic American Naturalist room is one in which there is a lot of exposed wood (furniture legs and wood floors). This living room demonstrates the warm look of wood with minimal upholstery.

"I worked for variety when I designed this room. Early Americans rarely acquired more than one piece at a time, so nothing matched. I try never to have more than two matching chairs in the same room. The living room here is dominated by red and sharp, angular furniture lines, so the black-and-white Windsor chairs against the wall, with their starkly contrasting colors and round shapes, act as a foil to the rest of the room. This contrast is heightened by the bare wood floor and abundance of visible furniture legs.

"I also tried to blend different colors and wood textures. Here a grain-painted chest, matte-black painted chairs, and pine and maple pieces together give an authentic, mixed flavor to the space.

"I encouraged the owners to take up the former floor rug and they marveled at the difference it made. All of a sudden, lines, textures, and colors that had been obscured by the rug became more noticeable.

"Since the room pictured is the first one you enter in the house, the family wanted it to set the right tone—one of informal warmth. The room carries that let's-gather-round-the-fire-and-crack-nuts feeling. All it needs is a sleeping dog on the hearth —and theirs often obligingly curls up on the swan hooked rug."

## Profile of a Naturalist Couple

**Names:** Beth and Howard
**Residence:** Three-room co-op apartment
**Setting:** urban
**Occupations:** Beth—museum curator; Howard—attorney
**Pets:** Two cats, Gwendolyn and Cecily
**Favorite furniture styles:** country primitive
**Decorative materials preferred:** cottons, quilts, old homespun
**Favorite color scheme:** blue and white

**Most creative interior endeavor:** finding an antique jam cupboard to house the stereo
**Most treasured objects:** Amish quilt collection
**Decorating pet peeves:** cutesy reproduction country furnishings and "commercial" folk art
**Dream house:** Howard—Revolutionary-period stone house along the Brandywine River; Beth—country farmhouse with ramshackle charm
**Favorite at-home entertaining:** casual dinner parties
**Pastimes:** sporting events (basketball, baseball), museum-going, antiquing
**Ideal getaway:** antiquing in New England, Pennsylvania
**Philosophy:** "What we like about the country look is that it's an easy-to-live-with style, one that allows us to create that warm, comfortable atmosphere we both want. When we come home at night we both like to change into casual clothes and unwind. Our decorating style helps us accomplish that."

The first piece of furniture Beth and Howard bought for their new apartment ten years ago was an old mahogany Chippendale-style secretary they found in a secondhand furniture store. "That first purchase set the tone for us," said Beth. "From that point on we knew we'd decorate in a traditional style."

The progression from formal Early American-style furniture to country was a natural one, growing out of their fondness for folk art and crafts, both antique and contemporary. Their initial country purchase was an antique buggy seat, which they fashioned, complete with needlepoint cushions, into a love seat.

As their collection of antiques grew, they found they were able to favorably use old elements to soften the more modern and utilitarian. For example, they threw an antique quilt over the back of the necessary contemporary sleep sofa, housed the stereo components in an old jam cupboard, and hung tieback curtains across the shower doors in the bathroom.

Their folk art collection also combines old and new, from antique baskets, nineteenth-century samplers, and worn weather vanes to contemporary primitive paintings. What gives them the greatest pleasure, though, is seeking out distinctive quilts, primarily Amish ones. For Howard, who admits to harboring contemporary tastes in art, the Amish quilts are the ideal synthesis. "Their rich, bold colors and abstract geometric patterns satisfy the modern side of me."

They feel another plus of the country style is its ability to harmonize with other looks. Both the bathroom, with its fresh blue-and-white motif and wicker accessories, and the bedroom, featuring a skirted table, country Victorian dresser complete with a pitcher and bowl set, and ruffled curtains, bear a touch of the sentimental. "We slept in a bed just like this one at a Vermont inn once," Howard noted, pointing to their white wrought-iron-and-brass bed. "And," he continued, "Beth was determined to find one just like it."

"We did," interjected Beth, "several years later, and it then took another two years to have the bed restored properly. Practically everything we've bought has a story to it."

Both Beth and Howard are more than willing to expend the necessary time and patience to find their furnishings. "For us," Beth explained, "outfitting our living space is more than just decorating. It's become a unifying factor in our lives. Weekend day trips and vacations are often planned around antiques shows and places where we know there are lots of good dealers."

Their most protracted search to date was recently rewarded when they found six matching antique painted country Windsor chairs to use with their country French dining table. "Sure, it took nine years to find them, but we had a lot of fun—and a lot of good memories—searching for them," Beth and Howard both agreed.

## *The Naturalist* Personality Window Treatments

Wallpaper border or hand-stenciled window trim.

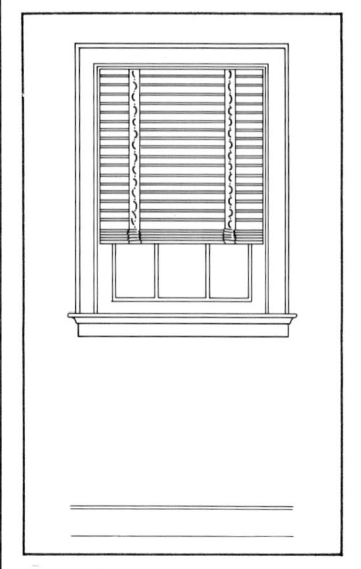

Wooden blinds with decorative cotton webbing tapes.

Reversible gingham swag with wooden pineapple hold backs.

Homespun café curtains combined with café-style shutters.

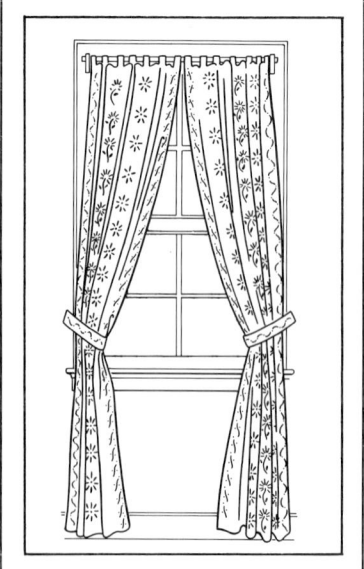

Plain muslin tie café curtain with swag.

Café curtains with swag.

## Major Furnishings

**Name:** Hutch table*
**Item no:** 1056
**Company:** Simms & Thayer Cabinet-makers, Inc.
**Dimensions:** 72"W X 34"D X 29"H
**Materials:** Pine
**Price range:** Moderate
**Note:** Available in oval or rectangular top.

**Name:** Hand-painted 1820 trunk
**Item no:** 14-0747
**Company:** Habersham Plantation Corporation
**Dimensions:** 38"W X 13"D X 23"H
**Materials:** Pine
**Price range:** Budget

**Name:** The Northampton wing chair*
**Company:** The Seraph
**Dimensions:** 23"W X 21-1/2"D X 47"H
**Price range:** Budget

|  | Major Furnishings | Accessories and Lighting |
|---|---|---|
| Budget | under $1,000 | under $100 |
| Moderate | $1,000-$2,500 | $100-$300 |
| Top-of-the-Line | over $2,500 | over $300 |

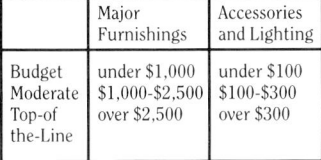

*Designates mail order

69

**Name:** The Granby sofa*
**Company:** The Seraph
**Dimensions:** 66"W, 72"W or 86"W X 21"D X 33"H
**Price range:** Budget

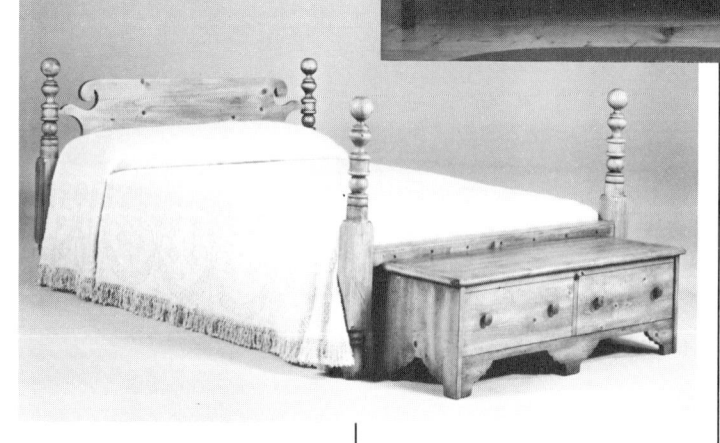

**Name:** Cannonball bed; two drawer chest
**Item nos:** 675-38 (bed); 4945-33 (chest)
**Company:** The Lane Company
**Dimensions:** 65"W X 89-1/2"D X 40-1/4"H (bed); 54"W X 16"D X 16-1/2"H (chest)
**Materials:** Pine (both)
**Price range:** Budget (both)

**Name:** Pie safe
**Item no:** 23-1437
**Company:** Habersham Plantation Corporation
**Dimensions:** 39"W X 14"D X 60"H
**Materials:** Pine
**Price range:** Budget (painted or stained)

**Name:** Shaker desk top and bottom
**Item no:** 53-2201
**Company:** Habersham Plantation Corporation
**Dimensions:** 34"W X 21"D X 67"H
**Materials:** Pine
**Price range:** Budget (stained); Moderate (painted)

**Name:** Mt. Lebanon settee*
**Item no:** F241
**Company:** Shaker Workshops
**Dimensions:** 43-1/4"W X 19"D X 37-1/2"H
**Materials:** Maple, cotton canvas seat tape
**Price range:** Budget

**Name:** Settle*
**Item no:** 2040
**Company:** Simms & Thayer Cabinet-makers, Inc.
**Dimensions:** 48"W X 17"D X 48"H
**Materials:** Pine
**Price range:** Moderate

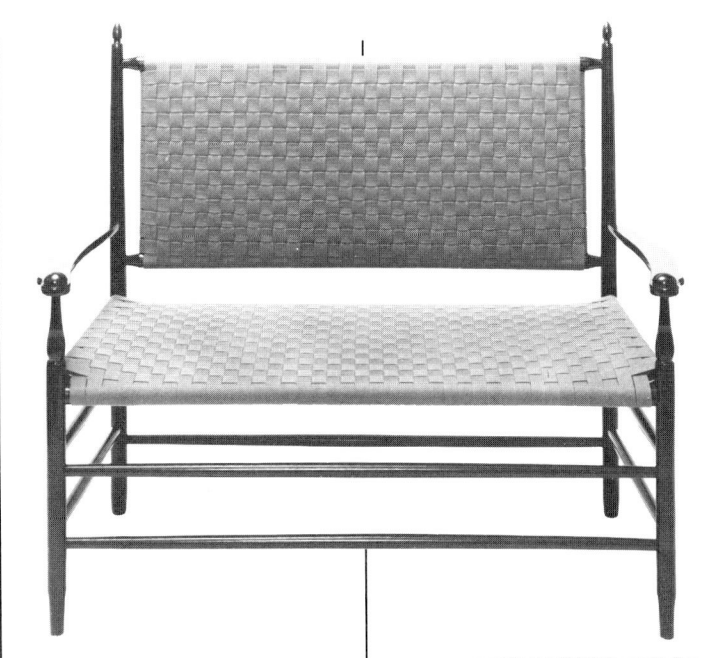

**Name:** Armoire
**Item no:** 17-0830
**Company:** Habersham Plantation Corporation
**Dimensions:** 48"W X 23"D X 79"H
**Materials:** Pine
**Price range:** Moderate (painted or stained)

71

**Name:** Trestle table*
**Company:** Shaker Workshops
**Dimensions:** 5', 6', 7', 8'W X 33"D X 29"H
**Materials:** Pine, maple
**Price range:** Budget

**Name:** Windsor comb-back armchair*
**Company:** William H. James Co./Stephen A. Adams, Furnituremakers
**Dimensions:** 17"W X 47"H
**Materials:** Maple; pine
**Price range:** Budget

**Name:** Twig canopy bed*
**Item no:** 5000
**Company:** Amish Country Collection
**Dimensions:** Available in twin, double, queen, and king.
**Materials:** Hickory twig
**Price range:** Moderate

**Name:** Five-drawer chest*
**Company:** William H. James Co./Stephen A. Adams, Furnituremakers
**Dimensions:** 35"W X 18"D X 48"H
**Materials:** Curly maple
**Price range:** Moderate

**Name:** Connecticut cupboard*
**Item no:** 2025
**Company:** Simms & Thayer Cabinet-makers, Inc.
**Dimensions:** 61"W X 19-1/4"D X 81"H
**Materials:** Pine
**Price range:** Moderate

**Name:** Open hutch with china base
**Item nos:** 675-65 (hutch); 675-64 (base)
**Company:** The Lane Company
**Dimensions:** 60-3/4"W X 16"D X 46-1/2"H (hutch); 60-1/4"W X 18"D X 39"H (base)
**Materials:** Pine
**Price range:** Moderate (two pieces)

**Name:** Amish courting seat*
**Item no:** 700
**Company:** Amish Country Collection
**Dimensions:** 48"W X 37"D X 48"H
**Materials:** Oak, cherry or walnut with hickory
**Price range:** Budget

**Name:** Tall pie safe*
**Item no:** 3-18-3562
**Company:** Sturbridge Yankee Workshop
**Dimensions:** 14"W X 12-1/2"D X 47"H
**Materials:** Pine; punched tin
**Price range:** Budget

**Name:** Herb chest*
**Item no:** 2035
**Company:** Simms & Thayer Cabinet-
  makers, Inc.
**Dimensions:** 56"W X 12"D X 35"H
**Materials:** Pine
**Price range:** Moderate

**Name:** Queen Anne camelback sofa
**Item no:** 20-7163
**Company:** Ethan Allen Inc.
**Dimensions:** 81"W X 35"D X 35"H
**Materials:** Selected hardwoods
**Price range:** Moderate

**Name:** Tilt-top table
**Item no:** 19-9309
**Company:** Ethan Allen Inc.
**Dimensions:** 36" diameter X 29"H
**Materials:** Pine
**Price range:** Budget

**Name:** Hand-painted wedding chest
**Item no:** 17-2120
**Company:** Habersham Plantation Corporation
**Dimensions:** 52"W X 22"D X 29"H
**Materials:** Pine
**Price range:** Moderate

**Name:** The Country Classic love seat*
**Company:** The Seraph
**Dimensions:** 58"W, 74"W or 86"W X 20"D X 36"H
**Price range:** 58"W (Budget); 74"W and 86"W (Moderate)

**Name:** Pie safe*
**Item no:** 2030
**Company:** Simms & Thayer Cabinetmakers, Inc.
**Dimensions:** 40"W X 18"D X 57"H
**Materials:** Pine; punched tin
**Price range:** Budget

**Name:** William and Mary chest*
**Item no:** 2034
**Company:** Simms & Thayer Cabinetmakers, Inc.
**Dimensions:** 40-1/2"W X 20"D X 40-1/2"H
**Materials:** Pine
**Price range:** Moderate
**Note:** Available in different woods and with two or four drawers.

75

# Accessories

**Name:** American Legacy Residence folding screen
**Item no:** 59-1700
**Company:** Habersham Plantation Corporation, Licensee for "An American Legacy"
**Dimensions:** 67"W X 2"D X 78"H
**Materials:** Pine
**Price range:** Top of the line

**Name:** Salt-glazed pitcher*
**Item no:** 5035
**Company:** Neat and Tidy, Rowe Pottery
**Dimensions:** 8"H (one quart capacity)
**Materials:** Stoneware, blue cobalt design
**Price range:** Budget

**Name:** Shaker wood box*
**Item no:** F941
**Company:** Shaker Workshops
**Dimensions:** 23"W X 8"D X 32-1/4"H
**Materials:** Poplar painted old red
**Price range:** Moderate

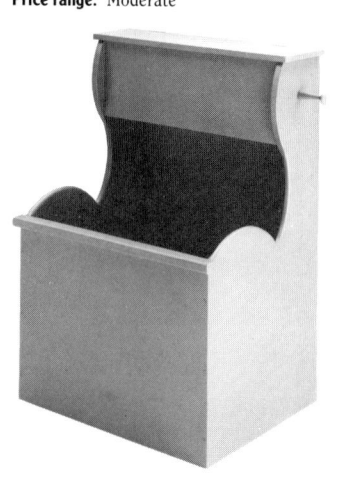

**Name:** Table-top desk
**Item no:** 53-0916
**Company:** Habersham Plantation Corporation
**Dimensions:** 24"W X 11"D X 20"H
**Materials:** Pine
**Price range:** Moderate (unpainted); Top of the line (painted finish)

76

**Name:** Sweet Elizabeth doll*
**Item no:** 6041
**Company:** Neat and Tidy
**Dimensions:** 21"H
**Materials:** Fabric
**Price range:** Budget

**Name:** Towel rack*
**Item no:** F211
**Company:** Shaker Workshops
**Dimensions:** 33-7/8"W X 13"D X 33-1/2"H
**Materials:** Pine
**Price range:** Budget

**Name:** North Star fireback*
**Item no:** FB002
**Company:** Pennsylvania Firebacks, Inc.
**Dimensions:** 21-1/2"W X 19-1/2"H X 3/4" thick
**Materials:** Cast iron
**Price range:** Moderate

**Name:** Heart quilt*
**Item no:** 4033
**Company:** Neat and Tidy
**Dimensions:** 20"W X 21"H
**Materials:** Assorted calicoes
**Price range:** Moderate

**Name:** Miniature rack*
**Item no:** 430
**Company:** Faith Mountain Country Fare
**Dimensions:** 12"W X 14"H
**Materials:** Sponge-painted wood
**Price range:** Budget

**Name:** Fan mirror
**Item no:** 19-9301
**Company:** Ethan Allen, Inc.
**Dimensions:** 24"W X 44"H
**Materials:** Pine
**Price range:** Moderate

# Lighting

**Name:** Chandelier*
**Item no:** 12B
**Company:** Gates Moore Early American Designs of Lighting Fixtures
**Dimensions:** 23" dia.; 11"H (at hook)
**Materials:** Pewter-coated distressed tin
**Price range:** Moderate

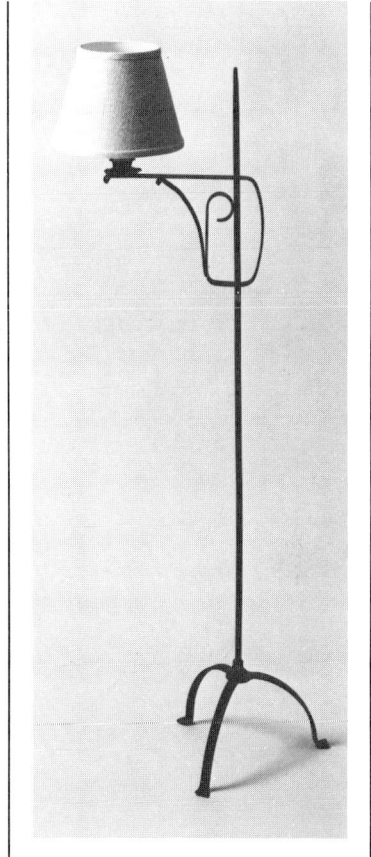

**Name:** Early candlestand lamp*
**Item no:** 488
**Company:** Cohasset Colonials
**Dimensions:** 52"H
**Materials:** Wrought iron, burlap shade
**Price range:** Budget

**Name:** Willow lamp*
**Item no:** 30130
**Company:** Lt. Moses Willard, Inc.
**Dimensions:** 16"W X 27"H
**Materials:** Tin
**Price range:** Budget

**Name:** Large storage jar lamp
**Item no:** 203
**Company:** Norman Perry
**Dimensions:** 23-1/2"H
**Materials:** Ceramic base, hardback paper shade
**Price range:** Moderate

**Name:** Wall sconce*
**Item no:** 8C
**Company:** Gates Moore Early American Designs of Lighting Fixtures
**Dimensions:** 8"W X 12"H
**Materials:** Pewter-coated distressed tin
**Price range:** Budget

**Name:** Hanging willow lantern*
**Item no:** 30141
**Company:** Lt. Moses Willard, Inc.
**Dimensions:** 8"W X 13-1/2"H
**Materials:** Tin
**Price range:** Budget

**Name:** Dedham table lamp*
**Item no:** 7184X
**Company:** Pot-pour-ri
**Dimensions:** 18"H
**Materials:** Dedham pottery, pleated linen shade
**Price range:** Budget (high)

**Name:** Animal chandelier*
**Item no:** 50151
**Company:** Lt. Moses Willard, Inc.
**Dimensions:** 24" dia. X 16"H
**Materials:** Wood, tin
**Price range:** Moderate

# *The Romanticist*
# Sourcebook

**The Romanticist** Nursery

## The Romanticist

Champions of personal expression in its most evocative form, Romanticists draw from an extensive and varied design reserve. They might warm to the look of an antique Renaissance-revival turn-of-the-century table with carved base and inlaid top, or to a reproduction wicker settee, fancifully scrolled, with pillows fashioned from garden-fresh chintz.

In spatial terms, a Romanticist setting can be achieved by placing wood upholstered furnishings in close, intimate groupings against a flurry of various paints, fabrics, and wallcoverings, in complex patterns and rich shades. Or, they may prefer something less cluttered, more akin to the mood of a weathered beachfront house, with exposed wood floors, little upholstery, a soft, muted color scheme, and a few furnishings in light materials. Both create an idyllic, almost nostalgic, mood, but in contrasting ways.

There's also a great diversity in the color and fabric preferences of Romanticists. Although most are partial to the pastel, ice-cream parlor shades, some may also respond to bolder crimsons, greens, and purples. Romanticists favor the warmth conveyed by yards of materials, be it skirted upholstery, ruffled pillows, tables with layered cloths, plush throws and wall-to-wall carpeting, needlepoint area rugs, or pastel dhurries. Brocades, velvets, organza, silk, damasks, polished cottons, needlepoint, lace—all are different in texture, but all convey a sensuousness that is the badge of the Romanticist decorating personality.

Romanticists' love affair with material extends into their window treatments as well. These take the form of deeply ruffled tiebacks, shirred valances, sheer panels paired with lace or velvet draperies or held back with ornamental tassels, cord, and porcelain knobs, or balloon shades in fabrics like taffeta.

Lighting adds to the overall mood, with dainty boudoir and wall-mounted lamps with painted or etched-glass shades, luxurious crystal chandeliers, and candles—lots of them, not just for special occasions, but for everyday use—set in silver candleholders or glass candelabras with hanging crystal prisms.

If you are a true Romanticist you wear your personality

Pictured Opposite: *Painted trompe l'oeil bow border on walls. Bouffant draperies with gathered, pleated valance. Skirted love seat. Eyelet-draped bassinet. Collections of antique picture frames, band boxes, and silver ornaments. Portuguese needlepoint rug. Frosted-glass night lamp. Painted china cabinet with trompe l'oeil painted trellis.*

mantle with confidence in your decorating *and* in your life. You have a keen sensitivity to detail, whether you're setting a table for a dinner party with a creative mixture of unmatched painted porcelain and handwritten placecards, or accessorizing an outfit with frilly jabots, picture hats, and antique jewelry.

In their interiors, Romanticists might frame a collection of crocheted gloves or fans in a gold-leaf flea-market frame and display it in the bedroom. Or they might decorate their kitchen with a collection of heart-shaped cookie cutters above the sink, an assortment of hand-embroidered towels on a display rack, and eyelet dresser scarfs for café curtains.

Collectibles, mementos, clothing, furnishings—all are incorporated into the Romanticist decor in exciting and imaginative ways.

Rich in detail, color, and fabric, the range of Romanticist furnishings shown here will express your personal style. Whether you prefer the more ornate atmosphere typical of a Victorian parlor or the lighter mood characterized by a wraparound summer porch, we think you'll find plenty from which to choose.

## Stanley Hura Talks About the Romanticist

Debra J. DeBoise

"I think the Romanticist would feel very ill at ease in a stark white setting sparsely furnished. Theirs is a more intricate and lavish look—an interior landscape that enhances both them and the possessions they cherish.

"Above all, Romanticists strive to create an atmosphere of beauty in their surroundings, one they can then draw their friends into, to enjoy and appreciate. Details play a key role, whether it's juxtaposing textures and colors or adding shirring or a bow in an unexpected place, which will ultimately catch the eye.

"Romanticists often have a few surprises up their lacy sleeves. They're devotees of period novels and parasol strolls, but they might just as easily embark on a rigorous canoe trip or keep abreast of contemporary theatre.

"I think they tend to be just as creative and unpredictable in their shopping habits, too. They might deplete their clothing allowance on good quality carpet or a rug, but then find a pile of old lace and a leather trunk at a bazaar for a pittance and do something smashing with them in the same room as the pricey floorcovering.

"This underlying contrast is evident in our room here. The

prevailing tempo certainly evokes all that is soft and alluring. Yet notice how the dark Chippendale chairs add to this sensuous mood while also serving as a kind of counterpoint to the white iron bed and light woods. The same can be said for the Venetian mirror next to the scrubbed pine piece. Yet these seemingly diverse elements are orchestrated in such a way that they all work together.

"Even though there is a lot happening in this room—it really explodes with detail and objects—I don't think it's what you would call cluttered. A sense of overall organization reigns here. Romanticists pursue a leisurely order that harks back to a less frenetic time. And color has a major role.

"In this room the soft blues and mauves of the walls, bedding, and skirting are elegant looking, but because the fabric is affordable sheeting, the result is an accessible, practical one. Price does not dictate or inhibit the design flair of the Romanticist.

"What I particularly like about this room is that even if it isn't your cup of tea and crumpet, there's a reassuring unfussiness about it that makes you want to visit, get to know the occupant, walk around and explore—and that's what successful, rewarding personal decorating is all about."

## Profile of a Romanticist Couple

**Names:** Allison and Tom
**Residence:** co-op duplex, built in the 1880s
**Setting:** urban
**Occupations:** Allison—writer; Tom—attorney
**Pet:** one dog, Tai, a Chinese Sharpei
**Favorite furniture styles:** high Victorian (Renaissance and Louis XV rococo revivals), Duncan Phyfe
**Decorative materials preferred:** velvet, lace, silk damask, satin, fringed and tasseled materials, brocaded and embroidered fabrics
**Favorite color schemes:** jewel tones—burgundy, rose, emerald green, accented with ivory and black; sage green and cream; apricot and ivory
**Most creative interior endeavor:** renovating the bathroom to give it an opulent nineteenth-century mood and twentieth-century convenience
**Most treasured object:** nineteenth-century Baccarat chandelier
**Decorating pet peeves:** rooms stripped of all personal mementos, 1950s styles, museumlike period looks in houses
**Dream house:** mid-nineteenth-century carriage house
**Favorite at-home entertaining:** small dinner parties, dessert get-togethers
**Pastimes:** restoring their co-op, horseback riding, antiquing, going to the ballet

**Ideal getaway:** "anywhere with good riding and antiquing, especially restored inns and ranches."

**Philosophy:** "We came to our decorating style via the antique doll houses Allison has been collecting and furnishing with nineteenth-century pieces for more than fifteen years. We love the highly decorative and visually stimulating look achieved by mixing different textures like dark, carved woods, lace, velvet, and gilding. And when we moved into our 'antique' duplex, which was already rich in period detail, it all came together."

When Allison and Tom were first married, they were drawn to turn-of-the-century golden oak furniture. It was affordable, available, and worked well in their apartment.

"But when we moved into our duplex, we felt the oak was too rustic. We wanted a more formal look, and the decorative, carved woods of Victorian pieces suited us beautifully," pointed out Tom. Their first purchase for the new house, therefore, was an ornate mahogany pier mirror. That piece, with its marble and carving and gilding, proved to be a major influence on future purchases.

Some of the couple's most beloved furnishings have filtered down from their families. These include an abbreviated recamier sofa (which Allison's grandfather made), velvet pillows from her grandmother, sconces, and a "gout stool" from her parents.

Other pieces are auction and antiques show—even garage sale—finds. "We rescued a 1920s chair and had it restored," said Tom. "We discovered the frame was European. We had such fun doing research to select a compatible fabric for it. Now I know I have a unique chair—and that's important to me."

The uniqueness of individual furniture pieces is important, but different pieces must work together in the room to create a special mood. "I want the living room to be like a jewel box, full of elements that will dazzle and hold the eye—different textures, colors, and objects," Allison commented. The living room is rich indeed with sumptuous detail: a fur throw, lace curtains, satin upholstery, a leather-topped Duncan Phyfe table, velvet-tufted window seat (where Tai, their exotic dog, holds court), porcelain figurines, Allison's antique miniatures, and a splendid array of artwork, from feather pictures to mezzotints.

The Victorian era was, of course, a golden age of portraiture, and Allison and Tom avidly collect prints and paintings of horses and dogs and have themselves posed for formal-style portraits. A favorite of theirs is a primitive-style painting of the entire family, Tai included, depicting them in nineteenth-century garb.

The feeling in the rose-painted bedroom is luxuriously romantic, highlighted by a marble-topped chest, dark wicker bedside table, and a valentine-patterned brass bed with a brilliant Victorian crazy quilt on the wall overhead.

A recent "jewel box" renovation involved a five-by-five-foot (exclusive of tub) bathroom. Although the space is small, Allison and Tom nonetheless managed to introduce the same elegant materials they used throughout the house—mahogany (vanity), brass (fixtures and accessories), crystal (chandelier), and lace (shower curtain).

Standing by her dollhouses, Allison observed, "When we're finished, our house will probably resemble one of my dollhouses. I feel I've done it all before. And that's fine—it's like bringing a fantasy to life."

## The Romanticist Personality Window Treatments

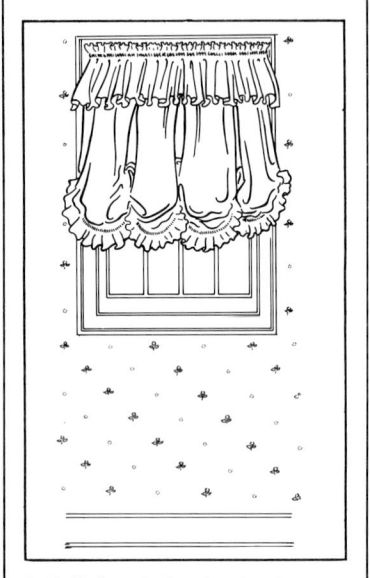

Ruffled balloon shade with gathered valance.

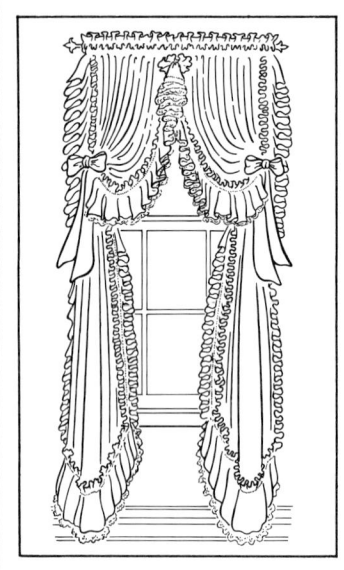

Double-ruffled curtains and bow tiebacks.

Lace divided panel with swag valance and porcelain hold-backs.

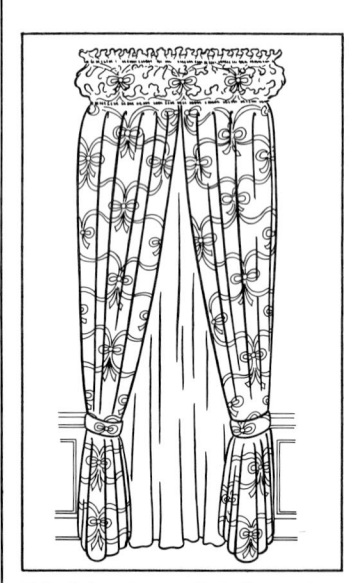

Tieback draperies, smocked valance with underlayer sheers.

Eyelet café curtains with wallpaper border trim (or stencil).

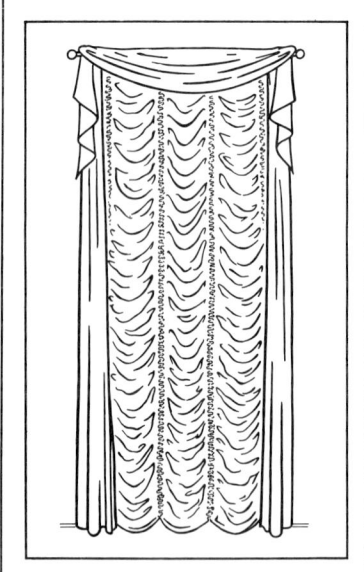

Floor-length Austrian shade with swag valance.

88

## Major Furnishings

**Name:** Carved armchair
**Item no:** 6055
**Company:** Casa Stradivari
**Dimensions:** 23"W X 24"D X 38"H
**Materials:** Beechwood frame
**Price range:** Budget

**Name:** The St. Louis bed
**Company:** The Charles P. Rogers Brass Bed Company
**Dimensions:** (King) 78-3/4"W X 89-1/2"D X 41-1/2"H (footboard) X 65"H (headboard)
**Materials:** Brass
**Price range:** Moderate

**Name:** Georgetown sofa
**Item no:** 77-7014
**Company:** Pennsylvania House
**Dimensions:** (outside) 88"W X 36"D X 33"H
**Materials:** Available in over 700 decorator fabrics.
**Price range:** Moderate
**Note:** Also available as a love seat.

|  | Major Furnishings | Accessories and Lighting |
|---|---|---|
| Budget | under $1,000 | under $100 |
| Moderate | $1,000-$2,500 | $100-$300 |
| Top-of the-Line | over $2,500 | over $300 |

*Designates mail order

**Name:** Double dresser
**Item no:** 5114
**Company:** O'Asian Designs, Inc.
**Dimensions:** 60"W X 22"D X 30"H
**Materials:** Woven rattan core
**Price range:** Moderate

**Name:** Beacon Hill chair, Laura Ashley Collection by Bridgeford
**Item no:** 7002
**Company:** Henredon Furniture
**Dimensions:** 32"W X 35"D X 32"H
**Price range:** Budget

**Name:** Great Hill Road secretary desk
**Item no:** 399
**Company:** Riverside Furniture Corporation
**Dimensions:** 34"W X 21"D X 57"H
**Materials:** Oak
**Price range:** Budget

**Name:** Rocking chair, Et Cetera Collection by Drexel
**Item no:** 584-274
**Company:** Drexel Heritage Furnishings, Inc.
**Dimensions:** 21-1/2"W X 42-1/4"D X 38"H
**Materials:** Wood, cane, wrought iron
**Price range:** Budget

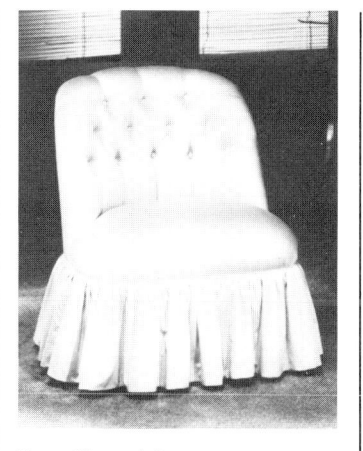

**Name:** Slipper chair
**Item no:** 968
**Company:** Hickory/KayLyn, the KayLyn, Inc. subsidiary
**Dimensions:** 30-1/2"W X 26"D X 32"H
**Price range:** Budget

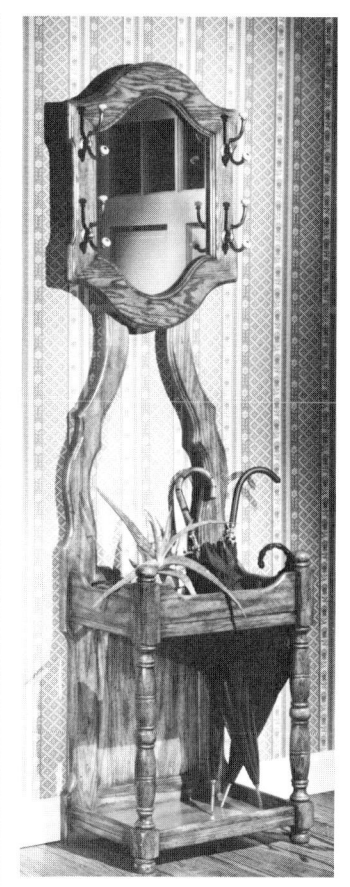

**Name:** Great Hill Road hall tree
**Item no:** 5311
**Company:** Riverside Furniture Corporation
**Dimensions:** 26"W X 14"D X 76"H
**Materials:** Oak
**Price range:** Budget

**Name:** Camelback sofa*
**Company:** Magnolia Hall
**Dimensions:** 73"W X 31"D X 40"H
**Materials:** Mahogany
**Price range:** Budget

**Name:** Junior dining room set
**Item no:** 1754
**Company:** Typhoon International
**Dimensions:** 60"W X 36"D X 29-1/2"H;
  side chair: 17"W X 20"D X 34"H;
  hostess chair: 22"W X 20"D X 34"H
**Materials:** Ratan core reed wicker, glass
  (cushions included)
**Price range:** Moderate (7 pieces)

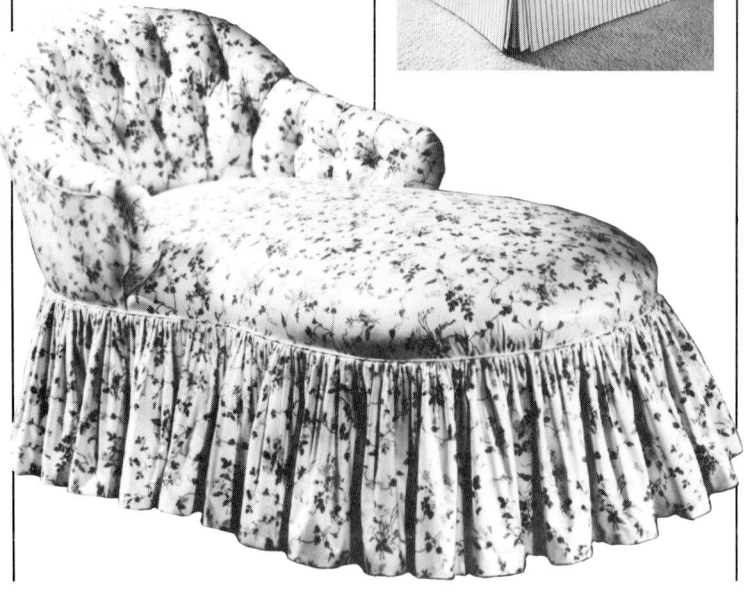

**Name:** Derby chair, Laura Ashley Collection by Bridgeford
**Item no:** 7057
**Company:** Henredon Furniture
**Dimensions:** 27"W X 34"D X 31"H
**Price range:** Budget

**Name:** Gents chair*
**Item no:** 50177
**Company:** Martha M. House
**Dimensions:** 27"W X 22"D X 38"H
**Materials:** Mahogany
**Price range:** Budget

**Name:** Chaise
**Item no:** 9619
**Company:** KayLyn, Inc.
**Dimensions:** 60"W X 29-1/2"D X 33"H
**Price range:** Moderate

**Name:** Carlisle chair and ottoman, Laura Ashley Collection by Bridgeford
**Item no:** 7022
**Company:** Henredon Furniture
**Dimensions:** 31"W X 34"D X 34"H
**Price range:** Budget (individually); Moderate (both)

**Name:** Abigail Walker Armless Chair*
**Company:** Magnolia Hall
**Dimensions:** 19"W X 23"D X 38"H
**Materials:** Mahogany
**Price range:** Budget

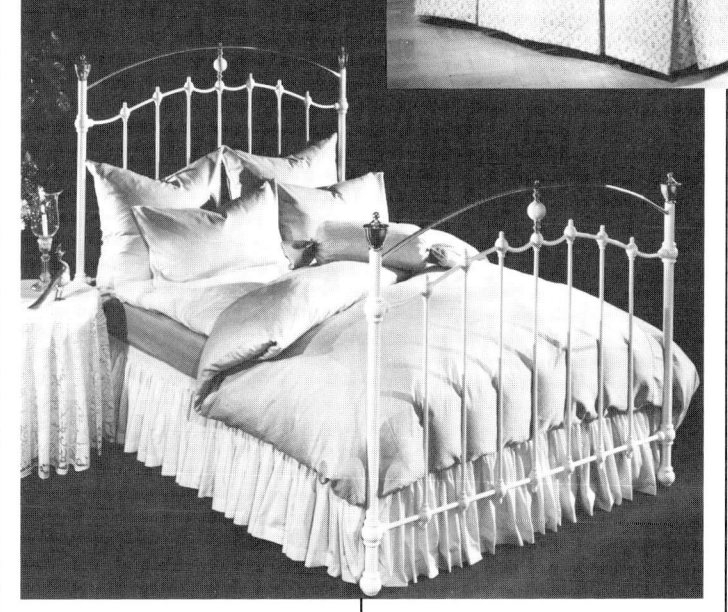

**Name:** Anniversary bed
**Designer:** Bella Ross
**Item no:** 504
**Company:** J/B Ross
**Dimensions:** (Queen) 64"H (headboard); 49"H (footboard)
**Materials:** White iron, brass
**Price range:** Budget

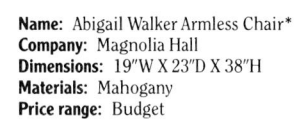

**Name:** Ashley sofa
**Item no:** 60-6601
**Company:** Pennsylvania House
**Dimensions:** (outside) 82-1/2"W X 34"D X 32-1/2"H
**Materials:** Available in over 700 decorator fabrics.
**Price range:** Moderate

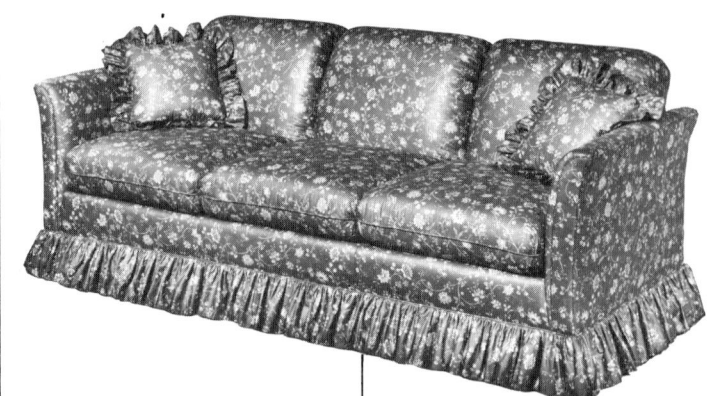

**Name:** Sofa and cocktail table
**Item nos:** 1285-95 (sofa); 1064 (cocktail table)
**Company:** O'Asian Designs, Inc.
**Dimensions:** 76"W X 34"D X 32"H (sofa); 37"W X 37"D X 16"H (table)
**Materials:** Woven rattan core
**Price range:** Budget (both)

**Name:** Ambiance dining chair
**Item no:** 405CU
**Company:** Ficks Reed Company
**Dimensions:** 28"W X 26"D X 32"H
**Materials:** Wicker
**Price range:** Budget

**Name:** Kent chair, Laura Ashley Collection by Bridgeford
**Item no:** 7017
**Company:** Henredon Furniture
**Dimensions:** 21"W X 33"D X 32"H
**Price range:** Budget

## Accessories

**Name:** Earthenware
**Item no:** Series 226
**Company:** Nora Fenton
**Dimensions:** 10"H (tallest piece)
**Materials:** Earthenware
**Price range:** Budget to moderate, variety of sizes

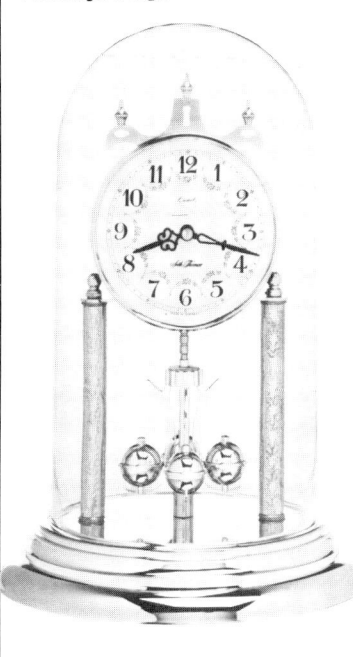

**Name:** Oak box*
**Company:** Jeanne Van Etten
**Dimensions:** 6-1/2" dia. X 2-3/4"H
**Materials:** Oak
**Price range:** Budget
**Note:** Also available in oval shape.

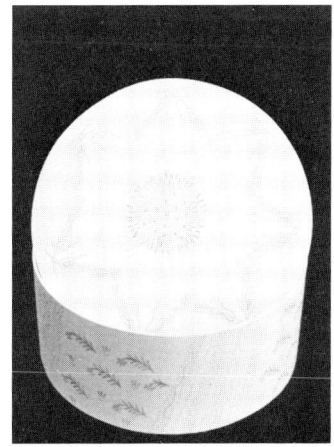

**Name:** Poise anniversary clock
**Item no:** 165
**Company:** Seth Thomas
**Dimensions:** 7-3/4" dia. X 11-3/8"H
**Materials:** Brass
**Price range:** Budget

95

**Name:** Painted basket*
**Company:** Jeanne Van Etten
**Dimensions:** 8" dia. X 14"H
**Materials:** Wicker
**Price range:** Budget

**Name:** Porcelain
**Item no:** Series 3800
**Company:** Nora Fenton
**Dimensions:** 6" dia. (box); 12"H (cachepot)
**Materials:** Porcelain
**Price range:** Budget to moderate

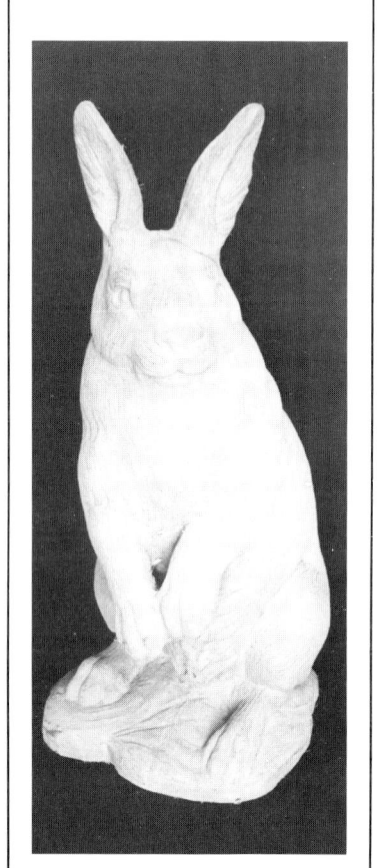

**Name:** French hare*
**Item no:** 63
**Company:** Ballard Designs
**Dimensions:** 21"H
**Materials:** Cement
**Price range:** Budget
**Note:** Also available in plaster.

# Lighting

**Name:** Calla lily chandelier
**Item no:** 21826AE
**Company:** Chapman Lamps
**Dimensions:** 33" dia. X 26"H; 3" chain length
**Materials:** Iron finish
**Price range:** Top of the line

**Name:** Table lamp*
**Item no:** T115
**Company:** Victorian Lighting Company
**Dimensions:** 20"H
**Materials:** Brass
**Price range:** Moderate

**Name:** Stained-glass table lamp*
**Item no:** 7163X
**Company:** Pot-pour-ri
**Dimensions:** 11"H
**Materials:** Porcelain, stained glass, brass
**Price range:** Moderate

**Name:** Table lamp*
**Item no:** T130
**Company:** Victorian Lighting Company
**Dimensions:** 15"H
**Materials:** Brass, glass
**Price range:** Budget

**Name:** Illuminated frosted glass lamp
**Item no:** L89
**Company:** Nora Fenton
**Dimensions:** 24"H
**Materials:** Italian handblown glass, silk shade
**Price range:** Moderate

**Name:** Table lamp*
**Item no:** T125
**Company:** Victorian Lighting Company
**Dimensions:** 27"H
**Materials:** Brass, glass
**Price range:** Moderate

**Name:** Wall sconce*
**Item no:** 0060-1
**Company:** Victorian Lighting Company
**Dimensions:** Projects 11"
**Materials:** Brass, glass
**Price range:** Budget

**Name:** Oak library lamp*
**Item no:** 1-16-0910
**Company:** Sturbridge Yankee Workshop
**Dimensions:** 15"H
**Materials:** Stained glass, brass, velvet-lined well
**Price range:** Moderate

**Name:** Broadmoor wall lamp*
**Item nos:** 30520 (green shade); 30521 (amber shade)
**Company:** Renovator's Supply
**Dimensions:** 5-3/4" dia. X 13" projection
**Materials:** Brass, glass
**Price range:** Budget

**Name:** Gas wall lamp*
**Item no:** 30519
**Company:** Renovator's Supply
**Dimensions:** 7-1/2"W X 12" projection
**Materials:** Brass, diamond daisy shade
**Price range:** Budget

**Name:** Windsor wall lamp*
**Item nos:** 30516 (green shade); 30517 (amber shade)
**Company:** Renovator's Supply
**Dimensions:** 13" projection
**Materials:** Brass, glass
**Price range:** Budget

**Name:** Two-light wall bracket
**Item no:** P2924
**Company:** Progress Lighting
**Dimensions:** 16"W; 9-1/2"H; extends 8-3/4"
**Materials:** Glass, brass
**Price range:** Moderate

**Name:** Lace hanging lamps*
**Item nos:** Left: KHL (white); Center; ZHL (white or beige); Right: DHL (white or beige)
**Company:** Rue de France
**Dimensions:** 14" dia. X 5"D
**Materials:** Lace, wire frame, white cord
**Price range:** Budget

**Name:** Iris Spring tablelamp
**Item no:** 4407
**Company:** Alsy Corporation, Cycle II Division
**Dimensions:** 27-1/2"H
**Materials:** Clear crystal, brass, white shirred shade
**Price range:** Moderate

**Name:** Gaslight parlor fixture*
**Item no:** 32502
**Company:** Renovator's Supply
**Dimensions:** 24″ dia. X 28-1/2″H
**Materials:** Brass, diamond daisy shade
**Price range:** Top of the line

**Name:** Double-arm swivel bracket*
**Item no:** 23198
**Company:** Renovator's Supply
**Dimensions:** 5-1/2″ dia. X 25″ projection
**Materials:** Brass, ruffled gas shade
**Price range:** Budget

**Name:** Table lamp*
**Item no:** T140
**Company:** Victorian Lighting Company
**Dimensions:** 16″H
**Materials:** Brass, glass
**Price range:** Moderate

**Name:** Flexible-arm table lamp*
**Item no:** T135
**Company:** Victorian Lighting Company
**Dimensions:** 14″H (flexed)
**Materials:** Brass, glass
**Price range:** Moderate

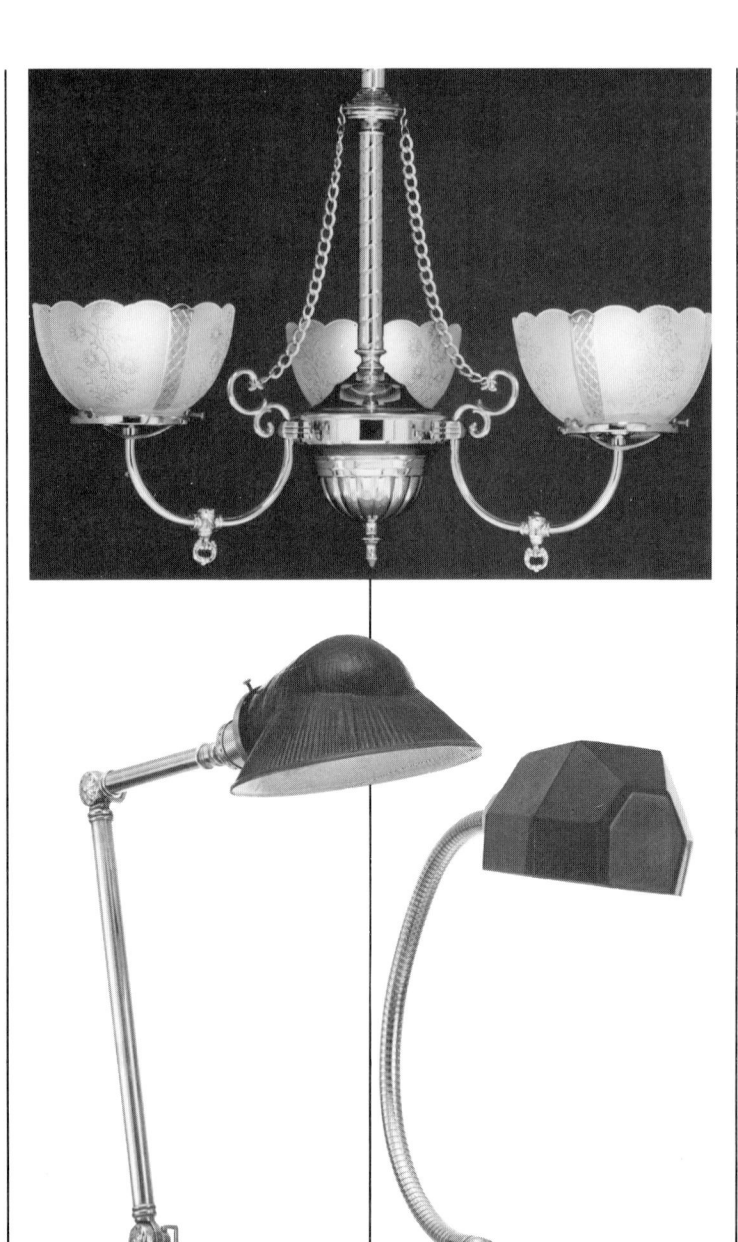

100

# *The Traditionalist* Sourcebook

## The Traditionalist Office/Study

## The Traditionalist

Traditionalist decorating personalities have a strong appreciation of the rich heritage of interior styles of the past. In designing their homes, they draw from several different looks, yet in such an uncontrived way that everyone who enters feels at ease. And most people who decorate in this style will probably have entertaining stories behind some of their favorite pieces, be it a silver tea set, a piece of antique porcelain, or a prized portrait.

In fact, there's so much latitude within this style that the possibilities are far-ranging. Traditionalists' love of color and fabrics extends from a more subdued seafoam and peach to emboldened forest green and oxblood, in woven fabrics (jacquards, nubby linens, wool plaid), smooth, glazed cottons like chintz, and documentary fabrics reproduced from those found in historic homes.

The Traditionalist prototype room, the apartment of designer Georgina Fairholme, encompasses many of the elements we expect to see in these personality settings—a bounty of fabrics, comfortable seating, often skirted, and displays of family and travel mementos and collectibles. Yet she has added her own personal touch by lending a light, airy delicacy to the room. Perhaps many might consider the style of Miss Fairholme's living room to be a mixture of a number of different looks. Well, we believe that good Traditionalist decorating is very often a result of this tasteful pastiche of more than one style.

Many Traditionalists might feel comfortable with wooden or ornamental valances (often coordinated with wallcoverings and upholstery fabrics) and fuller-than-full draperies (energy-saving, too!). Fabric-covered shades, painted shutters, tiebacks, and draperies over sheers are also successfully incorporated into Traditionalist rooms.

Because Traditionalists often have an assortment of friendly niches in their homes, they are able to take advantage of a wide repertoire of lighting fixtures. These might include a pharmacy lamp on a desk, a brass shell floor light for reading next to a wing chair, a wooden or pewter chandelier over the dining room table, a picture light illuminating an oil (perhaps an "ancestor" portrait), swing-arm lamps with soft shades

Pictured Opposite: *English rolltop desk. Red glazed walls. Antique hutch for storage (glass set in bottom doors). Metal campaign chest mounted on legs. Schoolhouse regulator clock. Green pull-down shades with natural oak shutters. Duxbury swivel desk chair. Antique model car collection. Pewter oil lamp. Reproduction Colonial Turkish rug. Tufted leather sofa. Green-cased-glass-and-brass desk lamp. Victorian frosted glass-and-brass ceiling fixture.*

over the bed, and ceramic-based table lamps in the living room.

If you are a Traditionalist, you love the comforts of home and enjoy opening it to others. You may throw a holiday brunch for a crowd, but prefer dinners for six or so. You may also enjoy working on home-related projects, sewing curtains for a child's room, or redoing a small bathroom yourself.

But most of all, you want your surroundings to reflect the appreciation you have of integrating good design in furniture, accessories, and fabrics. Because of this, you're always attuned to new ideas—such as the way chairs are arranged in the library of an inn where you're vacationing.

The Traditionalist directory that follows is as varied as the Traditionalist decorating personality. Featured is an assortment of styles in well-made reproduction adaptations. Yet Traditionalists also appreciate modestly priced antiques and may spend hours visiting antiques shows and shops looking for that right accessory. Should you prefer a more casual look (perhaps in the family room), consult the Naturalist directory for ideas; or, for a more formal space, such as the dining room, browse the Classicist directory. And, for a bedroom (yours or a guest room), a bit of the Romanticist might inspire you!

## Georgina Fairholme Talks About the Traditionalist

Tom Bernsten

"Before I moved into my highrise apartment a couple of years ago, I'd always lived in places characterized by period details like elaborate moldings and fireplaces. This is my first modern living space, and it was in many ways a refreshing challenge.

"The rooms, with their boxy conformity, lacked any real architectural interest, but I was attracted to the strong light that poured in through the windows. I also like the clean, unfettered lines of the rooms, which didn't dictate any choice of style.

"Basically I wanted to keep the apartment simple and use an abundance of color. I chose shades I've always liked but never had a chance to work with in my earlier homes. I decided to sponge-glaze the walls a cool lime green since the west light is so strong. The green works just as well in summer as in winter.

"The apartment is really a blend of old and new in a modern setting. To give the living room a finished—and more traditional—

look, I added a cornice molding. Many of the pieces are antiques, but there are a few new ones, too. The slipper chair and rug are new, but the coffee table and newly covered chintz chair are old friends. Like many Traditionalists, I like to combine favorite old furnishings with newly acquired pieces.

"I'm a collector, as you can see; many of the objects have been in my family. It's comforting to have them around me to care for. Who else will look after them if family won't! The portraits over the sofa (which is new, by the way) are of my great-great-aunts and are always placed prominently wherever I live. I've found that Traditionalist decorators often share these feelings about treasuring family possessions.

"I needed a place for my china and book collections, so I came up with the idea of the alcove. In most apartments like this, the space is usually used as a dining area because of its proximity to the kitchen. For me the alcove adds interest to the room, is practical (the divan is a bed), and it gives me the display space I need.

"Everyone who sees my apartment comments on how they're struck by the atypical mood it conveys. Well, I suppose that's what makes it so personal—I've put my English stamp on a New York high-rise urban apartment."

## Profile of a Traditionalist Couple

**Name:** Jane and David
**Children:** Becky, age 13, and Allan, age 7
**Residence:** brownstone, built 1877
**Setting:** urban
**Occupations:** Jane—homemaker, part-time teacher; David—business executive
**Pet:** One dog, Fudge, a poodle
**Favorite furniture styles:** Queen Anne, Chippendale
**Decorative materials preferred:** cotton shirting, striped satins, heavy linens
**Favorite color schemes:** rose, gray, and white; red, white, and blue
**Most creative interior endeavor:** building window seats for two bedrooms with storage areas underneath and upholstering the seats
**Most treasured object:** early-nineteenth-century cupboard inherited from Jane's family
**Decorating pet peeves:** angling major pieces in the corners of rooms; anything Art Deco
**Dream house:** new, nineteenth-century-inspired shingle-style with porch and cedar-shake roof
**Favorite at-home entertaining:** brunches, large and small (a traditional

one is on New York City Marathon day, when runners go right by their house)

**Pastimes:** Jane—redecorating the house, entertaining; David—gardening, entertaining

**Ideal getaway:** Sea Island, Georgia; cruise to Bermuda; their seaside summer house

**Philosophy:** "I love our house and taking care of the things in it, especially those pieces from our families. I try to create an elegant but comfortable look, a mood that's romantic without ruffles and lace, rooms that are inviting without being too casual or lived-in."—Jane

An inviting, caring sense of the past permeates the rooms of Jane and David's three-story brownstone, set on a busy urban street. For when they moved here, their first house, both sets of parents gave them several pieces of traditional furniture, with which Jane and David had each grown up. These furnishings then became the loving focal point of their decor.

"You could say David and I were both steeped in a traditional background, but it's a look we feel at ease with—and many of the pieces are very special to us." Jane observed.

In particular, the way Jane decorates is strongly tied to her fond memories of her childhood. The Sheraton-style cupboard, now in their living room, is a good example. "I remember how my father used to periodically take out the objects and show them to my sister and me," Jane recalled. "I think he hoped that one day we would love them as much as he and Mother did."

The classic cupboard shares the room with a more opulent Victorian armchair and matching love seat, both upholstered in blue velvet, as well as an eighteenth-century Chippendale-style wing chair covered in a reproduction print fabric. The different periods appear wonderfully at home in the high-ceilinged room with its ornamental white marble fireplace and French doors leading out to the deck and small garden below.

The easy formality of the house is punctuated here and there with a few rustic touches. Accenting the dark mahogany Duncan Phyfe table and chairs in the dining room are two quilts hanging on facing walls, one made by a former hometown neighbor.

Throughout the house is evidence of Jane's sewing ability and creative energies. She upholstered the dining room chairs, sewed curtains for all the windows, and made seat cushions for the bedroom window seats. "Because of my part-time job, I don't have as much time as I'd like to fix up the house, but I love doing it when I get the chance," Jane said.

With Jane's background in art history to guide them, the couple enjoys adding to their art books, paintings, and prints, as well as to their growing collection of porcelain and ornamental objects. "We can't afford the furniture at the antiques shows we go to, but we usually manage to find an affordable box or print," commented David.

Although Jane and David both take pleasure in acquiring and displaying their possessions, Jane fantasizes about one day living in a house with "maybe only one object on each tabletop and few, if any, rugs. "But," she added, "we probably couldn't live like that—we're too attached to the things we've collected over the years. And someday, we hope, the children will have them to look after."

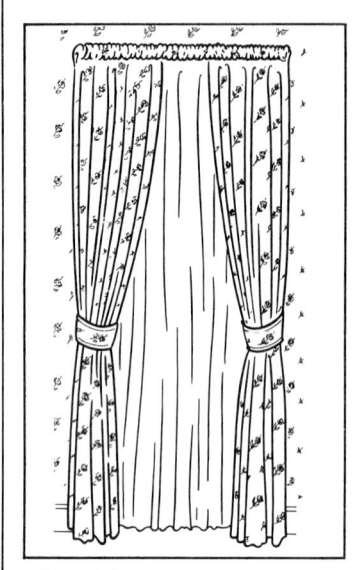

## The Traditionalist Personality Window Treatments

Full-length draperies with piped tiebacks and tightly shirred valance.

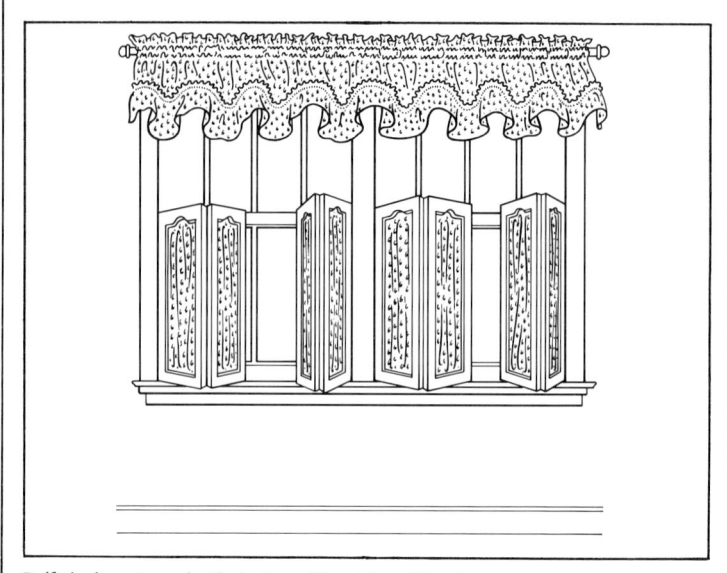

Ruffled valance teamed with shutters with matching fabric insets.

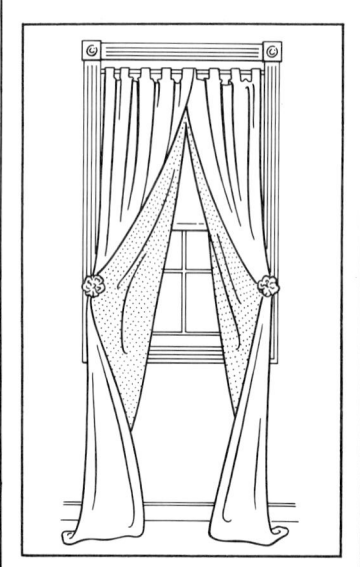

Fold-back tab draperies with contrasting lining.

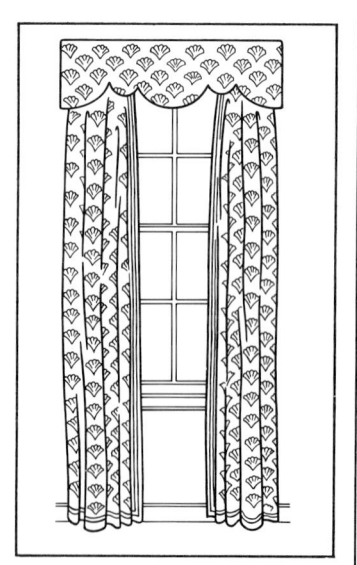

Coordinated scalloped cornice set over draperies with ribbon trim.

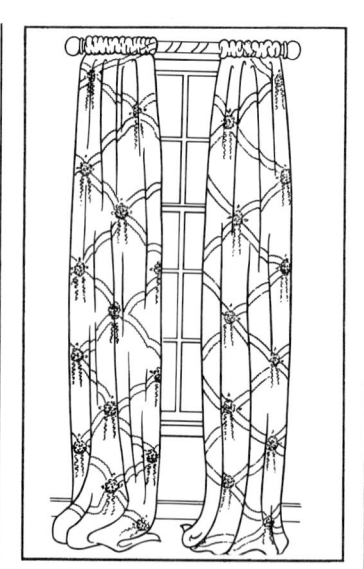

Oversize wooden rod trompe l'oeil painted, with tightly gathered draperies.

# Major Furnishings

**Name:** Sofa
**Item no:** 1005
**Company:** Harden
**Dimensions:** (outside) 83"W X 32-1/2"D X 32"H
**Price range:** Moderate

**Name:** Tufted leather sofa
**Item no:** 22-936
**Company:** Century Furniture Company
**Dimensions:** 86-1/2"W X 36"D X 33"H overall; arm height 28"
**Materials:** Leather, wood (feet and frame)
**Price range:** Top of the line

**Name:** Lowboy
**Item no:** 71-701
**Company:** Century Furniture Company
**Dimensions:** 33"W X 19"D X 31-1/2"H
**Materials:** Oak solids and veneers
**Price range:** Moderate

**Name:** Yorke lounge chair and ottoman
**Item no:** 60-1726 (chair); 60-2759 (ottoman)
**Company:** Pennsylvania House
**Dimensions:** (outside) 31-1/2"W X 33"D X 36"H (chair); 25-1/2"W X 24"D X 19"H (ottoman)
**Materials:** Available in over 700 decorator fabrics.
**Price range:** Budget (both)

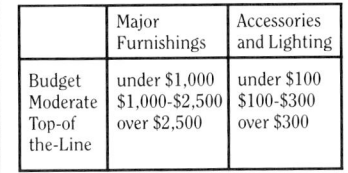

|  | Major Furnishings | Accessories and Lighting |
|---|---|---|
| Budget | under $1,000 | under $100 |
| Moderate | $1,000-$2,500 | $100-$300 |
| Top-of-the-Line | over $2,500 | over $300 |

*Designates mail order

109

**Name:** Regal Buckingham sleep sofa
**Company:** Castro Convertibles
**Dimensions:** (Twin beds) 88"W X 35"D X 27"H
**Materials:** Wood frame, polydacron cushion, cotton upholstery
**Price range:** Moderate

**Name:** Chippendale dining table, Georgian Court
**Item no:** 11-6063
**Company:** Ethan Allen
**Dimensions:** 70"W X 42"D X 29"H closed; 106"W X 42"D leaves open
**Materials:** Solid cherry
**Price range:** Moderate

**Name:** Upholstered host dining chair
**Item no:** 11-883
**Company:** Century Furniture Company
**Dimensions:** (overall) 26"W X 29-1/2"D X 50"H
**Materials:** Upholstered frame
**Price range:** Moderate

**Name:** Corner china cabinet
**Item no:** 11-6226
**Company:** Ethan Allen, Inc.
**Dimensions:** 42"W X 22"D X 76"H
**Materials:** Cherry
**Price range:** Moderate

**Name:** Wing chair
**Item no:** 942
**Company:** Harden
**Dimensions:** (outside) 24-1/2"W X 23"D X 31-1/2"H
**Materials:** Cherry (legs)
**Price range:** Budget

**Name:** Pencil-post canopy bed
**Item no:** 71-175, 5/0 size
**Company:** Century Furniture Company
**Dimensions:** 65"W X 87"D X 84"H
**Materials:** Oak solids and veneers
**Price range:** Moderate

**Name:** Eighteenth-century dresser
**Item no:** 17-2116
**Company:** Habersham Plantation
**Dimensions:** 68"W X 21"D X 37"H
**Materials:** Cherry
**Price range:** Moderate

**Name:** Queen Anne highboy*
**Company:** The Bartley Collection, Limited
**Dimensions:** 40-1/2"W X 22-1/4"D X 74"H
**Materials:** Cherry or mahogany
**Price range:** Top of the line

111

**Name:** Cabriole coffee table*
**Company:** Richard Bissell Fine Woodworking
**Dimensions:** 42"W X 18"D X 16"H
**Materials:** Cherry
**Price range:** Budget

**Name:** Shansi dining table and chairs
**Item nos:** 330-12-3 (table); 331-61-3 (armchair); 331-62-3 (side chair)
**Company:** White of Mebane
**Dimensions:** 74"W X 44"D (table); 23-1/2"W X 17"D X 39-1/2"H (armchair); 20-1/2"W X 16"D X 39-1/2"H (side chair)
**Materials:** Rock maple (hand-padded finish, mandarin or sand)
**Price range:** Table (moderate); chairs (budget)

**Name:** Console/game table*
**Company:** The Bartley Collection, Limited
**Dimensions:** (closed) 31"W X 15"D X 29"H
**Materials:** Cherry or mahogany
**Price range:** Budget

**Name:** Chaise
**Item no:** 11-615
**Company:** Century Furniture Company
**Dimensions:** (overall) 31-1/2"W X 63"D X 35"H
**Materials:** Upholstered frame
**Price range:** Moderate

**Name:** Queen Anne side chair
**Item no:** 1760-82
**Company:** Hickory Manufacturing Company, "The American Masterpiece Collection"
**Dimensions:** 24"W X 22-1/2"D X 39"H
**Materials:** Mahogany finishes
**Price range:** Budget
**Note:** Also available with hand-painted Chinoiserie finish.

**Name:** Cocktail table, Vintage Cherry Collection by Drexel
**Item no:** 184-157
**Company:** Drexel Heritage Furnishings, Inc.
**Dimensions:** 46"W X 18"D X 18"H
**Materials:** Cherry woods
**Price range:** Budget

**Name:** Queen Anne wing chair
**Item no:** 20-7613-5
**Company:** Ethan Allen
**Dimensions:** 34"W X 31"D X 44"H
**Materials:** Cherry legs
**Price range:** Moderate

**Name:** Tall lingerie chest, Vintage Cherry Collection by Drexel
**Item no:** 124-400
**Company:** Drexel Heritage Furnishings, Inc.
**Dimensions:** 24"W X 17"D X 54"H
**Materials:** Cherry woods
**Price range:** Budget

**Name:** Console table
**Item no:** 1777
**Company:** Schott Furniture
**Dimensions:** 29"W X 16-1/2"D X 28"H
**Materials:** Mahogany
**Price range:** Budget

**Name:** Upholstered dining chair
**Item no:** 11-880
**Company:** Century Furniture Company
**Dimensions:** (overall) 25"W X 28-1/2"D X 39-1/2"H
**Materials:** Upholstered frame
**Price range:** Budget

**Name:** Armoire, Vintage Cherry Collection by Drexel
**Item no:** 124-440
**Company:** Drexel Heritage Furnishings, Inc.
**Dimensions:** 50-1/2"W X 21"D X 74-1/4"H
**Materials:** Cherry woods
**Price range:** Moderate

**Name:** Queen Anne powder table and bench
**Item no:** 124-310
**Company:** Drexel Heritage Furnishings, Inc.
**Dimensions:** 45"W X 20-1/2"D X 29-1/2"H
**Materials:** Cherry woods
**Price range:** Budget (Individually); Moderate (both)

**Name:** Chest on chest
**Item no:** 17-2145
**Company:** Habersham Plantation
**Dimensions:** 40"W X 22"D X 72"H
**Materials:** Solid ponderosa pine, brass
**Price range:** Moderate

## Accessories

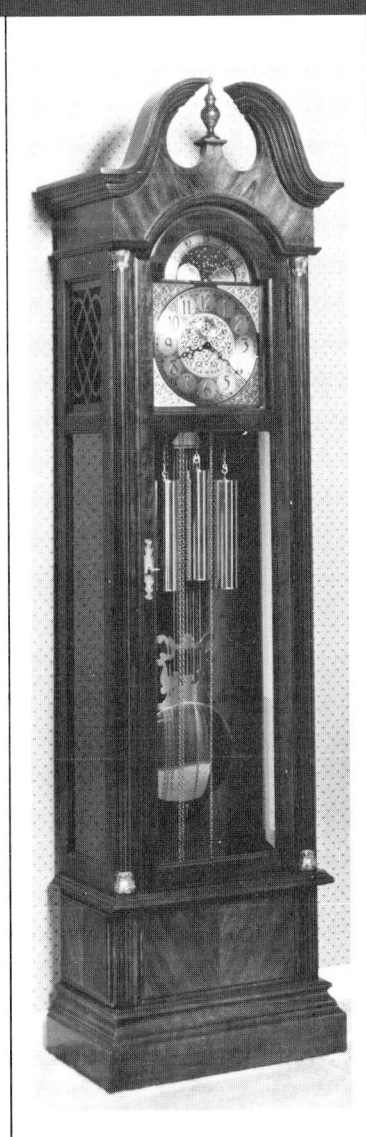

**Name:** Schoolhouse clock
**Item no:** 2367
**Company:** Seth Thomas
**Dimensions:** 14"W X 3-3/4"D X 21-1/2"H
**Materials:** Pine
**Price range:** Moderate

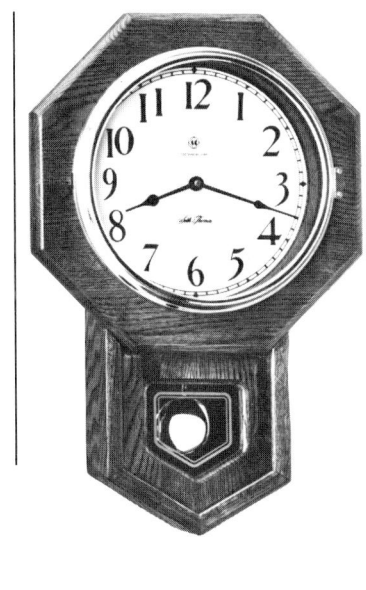

**Name:** Gallery rail
**Item no:** C-965-BB
**Company:** Amerock Corporation
**Dimensions:** 20"W; (5) 2-1/2" posts
**Materials:** zinc die cast
**Price range:** Budget

**Name:** Brandeis grandfather clock
**Item no:** 610-305
**Company:** Howard Miller Clock Company
**Dimensions:** 23-1/4"W X 13-1/2"D X 82-3/8"H
**Materials:** Cherry, brass
**Price range:** Top of the line

**Name:** Globe
**Item no:** 4700120
**Company:** S.P. Skinner Company
**Dimensions:** 12"W X 21"H
**Materials:** Wood base and frame; Old World map
**Price range:** Moderate

**Name:** Wall cabinet
**Item no:** 1016
**Company:** Schott Furniture
**Dimensions:** 24"W X 8-1/2"D X 33"H
**Materials:** Mahogany
**Price range:** Top of the line

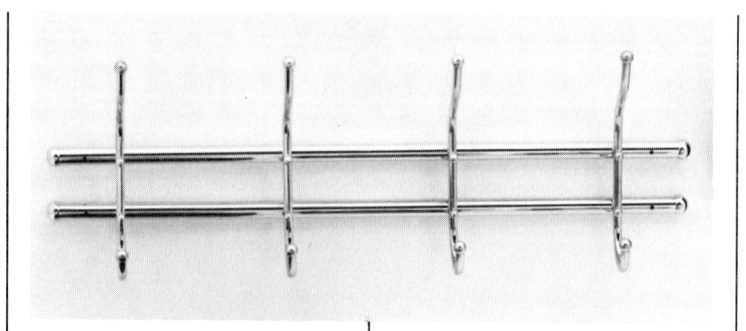

**Name:** Four-hook wall rack
**Item no:** 1214020
**Company:** S.P. Skinner Company
**Dimensions:** 36"W X 13"H
**Materials:** Brass
**Price range:** Moderate

**Name:** Calligraphic box
**Item no:** 43-5041
**Company:** Ethan Allen, Inc.
**Dimensions:** 19"W X 11-1/2"D X 12"H
**Materials:** Wood, brass
**Price range:** Moderate

**Name:** Costumer
**Item no:** 076075
**Company:** S.P. Skinner Company
**Dimensions:** 73"H
**Materials:** Brass
**Price range:** Moderate

**Name:** McKnight wall clock
**Item no:** 612-672
**Company:** Howard Miller Clock Company
**Dimensions:** 13-5/8"W X 7"D X 30-5/8"H
**Materials:** Solid cherry, elm burl, brass, beveled glass
**Price range:** Top of the line

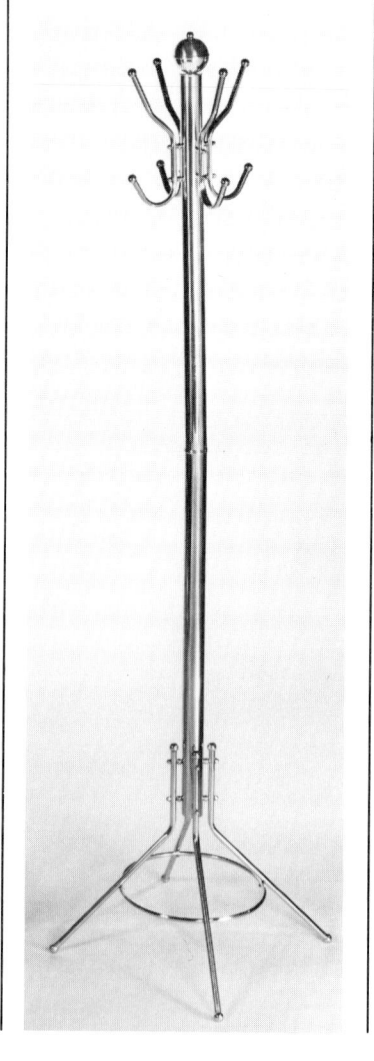

**Name:** Tea caddy*
**Item no:** CW102
**Company:** WILLIAMSBURG ®
Reproduction by Virginia Metalcrafters, Inc.
**Dimensions:** 10"W X 6"D X 6"H
**Materials:** Mahogany, brass
**Price range:** Moderate

**Name:** Umbrella stand
**Item no:** 4960020
**Company:** S.P. Skinner Company
**Dimensions:** 10-1/2" dia. X 23"H
**Materials:** Distressed wood, brass
**Price range:** Moderate

**Name:** McCabe-Marlowe wall clock
**Item no:** 612-218
**Company:** Howard Miller Clock Company
**Dimensions:** 14-1/4"W X 8-1/8"D X 25-5/8"H
**Materials:** Mahogany, inlaid ebony and maple, brass, glass
**Price range:** Top of the line

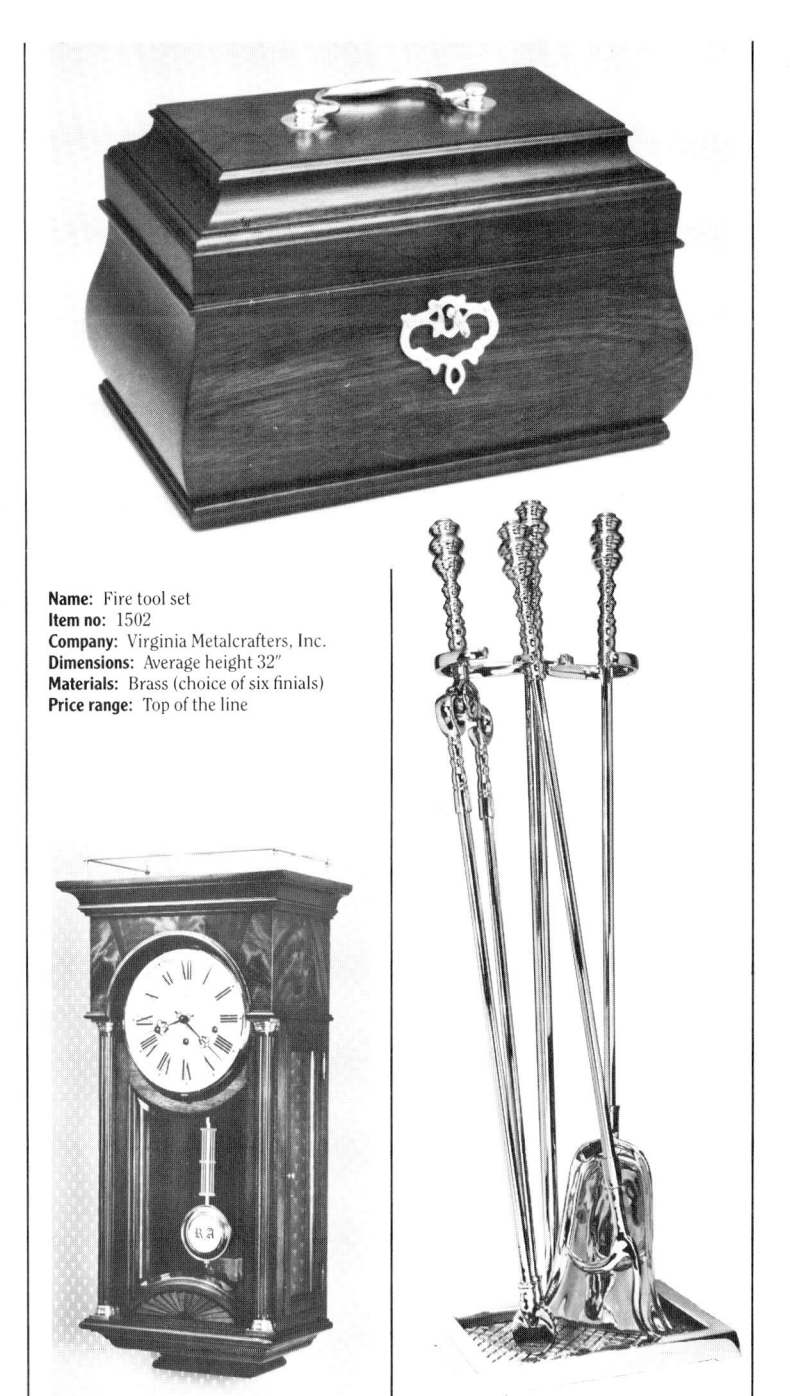

**Name:** Fire tool set
**Item no:** 1502
**Company:** Virginia Metalcrafters, Inc.
**Dimensions:** Average height 32"
**Materials:** Brass (choice of six finials)
**Price range:** Top of the line

# Lighting

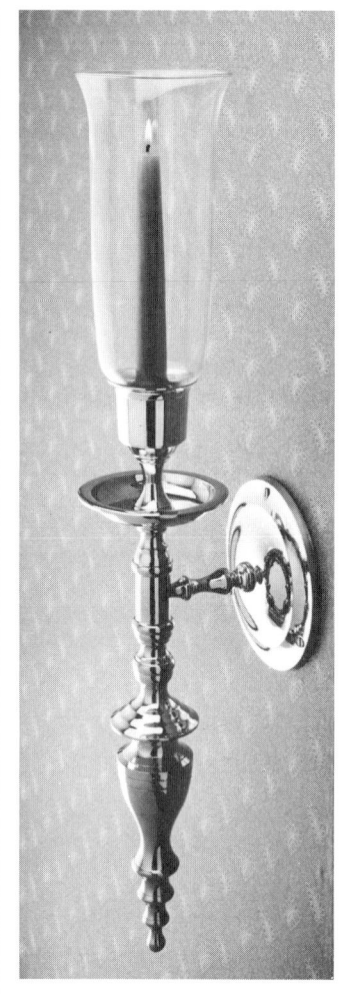

**Name:** Georgian sconce*
**Item no:** 1-16-1888
**Company:** Sturbridge Yankee Workshop
**Dimensions:** 26"H (extends 6")
**Materials:** Brass, handblown crystal
**Price range:** Budget

**Name:** Charleston Rose lamp (Historic Charleston Reproduction)
**Item no:** HC22
**Company:** Norman Perry
**Dimensions:** 29"H
**Materials:** Hand-painted porcelain, wood base, linen shade
**Price range:** Moderate

**Name:** Tankard chandelier
**Item no:** 3922 antique brass (shown); 3923 polished brass
**Company:** Lightolier
**Dimensions:** 25-1/2" dia. X 12"H (at candles) X 42"H overall
**Materials:** Solid brass, glass
**Price range:** Moderate

**Name:** Polished brass and lacquer table lamp
**Item no:** 2027-307
**Company:** Paul Hanson Company
**Dimensions:** 18"W (shade) X 20"H
**Materials:** Brass, red lacquer, lacquered shade
**Price range:** Moderate

**Name:** Tin chandelier (electrified or candles)*
**Item no:** CW12580
**Company:** WILLIAMSBURG ® Reproduction by Virginia Metalcrafters, Inc.
**Dimensions:** 24" dia. X 27"H (12" chain)
**Materials:** Steel (antique tin or black finish)
**Price range:** Moderate

**Name:** Student lamp*
**Item no:** 31051
**Company:** Renovator's Supply
**Dimensions:** 15"W X 6-1/2" dia. (base) X 22"H
**Materials:** Solid brass, green cased glass
**Price range:** Moderate

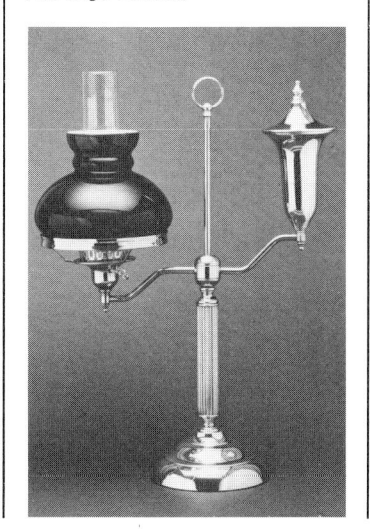

**Name:** Hand-carved walnut classic column lamp
**Item no:** 1808-125
**Company:** Paul Hanson Company
**Dimensions:** 17" (shade) X 33"H
**Materials:** Solid walnut, Flemish brass, silk shade
**Price range:** Top of the line

**Name:** Leather lamp
**Item no:** 6025-V
**Company:** The Stiffel Company
**Dimensions:** 29-1/2"H
**Materials:** Brass, leather shade (fabric also available)
**Price range:** Top of the line

**Name:** Wall-mounted, swing-arm lamp
**Item no:** 1440/3 (solid brass); 1440/6 (chrome)
**Company:** Alsy Corporation
**Dimensions:** 18" arm span X 7-1/4"H
**Materials:** Brass or chrome, Lucite fittings
**Price range:** Moderate

**Name:** Crystal three-arm candelabra
**Item no:** 5366
**Company:** Paul Hanson Company
**Dimensions:** 12"H
**Materials:** Crystal
**Price range:** Budget

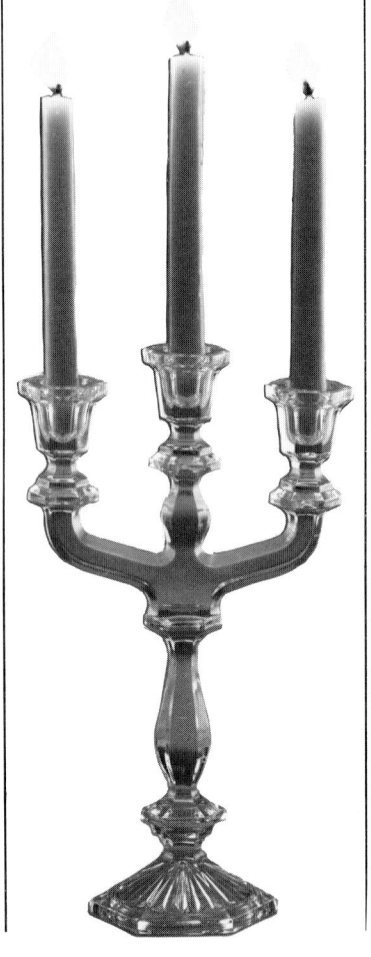

**Name:** Wall-mounted lamp
**Item no:** 228-V
**Company:** The Stiffel Company
**Dimensions:** 15"H
**Materials:** Brass, leather shade (fabric also available)
**Price range:** Moderate

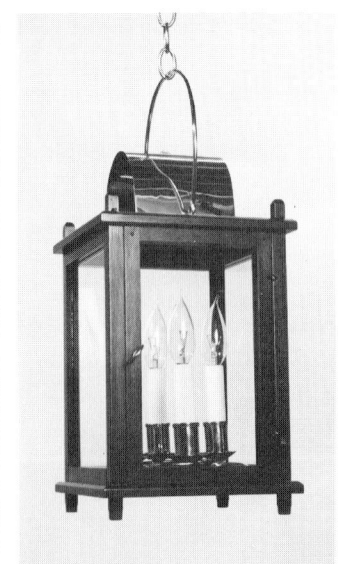

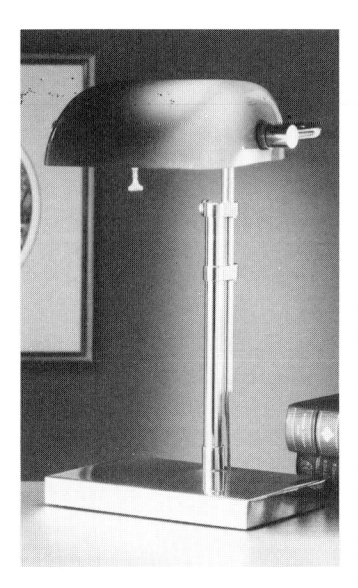

**Name:** Adjustable cased-glass desk lamp
**Item no:** 1959
**Company:** Paul Hanson Company
**Dimensions:** 14"–21"H
**Materials:** Solid brass, green cased-glass shade
**Price range:** Moderate
**Note:** Also available in white satin glass or butterscotch cased glass.

**Name:** Shenandoah hanging lantern (electrified)
**Item no:** 2120
**Company:** Virginia Metalcrafters, Inc.
**Dimensions:** 8-3/4" X 20"H (24" chain length)
**Materials:** Mahogany, brass
**Price range:** Moderate

*The Classicist*
**Sourcebook**

# The Classicist Living Room

## The Classicist

Pictured Opposite: *Silk brocade draperies with ball-fringed swag and cascades, fabric rosettes, and tassel cord tiebacks. Chippendale-style, gold-leaf metal mirror. Pembroke side table with pistol-handled porcelain urn lamp. Blue Canton vase lamp on drop-leaf Pembroke breakfast table. Chinese chippendale carved armchair. Queen Anne damask-covered, satin-striped wing chair. Queen Anne tea table with pull-out trays. Cove ceiling moldings. Eighteenth-century Philadelphia Chippendale-style sofa. Recessed, built-in niche with classical details. Chinese export porcelain collectibles. Oriental-style rug.*

Exacting, detailed people, Classicists often buy their furnishings from antiques dealers or at museum reproduction shops rather than at department or furniture stores. Those pieces that are not antiques or fine reproductions are chosen to offset those that are, in helping to create their setting.

Classicists will, of course, try to seek out homes that suit their period of interest (and will often get very involved in the accurate restoration of an old house). But their strong feelings for the past, and their passion for building a mood, if not an actual re-creation of a period, can give even a newly built house the atmosphere of a century-old structure.

While few people can afford museum-quality antique furnishings, savvy Classicists have learned that auction houses, antiques dealers, even flea markets are all excellent sources for formal pieces from many periods of the past, such as secretary-bookcases, highboys, desks, and dining tables. Classicists who don't collect antiques have been greatly aided by the reproduction programs, increasingly popular among American manufacturers in recent years, that have made both furnishings and accessories based on original pieces more available.

As Classicists know, color was an important element in the decoration of Early American as well as European homes. (It's a myth to think that all colonial homes were painted neutral hues inside and out!) The bold, even intense, colors favored by Classicists—marigold, viridian green, oxblood, regal blue—may, therefore, be surprising to those who may not be familiar with historical interior design. Frequently, these colors are seen in fabrics and wallpapers that have been copied from documented textiles and papers of a particular period.

Window treatments can be elaborate or simple, depending on the period and the window itself. Wood venetian blinds, often paired with elaborate fabric valance swags and jabots, were extremely popular in drafty Early American houses, and are also seen in many Classicist homes today. Window treatments are also often finished off with beautiful details, such as finials, elaborate rods and poles, and metal or fabric rosettes for tiebacks.

Our prototype Regency-style Classicist dining room is lit solely by candles—as it would have been in the early-nineteenth-century England. Classicists also favor lighting made from porcelains (both antique and reproduction), electrified lanterns and chandeliers, and lots of brass or other metal bases. It is of utmost importance to many Classicists that their important artwork and collections (both small-scale objects and large furniture) are lighted so that they can be truly seen and appreciated.

Classicists are our most formal decorating personalities. But this formality can take different guises. The owners of our prototype room, for example, like to serve elegant, sit-down dinners (the husband is a wine connoisseur), but both guests and hosts are usually in casual attire. In general, Classicists are sophisticated, knowledgeable people who pursue their interests with purposefulness and energy.

You won't find antiques in our Classicist shopping directories, but you will find reproductions and adaptations that indicate the styles Classicists prefer. These pieces can be purchased at better furniture and department stores or ordered by mail through museum reproduction catalogues such as Historic Charleston Reproductions.

## Nicholas Pentecost Talks About the Classicist

Anacleto Relaniza

"Working with the owners of this dining room was such a treat because they appreciated the personality of furniture styles like Regency or Biedermeier, which are considered a bit offbeat in today's decorating. And they were fun to work with because they furnished the house for their own pleasure and comfort, not to impress anyone.

"Basically, this is a Regency-period room with some later and earlier pieces, much like what you find in an English country house, where the furnishings have been accumulated over generations. The owners said they like to entertain fourteen for sit-down dinners and they liked everyone seated at one table. This meant we had to have a traditional pedestal-style table (as opposed to a round one). The one we found is English Regency and we also located a set of twelve Regency-period chairs to go with it. But since we needed two more chairs, we had them copied in old wood. The new chairs are so well done, you can't tell just by looking which is which!

"While the structure of the room is formal (the house is more than a hundred years old), it's also a very welcoming space, not at all intimidating, and I think the backgrounds have helped relax the mood. The scenic wallpaper, also of the type you would find in eighteenth- or early nineteenth-century England, has a primitive, not too serious quality about it. We felt it needed to be grounded, but didn't want an ordinary dado. And so an artist was hired to complete the scene. He painted the trompe l'oeil latticework dado around the bottom and also personalized the commercially available paper by adding birds in the air and the names of the family's children on the boats. This helps the room look like an old-fashioned dining pavilion, and at night, when the space is lit only by candles, it's very atmospheric.

"This is also a very *comfortable* room, and I think that is the key. I don't like rooms that are overworked or overdone, and I really think there's a spareness here. This is also more typical of the late eighteenth or early nineteenth century than the later Victorian era. But unlike a pure restoration that's rooted in a particular time, this home allows for people living here to add their own imprint over the years."

## Profile of a Classicist Couple

**Names:** Susan and Ronald
**Children:** Terrence, age twelve, and Samantha, age nine
**Residence:** federal-style white clapboard with shutters, circa 1830
**Setting:** rural
**Occupations:** Susan—volunteer work at museum; Ronald—store owner
**Pets:** two Scottish terriers, Tam and Bonnie
**Favorite furniture styles:** American federal, Empire, late Chippendale
**Decorative materials preferred:** chintz, satin, fine woods, woven textiles
**Favorite color schemes:** red and dark green; navy blue and mustard
**Most creative interior endeavor:** restoring the early-nineteenth-century fireplaces and the dining room mural
**Most treasured object:** antique Chinese Chippendale armchair, late-eighteenth-century clock
**Decorating pet peeves:** Insensitively built additions to old houses
**Dream house:** "the one we're living in"
**Favorite at-home entertaining:** formal sit-down dinners, garden parties
**Pastimes:** antiquing, tennis (both); Susan—jogging, needlework; Ronald—stamp and coin collecting, gardening
**Ideal getaway:** Northern Mexico, France

**Philosophy:** "We love the feeling we get when restoring old furniture—it's like bringing history alive. Whether we use antiques or reproductions, we try to recapture the mood of the past in our house, the same way a good period novel does."

Built around 1830, Susan and Ronald's federal-style house, with its Greek-inspired portico, commands a valley-sweeping view, from their terraced front to the river below.

After they bought the house, there was no question of the decorating style they would choose. "We wanted the interior to convey the same design spirit as the outside," said Susan. "But since our budget was strained after the purchase, we knew we'd combine antiques and quality reproductions."

In keeping with the exterior mood and the four elegant Classic-motif fireplaces, they naturally leaned toward styles of the late eighteenth and early nineteenth centuries. Two of these—federal and Empire—marry handsomely in the formal living room, highlighted by a richly ornamental federal mirror over a black marble fireplace, a carved Empire sofa, and full-length draperies with tassel-fringed swags.

It was in the dining room, though, that Susan and Ronald met their first real decorating challenge, in the form of a hundred-year-old painted wall scene depicting a busy nineteenth-century urban street scene. Ronald recalled the dilemma. "The wall mural was badly damaged, but we felt it was treasonous to cover it. So Susan found three interested students at a nearby art school who were willing to help restore it."

"They were so proud of the results—and so were we," Susan added.

The dining room also boasts two Regency reproduction dining chairs. "We found six antique side chairs for our Duncan Phyfe dining table from Ronald's family. But we needed two more," remarked Susan. "After much searching," she continued, "we located armchair reproductions that are a close match. There are some wonderful reproductions being made today, but like anything else, you have to shop knowledgeably or you may be disappointed."

In addition to the mural, their involvement in another interior project brought unexpected rewards, when they approached local weavers to make woven rugs. "We drove up on weekends to pick out the colors and then to watch the rugs grow. We became good friends with the weavers. The kids loved it, and now we have unique rugs that cost less than many you buy in department stores," said Ronald.

Their latest purchase—an antique Chinese Chippendale chair now in the master bedroom—is a great source of pride. "A couple of weeks after we found the chair we bid successfully on a small Chippendale stool at a local auction. It needed some repairs, but now, wearing the new needlepoint cover I made, it's the perfect companion to our favorite chair. It's one of those happy endings that make decorating such a rewarding experience," noted Susan.

## The Classicist Personality Window Treatments

Ruffled swag valance with descending cascades over side panels.

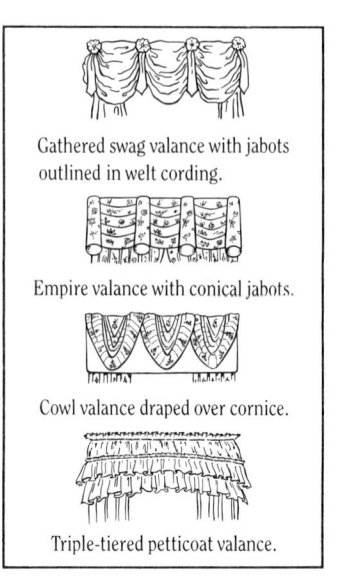

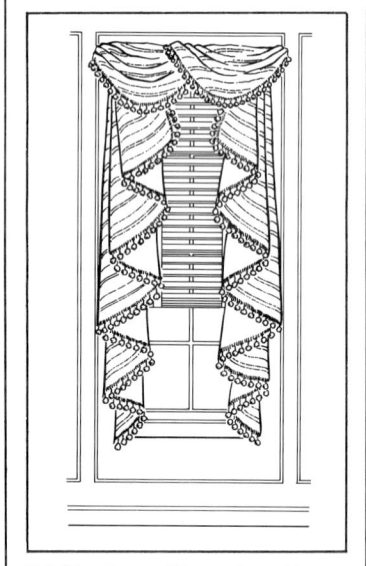

Gathered swag valance with jabots outlined in welt cording.

Empire valance with conical jabots.

Cowl valance draped over cornice.

Triple-tiered petticoat valance.

Ball-fringed swag with cascades as side panels, over wooden blinds.

Swag and deeply fringed cascades, braided cord tiebacks, and metal rod with classical-style finials.

128

# Major Furnishings

**Name:** Rhode Island desk and bookcase*
**Company:** Kindel Furniture Company (Winterthur Reproductions)
**Dimensions:** 25-5/8"W X 26"D X 98"H
**Materials:** Mahogany
**Price range:** Top of the line

**Name:** Regency dining table
**Item no:** 5038
**Company:** Baker Furniture (Stately Homes Reproduction)
**Dimensions:** 78"W X 48"D X 29"H
**Materials:** Mahogany, ebony and mahogany veneers
**Price range:** Top of the line

**Name:** Louis XVI chair
**Item no:** 8060
**Company:** Casa Stradivari
**Dimensions:** 26-1/2"W X 27"D X 36-3/4"H
**Materials:** Beechwood frame
**Price range:** Budget

**Name:** Charleston commode
**Item no:** 1925
**Company:** Baker Furniture (Historic Charleston Reproductions)
**Dimensions:** 34"W X 17-1/2"D X 34"H
**Materials:** Mahogany
**Price range:** Budget

**Name:** Cocktail table
**Item no:** 4005-40
**Company:** Henredon Furniture Industries, Folio 16 Collection
**Dimensions:** 40"W X 20"D X 15"H
**Materials:** Maple, maple and ash veneers
**Price range:** Moderate

|  | Major Furnishings | Accessories and Lighting |
|---|---|---|
| Budget | under $1,000 | under $100 |
| Moderate | $1,000-$2,500 | $100-$300 |
| Top-of-the-Line | over $2,500 | over $300 |

*Designates mail order

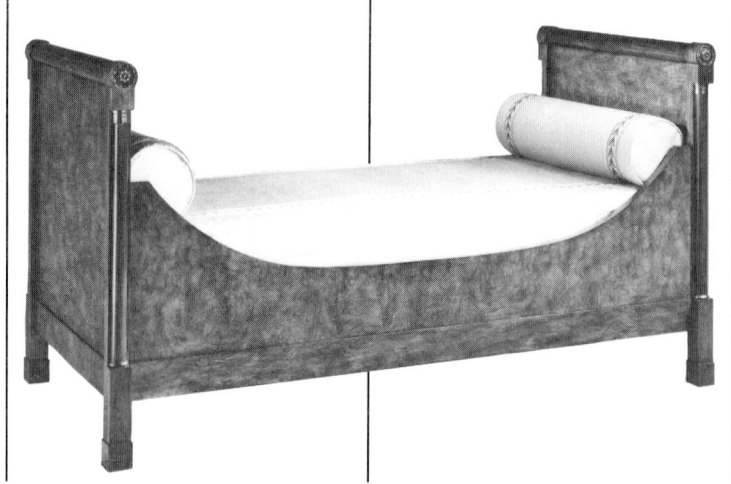

**Name:** Philadelphia lowboy
**Item no:** 1616
**Company:** Councill Craftsmen
**Dimensions:** 34-1/2"W X 19-1/4"D X 31-3/8"H
**Materials:** Mahogany
**Price range:** Moderate

**Name:** Dunlap highboy*
**Item no:** 5750
**Company:** Eldred Wheeler
**Dimensions:** 37"W X 18-1/2"D X 78"H
**Materials:** Cherry or maple
**Price range:** Top of the line

**Name:** Charleston sideboard
**Item no:** 1954
**Company:** Baker Furniture (Historic Charleston Reproductions)
**Dimensions:** 66"W X 23"D X 37"H
**Materials:** Mahogany, satinwood
**Price range:** Top of the line

**Name:** Daybed
**Item no:** 4116
**Company:** Baker Furniture, Continental Collection
**Dimensions:** 81-1/2"W X 39"D X 43"H
**Materials:** Maple solids, white ash burl veneers
**Price range:** Top of the line

**Name:** Philadelphia sofa*
**Item no:** 83-4980
**Company:** Kindel Furniture Company (Winterthur Reproductions)
**Dimensions:** 80"W X 33-1/2"D X 36-3/8"H
**Materials:** Mahogany
**Price range:** Top of the line
**Note:** Available in muslin, leather, or Winterthur fabric.

**Name:** Chest-on-chest
**Item no:** 1902
**Company:** Baker Furniture (Historic Charleston Reproductions)
**Dimensions:** 43"W X 22-3/4"D X 75-3/4"H
**Materials:** Mahogany; solid brass
**Price range:** Top of the line

**Name:** Breakfront china cabinet
**Item no:** 555
**Company:** Harden Furniture
**Dimensions:** 74"W X 18"D X 90"H
**Materials:** Cherry
**Price range:** Top of the line

**Name:** Chippendale bed
**Item no:** 5022
**Company:** Baker Furniture
**Dimensions:** 70"W X 90"D X 96"H
**Materials:** Mahogany
**Price range:** Top of the line

**Name:** Armchair
**Item no:** 943
**Company:** Harden Furniture
**Dimensions:** (outside) 29"W X 28"D X 37"H
**Materials:** Cherry (legs)
**Price range:** Budget

**Name:** China breakfront, Grand Palais Collection by Heritage
**Item no:** 064-455
**Company:** Drexel Heritage Furnishings, Inc.
**Dimensions:** 76"W X 16-1/2"D X 86"H
**Materials:** Walnut, satinwood, rosewood veneers
**Price range:** Top of the line

**Name:** Sheraton sofa
**Item no:** 1774
**Company:** Southwood Reproductions
**Dimensions:** 74"W X 30"D X 35"H
**Materials:** Mahogany
**Price range:** Top of the line

**Name:** Armoire
**Item no:** 3204-05
**Company:** Henredon Furniture, Villandry Collection
**Dimensions:** 48-1/2"W X 20"D X 82-1/4"H
**Materials:** Maple, myrtle veneer
**Price range:** Top of the line

**Name:** Chinese writing table
**Item no:** 9041
**Company:** John Widdicomb Company
**Dimensions:** 54"W X 26"D X 31"H
**Materials:** Wood, lacquer, brass
**Price range:** Top of the line

**Name:** Camelback sofa
**Item no:** 20-7130-5
**Company:** Ethan Allen, Inc.
**Dimensions:** 82"W X 35"D X 36"H
**Materials:** Hardwood, leather
**Price range:** Moderate

**Name:** Philadelphia easy chair*
**Company:** Kindel Furniture Company (Winterthur Reproductions)
**Dimensions:** 38-1/4"W X 35"D X 44"H
**Materials:** Mahogany
**Price range:** Moderate
**Note:** Available in muslin, leather, or Winterthur fabric.

**Name:** Bonnet-top secretary desk*
**Item no:** 5955
**Company:** Eldred Wheeler
**Dimensions:** 35"W X 20"D X 88"H
**Materials:** Cherry or maple
**Price range:** Top of the line

133

**Name:** Rice-back armchair
**Item no:** 1955-15
**Company:** Hickory Chair Company
**Dimensions:** 21-3/4"W X 23"D X 33"H
**Materials:** Mahogany
**Price range:** Budget

**Name:** Empire armchair by Heritage
**Item no:** 1311
**Company:** Drexel Heritage Furnishings, Inc.
**Dimensions:** 23"W X 21"D X 35-1/2"H
**Price range:** Moderate

**Name:** Low chest, Vintage Cherry Collection by Drexel
**Item no:** 184-668
**Company:** Drexel Heritage Furnishings, Inc.
**Dimensions:** 24"W X 15-1/4"D X 24"H
**Materials:** Cherry woods
**Price range:** Budget

**Name:** Pembroke table, Duke of Argyll, Scottish
**Item no:** 5075
**Company:** Baker Furniture
**Dimensions:** (closed) 25"W X 26-1/8"D X 28-1/4"H
**Materials:** Laurel, tulipwood, rosewood, satinwood, holly, maple
**Price range:** Top of the line

**Name:** Sheraton cylinder desk
**Item no:** 5039
**Company:** Baker Furniture (Stately Homes Reproduction)
**Dimensions:** 30"W X 20-1/4"D X 39-7/8"H
**Materials:** Mahogany, rosewood and boxwood inlays, brass
**Price range:** Top of the line

**Name:** Lolling chair*
**Company:** Kindel Furniture Company (Winterthur Reproductions)
**Dimensions:** 26-1/4"W X 28-3/4"D X 43"H
**Materials:** Mahogany
**Price range:** Moderate
**Note:** Available in muslin, leather, or Winterthur fabric.

**Name:** Philadelphia Queen Anne armchair*
**Company:** Kindel Furniture Company (Winterthur Reproductions)
**Dimensions:** 26-3/4"W X 22-3/4"D X 42-1/2"H
**Materials:** Mahogany
**Price range:** Moderate
**Note:** Also available in matching side chair, both in muslin, leather, or Winterthur fabric.

**Name:** Chippendale corner chair
**Item no:** 715
**Company:** Southwood Reproductions
**Dimensions:** 30-1/2"W X 25-1/2"D X 32 1/4"H
**Materials:** Mahogany
**Price range:** Budget

**Name:** Massachusetts bombé desk*
**Company:** Kindel Furniture Company
(Winterthur Reproductions)
**Dimensions:** 36-7/8"W X 19-5/8"D
X 43-1/2"H
**Materials:** Mahogany
**Price range:** Top of the line

**Name:** Leather Queen Anne armchair
**Item no:** 20-7405
**Company:** Ethan Allen, Inc.
**Dimensions:** 26"W X 28"D X 43"H
**Materials:** Hardwood, Leather
**Price range:** Moderate

**Name:** Philadelphia tea table*
**Company:** Kindel Furniture Company
(Winterthur Reproductions)
**Dimensions:** 32-1/8"W X 20-1/8"D
X 29-3/4"H
**Materials:** Mahogany
**Price range:** Top of the line

**Name:** Tilt-top table
**Item no:** 560
**Company:** Schott Furniture
**Dimensions:** 18" X 26" (oval) X 25"H
**Price range:** Budget

## Accessories

**Name:** Charles R. Sligh Centennial grandfather clock
**Item no:** 204
**Company:** Sligh Furniture Company, designed by Tom Van Tamelen and David Warren
**Dimensions:** 26-3/4"W X 16"D X 85-3/4"H
**Materials:** Solid cherry and veneers, brass
**Price range:** Top of the line

**Name:** Queen Anne stool
**Item no:** 701
**Company:** Southwood Reproductions
**Dimensions:** 21-1/2"W X 14-1/2"D X 18"H
**Materials:** Mahogany
**Price range:** Moderate

**Name:** Delftware tobacco jar
**Item no:** HC275
**Company:** Mottahedeh
**Dimensions:** 14"H
**Materials:** Porcelain, brass
**Price range:** Budget

**Name:** Brass sconce
**Item no:** 42-1160
**Company:** Ethan Allen, Inc.
**Dimensions:** 12-1/2"H
**Materials:** Brass
**Price range:** Budget

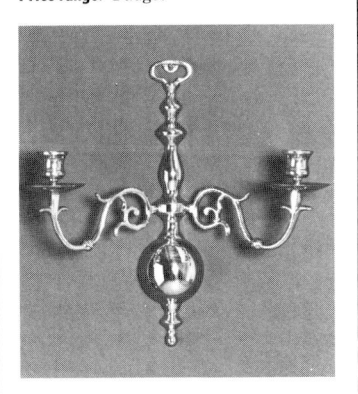

**Name:** Kangxi Hsi candlesticks
**Item no:** Y8391
**Company:** Mottahedeh (Metropolitan Museum of Art Reproduction)
**Dimensions:** 8"H
**Materials:** Blue-and-white porcelain
**Price range:** Moderate

**Name:** Ashley Hall Adam oval mirror*
**Item no:** 101G
**Company:** Friedman Brothers Decorative Arts (Historic Charleston Reproductions)
**Dimensions:** 25"W X 47"H
**Materials:** 23-karat gold leaf, hand-beveled glass, wood
**Price range:** Top of the line

**Name:** Cache pot monkey with drum
**Item no:** S4088A
**Company:** Mottahedeh
**Dimensions:** 7-3/4"W X 7-3/4"H
**Materials:** Glazed ceramic
**Price range:** Budget

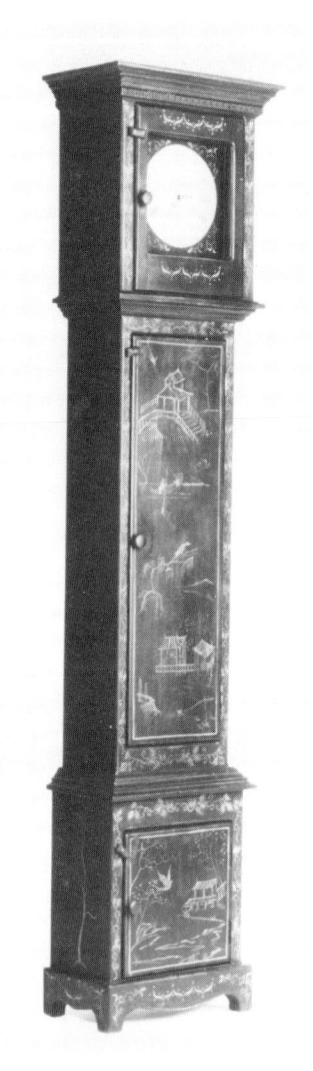

**Name:** Chinoiserie grandfather clock
**Item no:** 27-1630
**Company:** Habersham Plantation
**Dimensions:** 20"W X 11"D X 83"H
**Materials:** Pine
**Price range:** Top of the line

**Name:** Rabbit tureen
**Item no:** S5213
**Company:** Mottahedeh
**Dimensions:** 12"W X 9-1/2"H
**Materials:** Porcelain
**Price range:** Moderate

**Name:** Ginger jar*
**Item no:** HC241
**Company:** Mottahedeh (Historic Charleston Reproductions)
**Dimensions:** 10-5/8"H
**Materials:** Porcelain
**Price range:** Budget

# Lighting

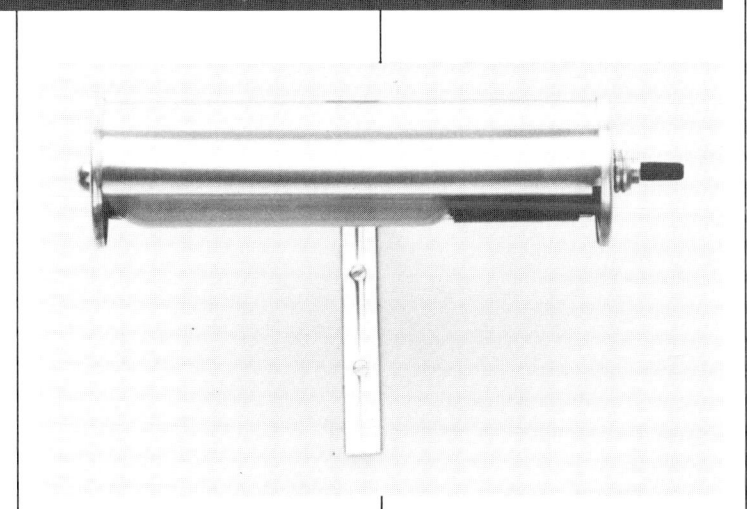

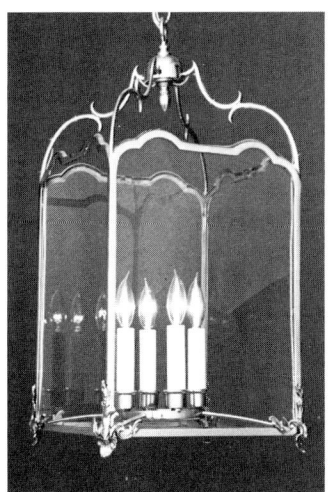

**Name:** Brush-Everard lantern (electrified)*
**Item no:** CW 11751
**Company:** WILLIAMSBURG® Reproduction by Virginia Metalcrafters
**Dimensions:** 10-1/2"W X 23"H (16" chain length)
**Materials:** Solid brass (polished or antiqued)
**Price range:** Top of the line

**Name:** Brass art lamp*
**Item no:** 24500
**Company:** Renovator's Supply
**Dimensions:** 6-1/2" shade; projects 7"
**Materials:** Brass
**Price range:** Budget
**Note:** Also available in 11-1/2" width

**Name:** Double-arm swan motif lamp
**Item no:** 15425A
**Company:** Chapman Lamps
**Dimensions:** 28-1/2"L
**Materials:** Brass
**Price range:** Top of the line

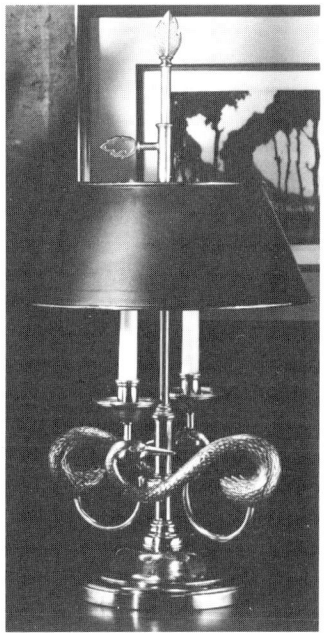

**Name:** Ebony black empire column table lamp
**Item no:** 1888-260
**Company:** Paul Hanson Company
**Dimensions:** 19" (shade) X 34"H
**Materials:** Bronze, black lacquer, shantung shade
**Price range:** Top of the line

**Name:** Table lamp*
**Item no:** T120
**Company:** Victorian Lighting Company
**Dimensions:** 24"H
**Materials:** Brass, glass
**Price range:** Moderate
**Note:** Also available in 11-1/2" width

**Name:** Regency hurricane lamp*
**Item no:** HC53
**Company:** Mottahedeh (Historic Charleston Reproductions)
**Dimensions:** 19"H
**Materials:** Solid brass, glass
**Price range:** Moderate

**Name:** Urn lamp
**Item no:** L45
**Company:** Nora Fenton
**Dimensions:** 21"H
**Materials:** Glazed earthenware
**Price range:** Moderate

**Name:** Tayloe House lantern (electrified)*
**Item no:** CW 11758
**Company:** WILLIAMSBURG® Reproduction by Virginia Metalcrafters
**Dimensions:** 10" dia. X 23"H (16" chain length)
**Materials:** Solid brass (polished or verdigris), lead crystal
**Price range:** Top of the line

# *The Individualist*
# Sourcebook

## The *Individualist* Sitting/Family Room

## The Individualist

If you're the kind of person who likes to creatively mingle different looks, whether it's period and contemporary, simple and fussy, bold and soft, light and dark, then you're an Individualist, at least to some degree.

Perhaps you enjoy collecting stoneware crocks and antique cooking implements (a favorite of Naturalist decorating personalities) but don't feel at ease with the colors, fabrics, and background usually associated with the Naturalist. Display your crocks and tools against a more contemporary gleaming ceramic tile, marble, and butcher block. You'll show your collection off to good advantage and feel you've made a personal statement in the process.

Individualist color choices include the bright, clean shades of blue and red, paired with white, along with more subdued peach, pink, and gray. An Individualist, for example, might downplay the old-fashioned look of a just-rescued-from-Grandma's-attic bench by painting it a glossy white or a soft matte gray and upholstering the seat in a semi-abstract geometric print fabric.

Fabrics that allow the Individualist to best express this design collaboration include bright polished cottons in simply designed patterns, durable sailcloth, and even lace. Lyn Peterson used lace curtains in the Individualist prototype room following page 24 to add softness and personality to a room void of architectural interest.

Lyn chose lace to make an Individualist statement for her window treatments, but others might want shutters, perhaps painted to coordinate with the walls, vertical blinds, or flat Roman shades. All are practical, understated, and offer good choices in rooms where different looks rub shoulders.

In general, Individualists select light fixtures to complement the prevailing mood of the room. That is, those with strong Modernist leanings would choose contemporary lighting fixtures such as recessed and track lighting and suspended cord lamps. Individualists more clearly in the period camp would pick fixtures like pharmacy lamps, table lamps with simple ginger jar bases, and swing-arm lamps. Or, they might like the look of a period-type lamp in a clean, modern space.

Pictured Opposite: *Plump club chairs with contemporary upholstery. Armless modular sofa. Wood-burning stove. Salt-glazed stoneware crock to hold firewood. Hamper-basket coffee table. Striped dhurrie rug. Lacquered wood end table. Reproduction printings. Painted double-tier café shutters. White ceiling fan.*

In the same way that Individualists juxtapose old and new in their interiors, they may also do the same in how they dress—a frilly ascot paired with a tweed jacket, for instance. And, in entertaining, they might combine country-style white ironstone dinner plates with glossy-black lacquered matchstick place mats.

Furnishings in the Individualist shopping directories encompass the spirit of both past and present. They include upholstered pieces with classic lines dressed in up-to-date fabrics, as well as stark, contemporary designs warmed by infusions of traditional colors and patterns. But it is the excitement generated by the meeting of these seemingly incompatible looks that inspires many Individualists to go a step further. In this regard, we suggest you check the personality style directories that correspond to those you identified with in the quiz. Then go on to build your *own* truly Individualist look.

## Lyn Peterson Talks About the Individualist

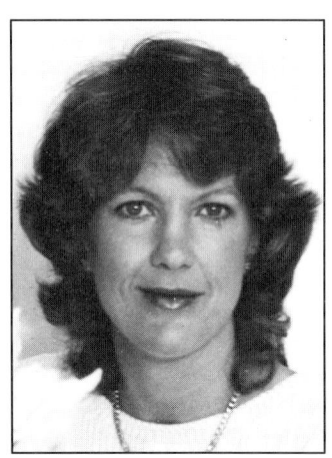

Adrienne Werle

"Expressing their preferences for different styles in innovative combinations is, I think, a hallmark of Individualists. And they do this without falling prey to the latest fads or giving in to extremes. This synthesis might take the form of marrying a Biedermeier-style chest in the same space with a Breuer chair. Or Individualists might clean up the period fussiness of floor-to-ceiling Victorian windows by introducing streamlined leather chairs; or adding the warm, soft curves characteristic of bentwood pieces to a contemporary ranch house. They're also drawn to furnishings that embody the past and the present—old-fashioned lines dressed in updated fabrics.

"The condominium bedroom pictured has several examples of this melding. Although modern in setting and basic inspiration, several Individualist elements have been introduced to underplay the stark modernity. Antiqued lace panels (former dresser scarves) at the windows admit filtered light and obscure the unsightly fire-escape view. The Art Deco–inspired headboard and the federal-style mirror (a bargain find at twenty-seven dollars) add fillips of period fantasy. The white-and-pink "Rosie's Crest" wallcovering provides a light, airy, and practical (washable, too!) surface and adds an affordable richness to the condo's drab drywalls. And the gray carpet keeps the whole effect from becoming too sticky-sweet for the young couple who live here.

"Space was at a premium in

the eleven-by-sixteen-foot room I designed and storage a major consideration. With the standard L-shaped Formica built-ins—incorporating bureau, bookcase, bed, and headboard—was a sleek and inconspicuous solution. The half-round dressing table (actually a full table sawed in half) and the small stool are both space-saving and appealing.

"I think people who are drawn to this look like the contrasts of varied designs that combine low maintenance with good looks. It all works in this room because the choices were so, well—Individualist."

## Profile of an Individualist Couple

**Names:** Nancy and Eric
**Residence:** contemporary cedar ranch, built 1980
**Setting:** secluded woodland
**Occupations:** Nancy—corporate marketing researcher; Eric—self-employed computer software writer and consultant
**Pet:** one dog, Dick, a mutt
**Favorite furniture styles:** Nancy—Art Deco, Shaker; Eric—anything comfortable
**Decorative materials preferred:** wool, silk, cotton, marble, tile
**Favorite color schemes:** beige, cream, and brown; peach and gray
**Most creative interior endeavor:** attached glass-enclosed "recovery room," with wood-burning stove, wet bar, changing room, and hot tub
**Most treasured object:** wood sculpture heron, contemporary handcrafted wineglasses
**Decorating pet peeves:** "sets" of anything
**Dream house:** architect-designed contemporary
**Favorite at-home entertaining:** "hot-tub" parties, dinner parties
**Pastimes:** tennis, skiing, theater, flying
**Ideal getaway:** Nancy—footloose tour of the Greek Islands; Eric—skiing the Bugaboos, Canada
**Philosophy:** "When we moved into the house, the first thing we wanted to do was to put some charm back into it, soften it, and add some curves in what was a very severe atmosphere. Had we bought an older house with inherent charm, we probably would have made it look more contemporary with elements like brass and glass. Striking a balance that suits our life-style is what we find exciting and challenging about decorating."

From the moment they purchased their brand new house, with its seventeen-foot-high cathedral ceilings and huge expanses of glass, Eric and Nancy have been concerned with subduing its modern lines. "Because of the house's wooded setting, we envisioned friends hiking or cross-country skiing up to the back door and then getting into the hot tub," Nancy pointed out. "But, on the other hand," Eric interrupted, "we love to entertain, especially dinner parties, so we didn't want to entirely transform the house into a Vermont ski chalet. It had to be a combination of relaxed casualness *and* formality."

By decorating with objects they've bought while antiquing with friends and when traveling, they've successfully added a distinctly personal stamp to their rooms. When you open the front door of their house you see evidence of this Individualist quality at once: the entryway, characterized by tile floor and cedar walls, also boasts a full-size, handmade country quilt hanging over an antique Windsor settee. The quilt's texture and color, together with the design interest of the wooden bench, lend an inviting warmth to the space.

The sunken living room is architecturally the most up-to-date looking room in the house. Yet even here, amid the low-pile wool rug, champagne-colored banquettes, and ottomans facing the wall-size fireplace, one finds hints of two personalities cozily rubbing shoulders, with quilt pillows on the banquettes and a colorful area rug placed over the wall-to-wall carpet. And in the far corner, gazing out majestically, is a five-foot-tall carved wood heron. "When we first saw the heron at a crafts show years ago we didn't buy it, but we finally tracked it down," Eric observed. "I like the idea of shaping a room around a beautiful object that we both love."

Here, and throughout their rooms, it's the warmth of certain pieces—be it contemporary crafts or Victoriana—that dresses up the house's spare architectural details.

The dining room contains several examples of this design duality. The Chinese-style dining table, paired with contemporary Italian side chairs, and a sleek, marble-topped sideboard are all offset by a fifteen-foot paisley wall hanging, a turn-of-the-century find from London, and a Victorian display cabinet from Eric's family, which they use to house their handcrafted wineglasses.

The process of furnishing the master bedroom has spawned friendly debate. Eric has cast his vote for a four-poster bed to complement the crisp blue-and-white wallpaper. But Nancy is doubtful. "That might be getting just a little *too* traditional for me. We've got to remember that balance," she smiled.

## *The Individualist* Personality Window Treatments

Café-style shutters.

Reversible or lined fabric curtains, tucked up.

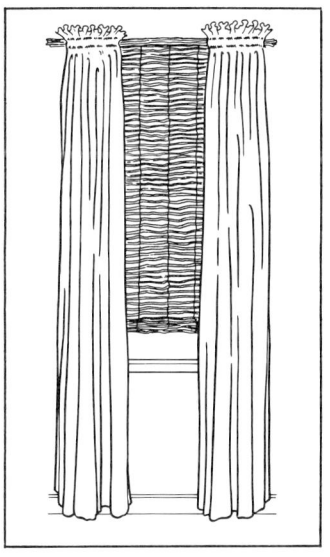

Matchstick, bamboo shades paired with full-length, tightly gathered sheers.

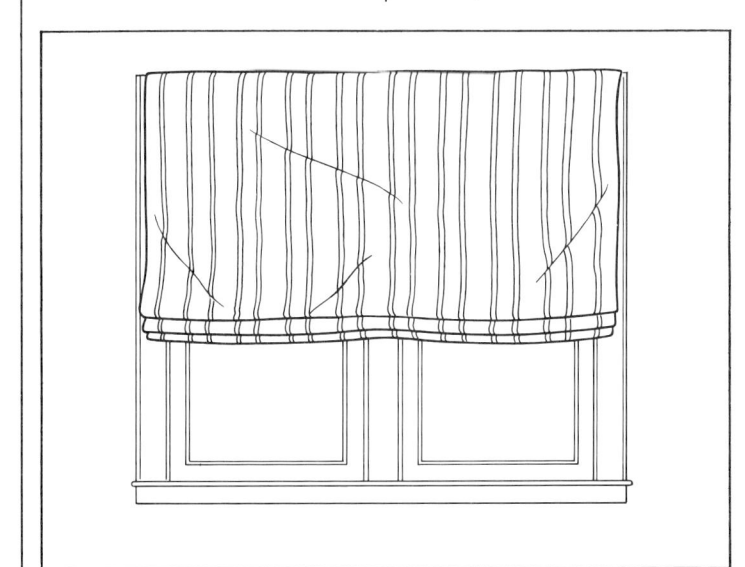

A flat fabric pull-up Roman shade.

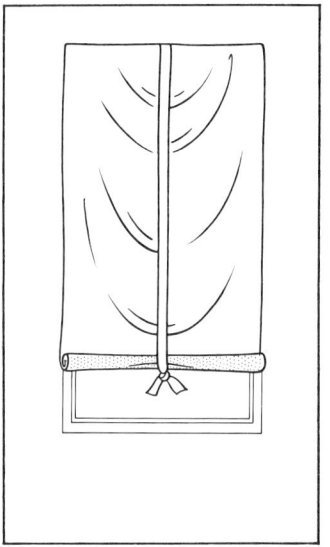

Neutral cotton duck and contrasting lining roll-up shade with fabric sash tie.

# Major Furnishings

**Name:** Facade Collection Rustication Bar
**Item no:** 5568
**Company:** Baker Furniture Co.
**Dimensions:** 48"W X 24-1/4"D X 87-3/4"H
**Materials:** Antique sandstone finish, taupe lacquer
**Price range:** Top of the line

**Name:** Continental wall system
**Company:** Scandinavian Design/Scandinavian Gallery
**Dimensions:** 100"W X 21"D X 77"H
**Materials:** Teak wood
**Price range:** Moderate

**Name:** Illusions East canopy bed
**Item no:** 730-48
**Company:** The Lane Company, Inc.
**Dimensions:** 65-3/4"W X 85"D X 84"H
**Materials:** Polymeric lacquer, synergite and maple solids
**Price range:** Moderate

|  | Major Furnishings | Accessories and Lighting |
|---|---|---|
| Budget | under $1,000 | under $100 |
| Moderate | $1,000-$2,500 | $100-$300 |
| Top-of-the-Line | over $2,500 | over $300 |

*Designates mail order

148

**Name:** Pine sleigh bed from the Replicas 1800 Collection
**Item no:** 16911-473
**Company:** Thomasville Furniture Industries
**Dimensions:** 43"W X 82"D X 32"H
**Materials:** Pine
**Price range:** Moderate

**Name:** Dragon table (MO)
**Item no:** 400A
**Company:** Ballard Designs
**Dimensions:** Top: 28" dia., 29"H
**Materials:** Base: plaster with rod iron supports, glass top
**Price range:** Budget

**Name:** Essence Collection stacking drawer chest
**Item no:** 20811-325
**Company:** Thomasville Furniture Industries, Inc.
**Dimensions:** 40"W X 18"D X 50"H
**Materials:** Honduras mahogany
**Price range:** Budget

149

**Name:** Pearson chaise
**Item no:** 2864
**Company:** The Pearson Company, Division of Lane
**Dimensions:** 62"W X 35-1/2"D X 30"H
**Materials:** Polymeric lacquer, synergite and maple solids
**Price range:** Moderate

**Name:** Sideboard
**Item no:** 5531
**Company:** Baker Furniture Co.
**Dimensions:** 66"W X 24"D X 29-1/2"H
**Price range:** Top of the line

**Name:** Card table
**Item no:** 5578
**Company:** Baker Furniture Co.
**Dimensions:** 38"W X 38"D X 29"H
**Materials:** Carpathian elm burl, brass, leather
**Price range:** Top of the line

**Name:** Chair
**Item no:** 2112
**Company:** Perfection Furniture Co., Inc.
**Dimensions:** 35"W X 30"D X 25"H
**Materials:** Hardwood frame, sinuous wire construction, polydac cushions
**Price range:** Budget

**Name:** Bar
**Item no:** 6903-2
**Company:** Erwin-Lambeth, Inc.
**Dimensions:** 46"W X 20"D X 80"H
**Materials:** Cherry
**Price range:** Top of the line

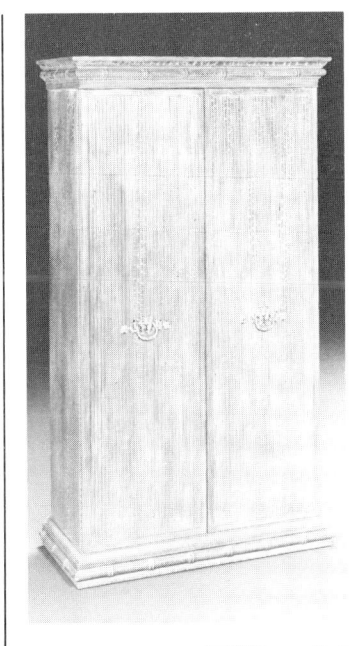

**Name:** Canopy bed from the Essence Collection
**Item no:** 20811-495
**Company:** Thomasville Furniture Industries
**Dimensions:** 60"W X 80"H
**Materials:** Honduras Mahogany
**Price range:** Moderate

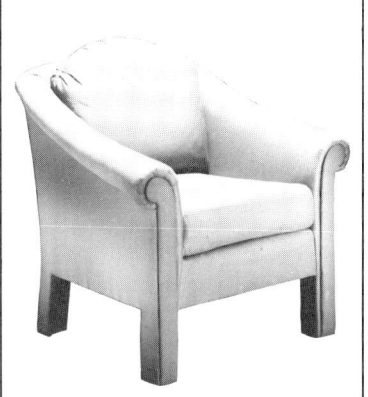

**Name:** Dressmaker slipper chair
**Item no:** 11-884
**Company:** Century Furniture Co.
**Dimensions:** 28"W X 37-1/2"H
**Materials:** Upholstered frame
**Price range:** Budget

**Name:** Parsons leg chair
**Item no:** 2107
**Company:** Perfection Furniture Co., Inc.
**Dimensions:** 34"W X 34"D X 32"H
**Materials:** Hardwood frame, sinuous wire construction, polydac cushions
**Price range:** Budget

**Name:** Rattan bed
**Item no:** RL-08
**Company:** O'Asian
**Designer:** Ralph Lauren
**Dimensions:** 60"W X 54"H (headboard)
**Materials:** Rattan
**Price range:** Moderate

**Name:** Square cocktail table
**Item no:** 7022-370
**Company:** Weiman
**Dimensions:** 42"W X 42"D X 15-1/2"H
**Materials:** Brass and glass
**Price range:** Moderate

**Name:** Lounge chair
**Item no:** 2111
**Company:** Perfection Furniture Co., Inc.
**Dimensions:** 31"W X 34"D X 31"H
**Materials:** Hardwood frame, sinuous wire construction, polydac cushions
**Price range:** Budget

**Name:** Parsons chair
**Item no:** 20-7604-5
**Company:** Ethan Allen, Inc.
**Price range:** Budget

**Name:** Illusions East cocktail table and sofa
**Item nos:** Table: 1260-19; sofa: 2861
**Company:** The Lane Company, Inc., and Pearson Company, Division of Lane
**Dimensions:** Table: 50"W X 26"D X 15"H; sofa: 74"W X 28"D X 30"H
**Materials:** Polymeric lacquer, synergite and maple solids
**Price range:** Table: budget; sofa: moderate

**Name:** Contemporary sofa
**Item no:** C2-2110
**Company:** Century Furniture Co.
**Dimensions:** 83-1/2"W X 37"D X 33"H
**Materials:** Upholstered frame
**Price range:** Moderate

**Name:** Bistro chair
**Company:** Palacek
**Dimensions:** 27"W X 23"D X 30-1/2"H
**Materials:** Wicker, available in many colors
**Price range:** Budget

153

**Name:** Taurus sofa
**Item no:** 8113
**Company:** New Horizons
**Dimensions:** 89"W X 38"D X 32"H
**Price range:** Moderate

**Name:** Trestle table
**Company:** Hancock Shaker Village, Inc.
**Dimensions:** Available in 5', 6', 7', or 8' lengths
**Materials:** Maple base, cherry or maple top
**Price range:** Budget (5' and 6'); Moderate (7' and 8')

**Name:** Chair
**Item no:** 218
**Company:** Erwin-Lambeth, Inc.
**Dimensions:** 31"W X 33"D X 34"H
**Price range:** Moderate

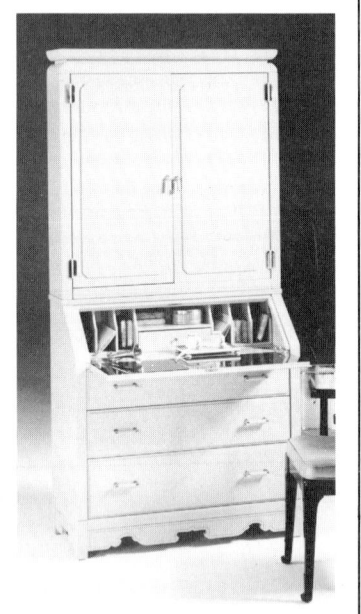

**Name:** Illusions East secretary
**Item nos:** top: 1294-38; drop-lid desk: 1294-50
**Company:** The Lane Company, Inc.
**Dimensions:** Secretary top: 36"W X 9"D X 38"H; secretary bottom: 36"W X 17"D X 36-1/2"H
**Materials:** Polymeric lacquer, synergite and maple solids
**Price range:** Secretary: moderate; chair: budget

**Name:** Newport sofa and loveseat
**Company:** Scandinavian Design/Scandinavian Gallery
**Dimensions:** Sofa: 88-1/2"W; loveseat: 66"W
**Materials:** Upholstered in neutral, cotton-blend fabric
**Price range:** Budget (both)

**Name:** Beauchene Collection cocktail table
**Item no:** 49340
**Company:** Casa Stradivari
**Dimensions:** 40-3/4"W X 40-3/4"D X 18-1/4"H
**Materials:** Oak
**Price range:** Moderate

**Name:** Bold wicker chaise lounge
**Company:** Palacek
**Dimensions:** 28"W X 60"L X 15"H (back, 33"H)
**Materials:** Wicker (available in six colors)
**Price range:** Budget

# Accessories

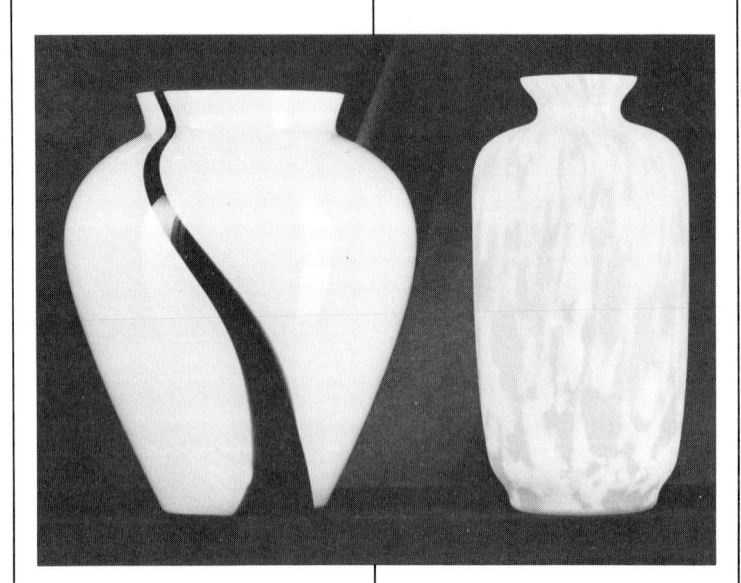

**Name:** "Swirl" (left) and "Da Vinci" (right) vases
**Item nos:** Swirl: 15497; Da Vinci: 4631
**Company:** Beaumont Glass
**Dimensions:** Swirl: 11"W X 12"H; Da Vinci: 6-3/4"W X 12-3/4"H
**Materials:** Handblown cased glass
**Price range:** Moderate (both)

**Name:** Italian glass vases
**Item nos:** Left to right: 1013, 1016
**Company:** Casa Bique, Ltd.
**Dimensions:** 1013: 9-1/2"L X 9-1/2"D X 20"H; 1016: 19"L X 19"D X 20"H
**Price range:** Moderate (all)

**Name:** Baker's rack*
**Item no:** 54346
**Company:** Pot-pour-ri
**Dimensions:** 12"W X 10-1/2"D X 58"H
**Materials:** Enameled steel
**Price range:** Budget

## Lighting

**Name:** Table lamps
**Company:** The Natural Light
**Dimensions:** 25" to 32"H
**Materials:** Wicker and rattan
**Price range:** Moderate (all)


**Name:** Art Nouveau table lamp
**Item no:** L6004-09
**Company:** Morris Greenspan Lamps
**Dimensions:** 31"H
**Materials:** China body; bronze cap and mounting; pleated luxon shade with rayon lining
**Price range:** Moderate

**Name:** Gooseneck floor lamp
**Item no:** 4602-W
**Company:** The Stiffel Co.
**Dimensions:** 47"H
**Materials:** Polished brass finished base with white opal or green cased shade
**Price range:** Moderate

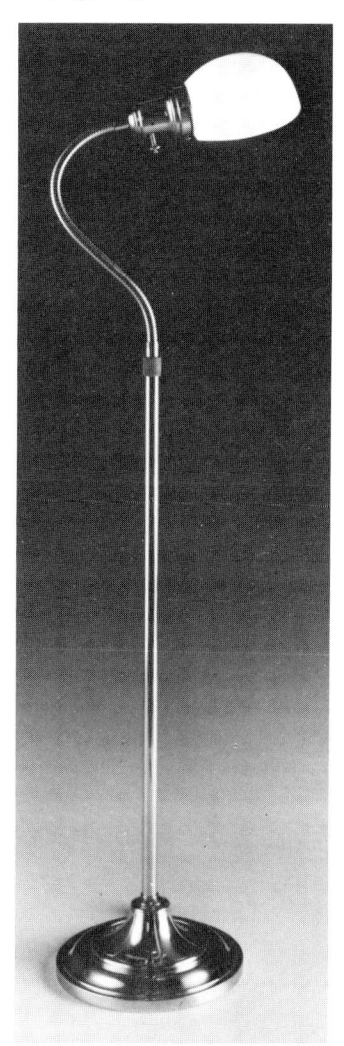

**Name:** Table lamps
**Item nos:** 2470P (left); 2467M (right)
**Company:** Casual Lamps of California, Inc.
**Dimensions:** 2470P: 9-3/4"W X 29"H;
 2467M: 7-3/4"W X 31"H
**Materials:** Ceramic bases
**Price range:** Moderate (both)

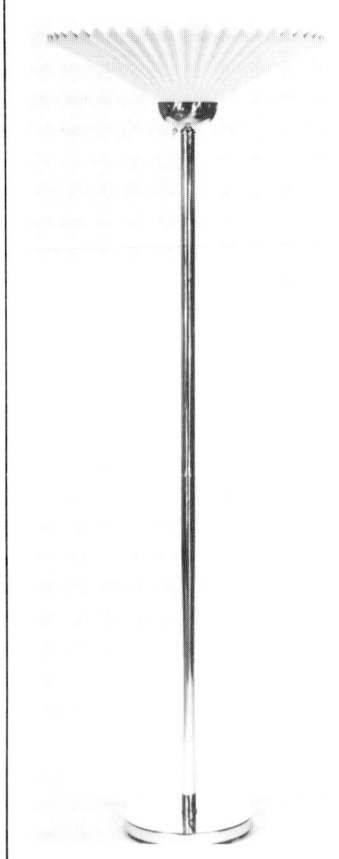

**Name:** Torchiere
**Item no:** 3655
**Company:** Alsy
**Materials:** Torchiere and base: brass finish; pleated acrylic shade
**Dimensions:** 66"H
**Price range:** Moderate

**Name:** Art Nouveau jar lamp
**Item no:** 1946-281
**Company:** Paul Hanson Co., Inc.
**Dimensions:** 27"H, shade 20"
**Materials:** Handpainted beige crackle porcelain, solid brass mountings; shade: beige butcher linen
**Price range:** Top of the line

**Name:** Rete floor and hanging lamp*
**Item nos:** Floor lamp: PNF 1506; hanging lamp: PNH 1522-OB
**Company:** Nessen Lamps Inc.
**Dimensions:** Floor lamp: 72"H, 15" glass dia.; hanging lamp: 19" glass dia.
**Materials:** Chrome, Murano glass
**Price range:** Top of the line

*The Young Professional* **Sourcebook**

## The Young Professional Kitchen

## The Young Professional

As active, career-oriented people, Young Professionals need a living environment that's as diversified as they are. And since, more often than not, they lack the space they'd like to have, they shop for pieces that both reflect the latest designs and can serve more than one purpose. For example, an extension on a desk opens out to provide a work area or place to set buffet dishes; a futon that affords comfortable seating unfolds to accommodate an overnight guest. Chairs collapse and slip out of sight into a closet; nested and drop-leaf tables expand and contract as the situation demands. Etagères house a basket of cosmetics, a pile of bright sweaters, a tape deck, and books. A willow trunk with a glass top doubles as a coffee table/storage area.

The primary shades favored by the Young Professional make a fine counterpoint to their furnishings, which are frequently fashioned from light-finished woods such as pine or beech, or white laminates. Quite often they will invest in one or two good classic pieces—a plump sofa or a leather lounge chair with ottoman, for example—that they'll be able to incorporate into another setting when they move and can afford to upgrade their furniture.

Budget-conscious Young Professionals want good-looking, durable pieces that are easy to maintain, in natural fabrics. Favorite accessories range from the whimsical, like a gumball machine, to the practical, such as stacked goblets and canisters, to a rainbow display of ceramic plates.

Since most people in this decorating personality live in small apartments, usually in busy neighborhoods, privacy is a major consideration when it comes to selecting window treatments. They therefore opt for heavy, pleated paper-vellum shades, Roman shades, or micromini metal blinds.

To illuminate the multipurpose nature of their space, Young Professionals employ wall spots mounted directly on walls (less expensive than track systems) to show off a series of contemporary art posters or photographs. Portable metal work lamps with adjustable necks conveniently clamp onto a desk or étagère, glass or metal pendants hang over a kitchen work area, and table lamps with ceramic bases and paper shades flank a love seat or a convertible sofa.

Pictured Opposite: *Maple butcher block table. Beechwood folding chairs with slatted seats. Melamine and pine rolling trolley. Plastic quartz wall clock. Pleated paper window shades. Painted-metal, suspended ceiling light fixture. Melamine and pine étagère. Painted check-patterned floor (high gloss primary shade). Decorative wallpaper border at chair-rail height. Multi-colored fiesta ware pitchers and kitchenware.*

In order to save time and money, Young Professionals might also cover a wall with inexpensive fabric, such as sheeting, instead of expensive wallpaper. Those with sewing skills may also use sheeting to make their own duvet cover for the bed (as our Young Professional designer did for the prototype room following page 24).

Young Professionals have a knack for combining good contemporary design, fresh colors, and duality in a setting. Most often their living areas incorporate many elements of their busy lives, from a workout space to a place to study or do business at home—and yet the elements are so attractively presented that they become an integral part of the room. When company comes, there's little to hide!

The directory that follows illustrates a bounty of smart-looking furnishings that are versatile, easy to maintain, and often disassemble for easy storage and moving—all priced within reach of the career-minded individual.

Bear in mind, too, that you don't have to be young *or* professional to take advantage of these furnishings. People outfitting second homes, those who've given up large homes in favor of smaller spaces, even someone who's furnishing a family or teen's room, all are excellent candidates for making use of the Young Professional shopping directory.

## James Bloor Talks About the Young Professional

James Levin

"I identify with this style. Being a young designer is a lot different from being one who has been in business for a long time and has been able to acquire expensive furnishings. I couldn't think of spending eight thousand dollars on a whole apartment, much less on one chair. But this whole apartment (see photo following page 24) can be done for under two thousand dollars.

"This is a basic studio apartment—a living, dining, sleeping, and working situation—and all those needs had to be taken care of. The storage units, for example, come with and without doors, so things like the typewriter can be hidden, while the dinnerware and glassware—items good-looking enough to function as decorative accessories—can be on display.

"And, it can all be put together in very little time, which is important to people who are busy concentrating on their careers. Everything can be bought in an afternoon. You wait two or three days for delivery, and the whole apartment can be done at the end of the week. If you start on Monday, you can have guests in for dinner on Saturday and entertain in style!

"I also like changing my apartment frequently. Change is a very important word in the vocabulary of the Young Professional. The person who lives in this apartment probably won't be here for a terribly long period of time, and will want to invest in furnishings that will work—maybe in a different configuration or in a different room—wherever she moves to. And the sheets on the wall represent, at tops, a two-hundred-dollar investment that can be easily changed if you get tired of the pattern or color or decide to move.

"The Young Professional will buy one or two really classic pieces to go with the flexible furniture, however. But even these don't have to be expensive originals, they can be knockoffs, but good knockoffs. In this room, the classic piece is the Le Corbusier chaise. It's a timeless piece—and, of course, a copy—that will look good anywhere for a long, long time."

## Profile of a Young Professional

**Name:** Mary
**Residence:** one-bedroom apartment, three-floor tenement, circa 1885
**Setting:** urban
**Occupation:** magazine associate art director
**Favorite furniture styles:** Scandinavian contemporary, butcher-block
**Decorative materials preferred:** printed cottons, linen, pine, oak
**Favorite color schemes:** blue, white, and rose; red, black, and gray
**Most creative interior endeavor:** making cushions and curtains; painting one living room wall a contrasting color
**Most treasured objects:** pine wardrobe, Japanese print, silver bonbonnière dish
**Decorating pet peeves:** poor lighting, slipcovers, synthetic fabrics
**Dream house:** brownstone in city
**Favorite at-home entertaining:** small dinner parties and brunches
**Pastimes:** museum shows, movies, concerts, cooking, walking, reading magazines
**Ideal getaway:** Cape Cod, Australia (future)
**Philosophy:** "My apartment is small, so the furnishings have to be functional and multipurpose. It's also important that the pieces are well designed because when I move into a larger space, I want to be able to use them again, perhaps in a guest room."

There's a snug yet uncluttered mood to Mary's living room, with its tall, old-fashioned framed windows and fireplace. Her first purchase for this space was two child-size futons, which are housed in a pine frame she had built for them. To harmonize with the solid periwinkle blue and pale plum futons, Mary made an assortment of polished cotton pillows, together with a round table skirt and square topper to match the miniprint lampshade on the table next to the futon. She rounded out her accessory purchases with a blue-and-rose geometric wool rug and muslin draperies, which she trimmed with a vertical floral border.

Mary's main concerns when buying furniture are versatility and size. "Believe it or not, I can seat eight people for dinner when the tabletop is folded out," Mary said, referring to the honey-colored pine table surrounded by pine director's chairs in nubby taupe cotton. The white melamine parsons table and wall shelf unit are also multifunctional and indispensable for storing books, the stereo, and the television.

Mary expressed great pleasure in her newest acquisition, a pine wardrobe, which meets both her practical and design requirements. "Since I've no closets to speak of, I hang my clothes in it, and the area behind it is perfect for stashing my extra director's chairs—plus, it's lovely to look at!"

When furnishing the large kitchen, Mary had a different set of priorities. "I wanted the kitchen to be organized and easy to maintain, so everything is stored away." To add a fillip to the all-white appliances, Mary chose bold red accessories and decorative storage canisters and containers.

Scattered throughout the apartment are indications of Mary's interests and her art background. Metallic-framed photographs that she took and one of her abstract college paintings hang in the living room and Lilliputian-size bedroom. Contemporary museum-show posters in brilliant tones add a flush of color to the otherwise spare kitchen. "I'm not an avid collector, but I display a few special objects given to me by family and friends, to add a homey touch," she said.

Mary feels comfortable in her surroundings, but she does look forward to moving into a place with closets and a bathroom that's not the size of one! "Yet," she remarked, "my next place will probably have much the same mood as this one—only the pieces will be more upscale in look, with more individuality."

## *The Young Professional* Personality Window Treatments

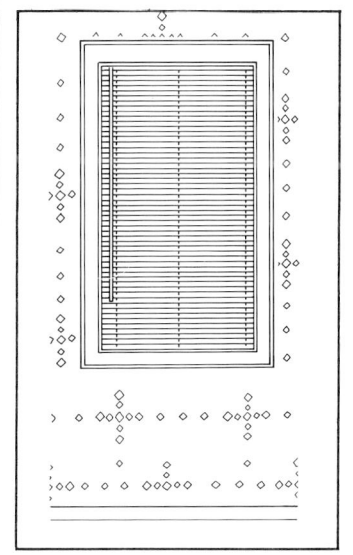

Mini-blinds.

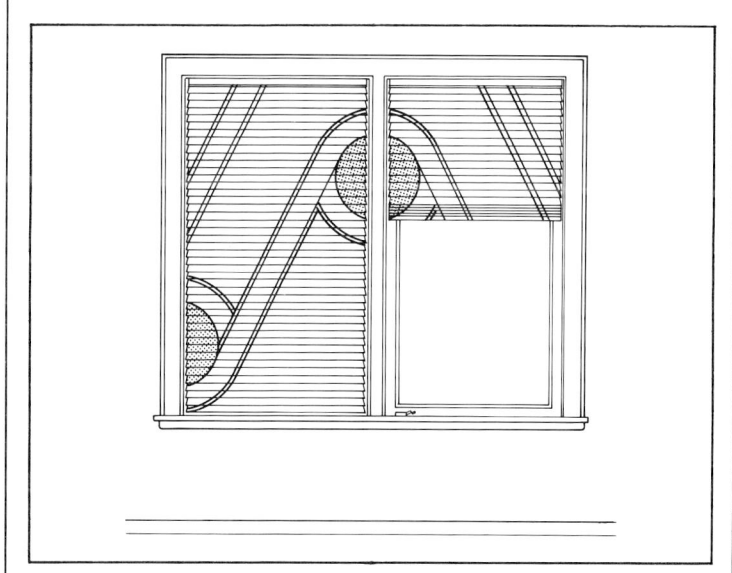

Blinds with bold graphic design (in closed position).

Roman shade with coordinated wallcovering.

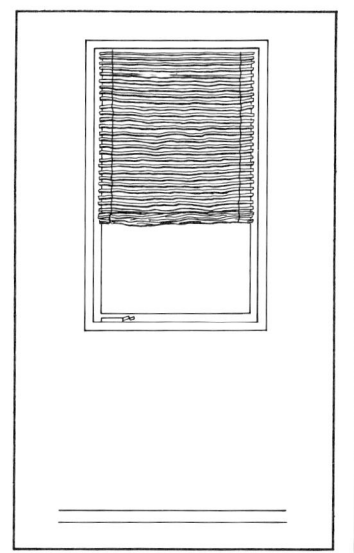

Matchstick blinds.

Café curtain with ruffled valance over color-coordinated pull-up window shade.

## Major Furnishings

**Name:** Contemporary fully upholstered sofa
**Item no:** 22-941
**Company:** Century Furniture Company
**Dimensions:** 81-1/2"W X 33-1/2"D X 33"H
**Materials:** Upholstered frame
**Price range:** Moderate

**Name:** IG-IG sofa sleeper
**Item no:** IG-62CVT
**Company:** The Sherwood Corporation
**Dimensions:** 63"W X 30"D X 30"H
**Materials:** Foam
**Price range:** Budget

**Name:** Triad chair
**Item nos:** TD-AC35 (chair)
**Company:** Tiffany and Tiffany for Atlantic Furniture Co., Inc.
**Dimensions:** 35"W X 33"D X 32"H
**Materials:** Hardwood frame
**Price range:** Budget

**Name:** Refectory dining table and Windsor-style chairs
**Company:** Workbench
**Materials:** Oak
**Price range:** Budget (all)

|  | Major Furnishings | Accessories and Lighting |
| --- | --- | --- |
| Budget | under $1,000 | under $100 |
| Moderate | $1,000-$2,500 | $100-$300 |
| Top-of-the-Line | over $2,500 | over $300 |

*Designates mail order

**Name:** Counter and stools*
**Item nos:** 7331X (counter); 7332X (stools)
**Company:** Pot-pour-ri
**Dimensions:** Counter: 42"W X 18"D X 36"H; stools: 28"H
**Materials:** Maple
**Price range:** Budget (all)

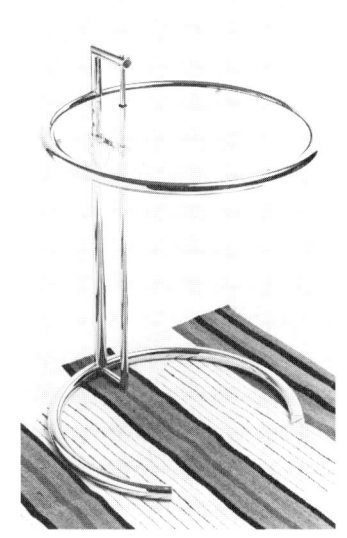

**Name:** Adjustable Chroma table*
**Item no:** 366854
**Company:** Conran's
**Dimensions:** 21-1/2" to 36-1/2"H, 20" dia.
**Materials:** Chromed steel with glass
**Price range:** Budget

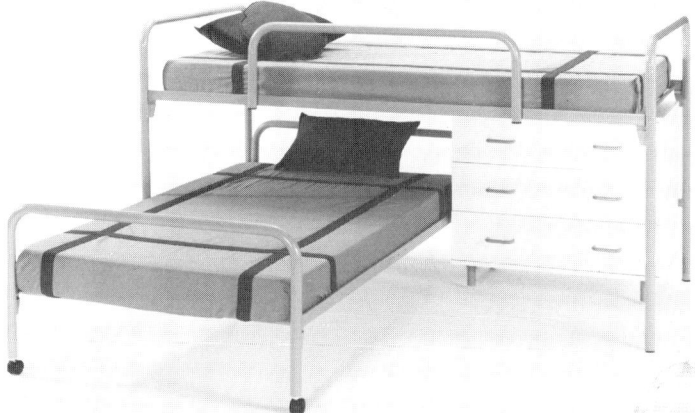

**Name:** Condo bed
**Item no:** 131 bed
**Company:** Amisco Industries
**Dimensions:** 41"W X 78"L X 41-3/4"H
**Materials:** Tubular steel with epoxy polyester powder finish
**Price range:** Budget

**Name:** Convertible bed*
**Company:** Arise Futon Mattress Co., Inc.
**Dimensions:** 39"W X 75"L (twin); 54"W X 75"L (full); 60"W X 80"L (queen)
**Materials:** Maple frame; cotton futon and cover
**Price range:** Budget

**Name:** Tivoli wall system
**Company:** Workbench
**Materials:** Oak or teak
**Price range:** Budget

**Name:** The "Excalibur" Option sofa sleeper*
**Company:** Castro Convertibles
**Dimensions:** Full size bed
**Materials:** Hardwood
**Price range:** Moderate

**Name:** Abacus bed*
**Item no:** 36604
**Company:** Conran's
**Dimensions:** 57"W X 78"D X 37"H (double; also available in queen)
**Materials:** Stained ash
**Price range:** Budget

**Name:** Castro's Aspen sofa sleeper*
**Company:** Castro Convertibles
**Dimensions:** 80"W X 34-1/2"D X 27"H (queen; also available in twin, full, and long line)
**Materials:** Wood frame, polydacron cushions; cotton cover
**Price range:** Budget

**Name:** Claremont bed with triple arch trim*
**Item no:** 433
**Company:** Landes
**Dimensions:** 54-1/2"W (double); 61-1/2"W (queen) X 33-1/2"H (at headboard)
**Materials:** Polyurethane coating on steel tubing
**Price range:** Budget

**Name:** Athena desk*
**Item no:** 659908
**Company:** Conran's
**Dimensions:** 49-1/2"W X 29"D X 29"H
**Materials:** White lacquered chipboard
**Price range:** Budget

169

**Name:** Double futon with large bolster*
**Item nos:** 21580 (futon); 1395 (bolster)
**Company:** Natural Design
**Dimensions:** Futon: 54"W X 75"L; bolster: 40"W X 9"D
**Materials:** Cotton
**Price range:** Budget (both)

**Name:** Layout rocker
**Item no:** LA-2 rocker
**Company:** The Sherwood Corporation
**Dimensions:** 27"W X 33"D X 26"H
**Materials:** Foam with wood panel back and base
**Price range:** Budget

**Name:** "Softly" armchair
**Company:** The Sherwood Corporation
**Dimensions:** 35"W X 36"D X 31"H
**Materials:** Wood panel arms and back, foam
**Price range:** Budget

**Name:** Mule ear side and arm chairs
**Item nos:** 041 (side chair); 045 (arm chair)
**Company:** Nichols & Stone, Gardner, MA.
**Dimensions:** Side chair: 20-1/2"W X 41"H; arm chair: 23-1/2"W X 41"H (arm)
**Materials:** Solid ash
**Price range:** Budget (both)

**Name:** Breuer-style armchair
**Item no:** AL 10A
**Company:** Workbench
**Dimensions:** 23"W X 20"D X 32"H
**Materials:** Chrome plated steel frame, beech, cane
**Price range:** Budget

**Name:** Roadster chair
**Item no:** ROAC32
**Company:** Tiffany and Tiffany
**Dimensions:** 32"W
**Materials:** Hardwood frame
**Price range:** Budget

**Name:** Sling chair
**Item no:** KJOKE
**Company:** Workbench
**Dimensions:** 24-1/2"W X 26"D X 29"H
**Materials:** Steel tubing, quilted gabardine fabric
**Price range:** Budget

**Name:** Beech dining chair
**Item no:** PISTO
**Company:** Workbench
**Dimensions:** 16"W X 16"D X 32"H
**Materials:** Beech with raffia or twill seat
**Price range:** Budget

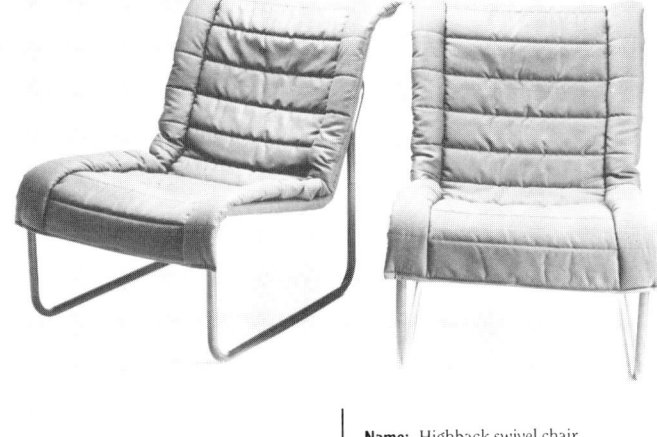

**Name:** Highback swivel chair
**Item no:** KG IRA
**Company:** Workbench
**Dimensions:** 25-1/2"W X 30"D X 36"H
**Materials:** Steel tubing frame, Trevira/viscose cover
**Price range:** Budget

# Accessories

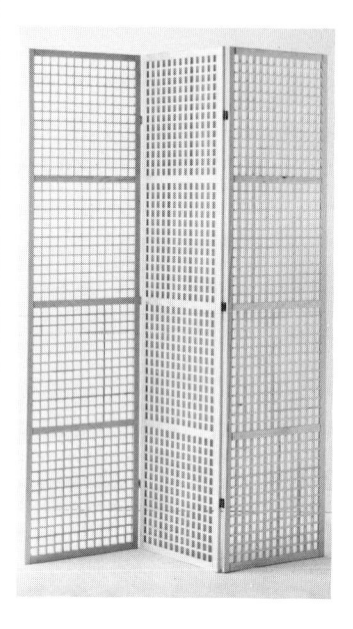

**Name:** Pine screen*
**Item no:** 995096
**Company:** Conran's
**Dimensions:** 59-1/2"W X 1/2"D X 67-1/4"H
**Materials:** Unfinished pine
**Price range:** Budget

**Name:** Quartz clock
**Item no:** 622-878 clock
**Company:** Howard Miller Clock Co.
**Dimensions:** 10-1/2" dia.; 1-5/8"D
**Materials:** Solid oak case
**Price range:** Budget

**Name:** Spanish willow trunk*
**Item no:** 447870
**Company:** Conran's
**Dimensions:** 19"W X 31"L X 17"D
**Materials:** White willow
**Price range:** Budget

**Name:** Rectangular planter with wheels
**Item no:** 5/4694
**Company:** Kartell USA
**Dimensions:** 13"W X 26"D X 13-3/4"H
**Materials:** Polyurethane
**Price range:** Moderate

**Name:** Northridge collection three-drawer unit*
**Item no:** 60
**Company:** Landes
**Materials:** Black steel frame; cotton or polyduck canvas drawers
**Price range:** Moderate

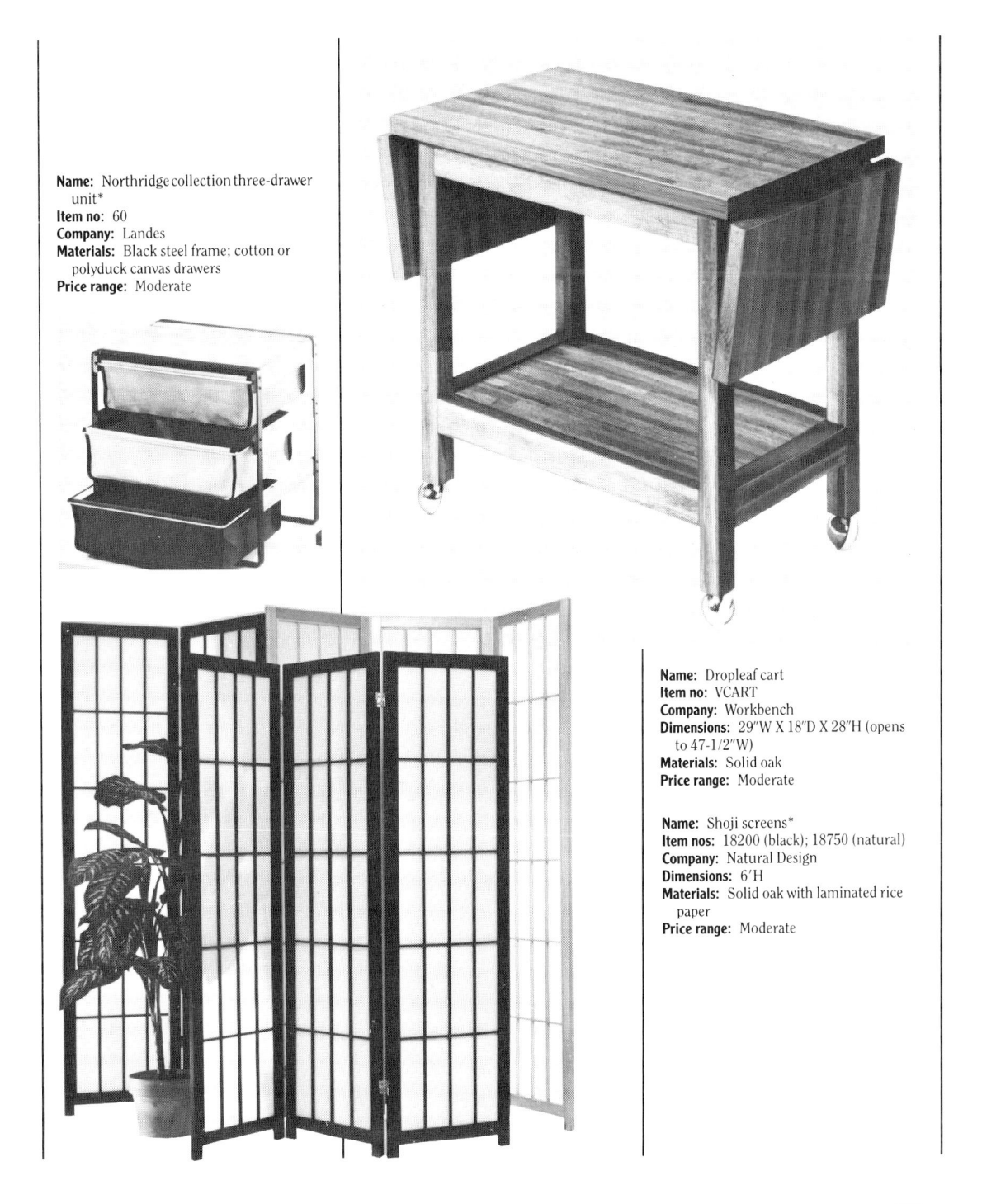

**Name:** Dropleaf cart
**Item no:** VCART
**Company:** Workbench
**Dimensions:** 29"W X 18"D X 28"H (opens to 47-1/2"W)
**Materials:** Solid oak
**Price range:** Moderate

**Name:** Shoji screens*
**Item nos:** 18200 (black); 18750 (natural)
**Company:** Natural Design
**Dimensions:** 6'H
**Materials:** Solid oak with laminated rice paper
**Price range:** Moderate

**Name:** Folding closet*
**Item no:** 248
**Company:** Landes
**Materials:** Steel frame; cotton canvas or polyduck
**Price range:** Moderate

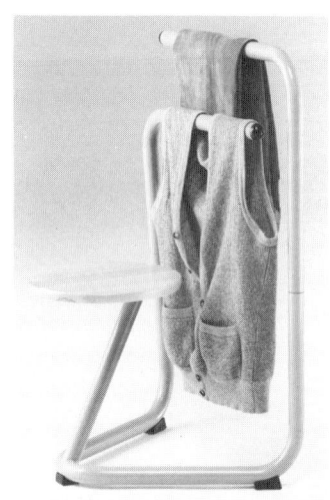

**Name:** Unishelf System
**Item no:** 4008
**Company:** Kartell USA
**Dimensions:** 30-3/4"W X 11"D X 59-1/4"H
**Materials:** Styrene
**Price range:** Moderate

**Name:** TV cart
**Item no:** E 8012
**Company:** Workbench
**Dimensions:** 32"W X 20"D X 27"H
**Materials:** Oak or teak or white lacquer
**Price range:** Moderate

**Name:** Valet
**Item no:** 688
**Company:** Amisco Industries
**Dimensions:** 23"W X 20"L X 34"H
**Materials:** Tubular steel with natural wood seat
**Price range:** Budget

## Lighting

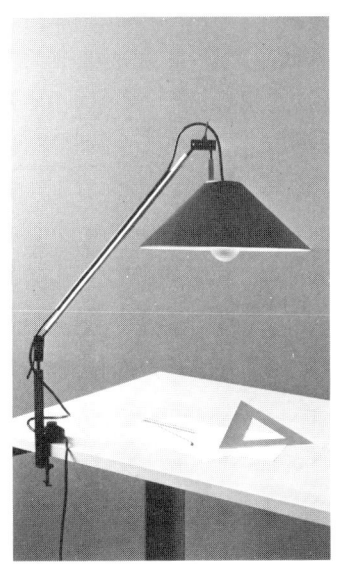

**Name:** Stoneware lamps
**Item nos:** GS12, GS13, GS14, GS15
**Company:** George Kovacs Inc.
**Dimensions:** GS12: 14-1/2"H; GS13: 18-1/2"H; GS14: 18-1/2"H; GS15: 28"H
**Materials:** Handcrafted ceramic stoneware
**Price range:** Moderate

**Name:** Aggregato clamp-on lamp
**Company:** Artemide, Inc.
**Dimensions:** 38"H maximum
**Materials:** Anodized aluminum and dark grey lacquered metal
**Price range:** Moderate

**Name:** Nessen/Augusti floor lamp*
**Item no:** NAF 60 with NAR 85 reflector
**Company:** Nessen Lamps Inc.
**Dimensions:** 48-3/4"H; 9-1/4" dia. base
**Materials:** Brass
**Price range:** Moderate

**Name:** Quad lighting*
**Item nos:** 541109 (wall light); 358975 (table light)
**Company:** Conran's
**Dimensions:** 10" dia.
**Materials:** Lacquered metal frame, etched glass
**Price range:** Budget

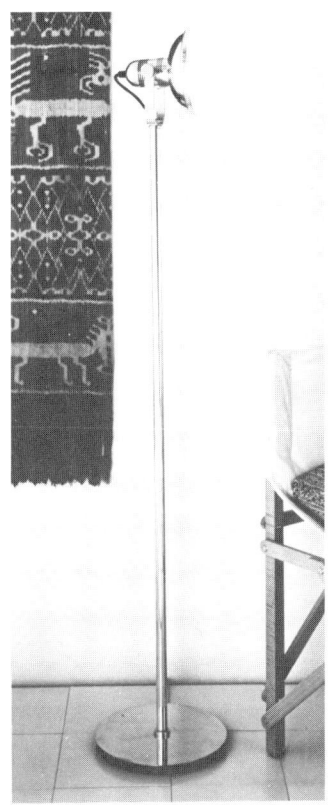

**Name:** Atlas work light*
**Item nos:** 353728 (white); 353736 (black)
**Company:** Conran's
**Dimensions:** 8″ dia.; extends 33″
**Materials:** Metal
**Price range:** Budget

**Name:** "Tuf Art" lamp
**Item no:** 2216
**Company:** Alsy
**Dimensions:** 20″H
**Materials:** Terra-cotta, silk shade
**Price range:** Budget

**Name:** Floor and desk lamps
**Item nos:** 6410, 6411
**Company:** George Kovacs Inc.
**Dimensions:** 6410, 42″H; 6411, 11″H
**Materials:** Metal painted white, black, or grey
**Price range:** Moderate

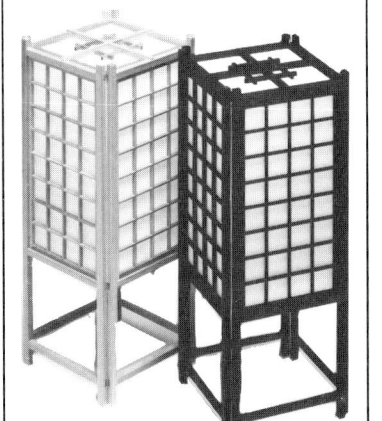

**Name:** Shoji lamp*
**Item nos:** 20680 (natural); 20700 (black)
**Company:** Natural Design
**Dimensions:** 7-1/2"W X 7-1/2"D X 18"H
**Materials:** Wood and reinforced rice paper
**Price range:** Budget

**Name:** Aggregato stelo table lamp
**Company:** Artemide Inc.
**Dimensions:** 22-1/2"H, base 7-1/2"W
**Materials:** Stem: anodized aluminum; base: grey thermoplastic coated metal; shade: metal or opline thermoplastic
**Price range:** Moderate

**Name:** Can light
**Item no:** 5055
**Company:** George Kovacs Inc.
**Dimensions:** 9-1/2"H, 5-3/4" dia.
**Materials:** Aluminum
**Price range:** Budget

177

# *The Modernist* Sourcebook

## *The Modernist* Bedroom

# The Modernist

Modernists have arrived: they are settled, secure, and very sure of their taste in almost everything. They're well aware of what's going on in the design world (garnered from the pages of *Architectural Digest* and *House and Garden*), but it would take a major revolution in popular style to get them to radically change the elegant, timeless-looking environment they have created for themselves.

Custom-made built-ins, created by a professional designer or a talented local carpenter, are an important part of the Modernist decorating repertoire. In fact, much of their furniture—from lacquered liquor cabinets to sleek sofas—was probably custom-designed or looks like it was. The Modernist taste in furniture does not vary much from the clean-lined, simple styles that have been in vogue for a number of years now (modular sofas, glass-and-brass tables, elegant wood storage pieces), although included in this personality are some newer trends, such as Art Deco revival and postmodern.

Accessories range from contemporary crafts to antique Oriental objets d'art, but such accents are usually limited to just a few select pieces. "Less is more" is the motto of this personality, and you won't find crowded tabletops or any fussy arrangements in a Modernist home.

Beige-on-beige is the quintessential Modernist color scheme (see Sybil Levin's beige living room, following page 24), but other strong monochromes (black, white, even red) and decorating plans that utilize compatible solids are also popular. These basic colors are often relieved with bright accent tones, such as gold or deep red. Postmodernists, who incorporate references to the past in their contemporary furnishings, often favor shades of pink with gray or black; mauve, peach, and seafoam green are other hues that have been increasingly used in Modernist settings in recent years. In general, however, color is a low-key element in a Modernist home, and is usually considered background for the interesting, vivid people who live and visit here.

Window treatments are also considered background, and frequently it's not possible to tell where a window begins and ends in a Modernist setting. For example, floor-to-ceiling

Pictured Opposite: *Floor-to-ceiling vertical blinds dyed to match walls. Recessed ceiling wallwashers. Surface-mounted track lighting. Thick-pile, velvet wall-to-wall carpeting. Adjustable brass swivel floor lamp. Built-in wall unit with recessed mirror, end tables, and platform bed. Linen-upholstered chaise in coordinated fabric. Glass-topped table with marble column legs. Stone sculpture collection. Glazed porcelain vases and urns.*

vertical blinds in a woven fabric that blends with the color of the wall may camouflage a small, ugly window. Similarly, simple drapes that extend from one wall to another can hide a bad view and expand the look of a narrow space. However, when the outlook, whether urban or rural, is beautiful, the Modernist will gladly forgo any window coverings so all can admire the view.

In Modernist homes, lighting is often an inconspicuous element as well, but it can also be dramatic—an important part of the design. Both recessed ceiling lights and spotlights on tracks can be put on dimmers so the level of illumination can be regulated. When aimed at artwork or furnishings, the lighting becomes an integral element in the design of a Modernist room.

Modernists like luxury, plush furnishings, and a supremely elegant and comfortable home. Included in the shopping directories is a wide range of furnishings—from glass-and-brass tables to plump, yet streamlined, sofas—that we feel will appeal to the Modernist. Yet because many may have a bit of the adventurist in them (as would be indicated by the Personality Quiz results), we suggest dipping into the Futurist directories for an accent piece or perhaps a lamp that will add an extra dimension to this look.

## Sybil Levin Talks About the Modernist

James Levin

"When my husband and I were first married, I moved from my traditionally decorated suburban home to our new Manhattan apartment. There was only one problem: my husband disliked traditional interiors. With this in mind, we decided to use the problem to our advantage by starting off with a clean slate. Neither of us contributed any major pieces from our earlier homes.

"We collaborated and compromised. He knew that it was important to me to keep many of my treasures, and I recognized his need for a tailored, uncluttered environment. We mutually agreed upon a neutral color scheme for the walls, furniture, carpeting, and contemporary-style major furnishings. The collectibles and Oriental artwork I had accumulated over the years added color and interest; I was delighted at how striking they appeared in the monochromatic setting.

"I guess you could say, therefore, that I'm a modernist by marriage. Yet I found it surprisingly easy to adapt to the more pared-down contemporary look. Since I'm inundated with a riot of color and pattern in my work as an interior designer, it's relaxing to open the door at day's end and be greeted by subdued, quiet surroundings.

"I think there are both aesthetic and practical advantages to the Modernist decorating personality, especially for career people with modest-size rooms. The single color scheme has a unifying effect, which, in turn, makes the rooms appear more spacious; the neutral background also creates an ideal foil against which to view collectibles and art, which lend personality. And it's easy and economical to change the mood of a space simply by buying new pillows or hanging a different piece of art."

## Profile of a Modernist Couple

**Names:** Pamela and John
**Children:** two, both grown, and two grandchildren
**Residence:** architect-designed contemporary ranch, built 1960
**Setting:** suburban, waterfront
**Occupations:** Pamela—volunteer work; John—stockbroker
**Favorite furniture styles:** designer contemporary, Oriental, modern Italian
**Decorative materials preferred:** woven cotton, leather, marble, metal, glass
**Favorite color schemes:** neutral backgrounds accented with red, yellow, coral
**Most creative house endeavor:** Japanese-style swimming pool
**Most treasured objects:** modern art collection
**Decorating pet peeves:** gold and glittery interiors, a highly "decorated" look
**Dream house:** city penthouse
**Favorite at-home entertaining:** informal catered buffets
**Pastimes:** Pamela—swimming, tennis, needlework; John—gardening, tennis, boating
**Ideal getaway:** barge trip down French canals
**Philosophy:** "We want our rooms to be light and open, to exemplify our love of neutral and primary colors, geometric shapes and orderliness. It's also vital that our interior provide the right backdrop for our art objects."

Inspired by their inclination toward bold colors and clean lines, Pamela and John have designed their rooms to set off the dramatic views of the water and their equally dramatic paintings and sculpture.

Although the one-floor house, built of white-glazed brick, has an Oriental look to it, it was actually modeled after ancient Roman houses. Located one hundred yards from the water, with an all-glass front facing the bay, they both admit that it was "the setting that convinced us to buy the house."

The front door opens onto the entryway, in the center of which is a glass, open-roof atrium. Here flourishes a beautifully designed microcosm of shrubs, trees, and a fish pond under a rock ledge.

The dining area, behind the atrium, is decorated sparely with a table and six Italian-style upholstered side chairs. "One day I got tired of the cherry wood on the table, so I bought some natural linen and had the table covered and then lacquered," Pamela told us. Her decorating innovativeness is also exemplified by the ceiling light fixture in this space. Tucked between the levels of a large metal sculpture are small canister downlights, which can be dimmed or brightened as the occasion warrants. "Both John and I find chandeliers very unflattering to people and space."

The coral and black fabric of the chairs is echoed in the large abstract painting bought a number of years ago, which hangs on the facing wall. "We love the thrill of discovering the work of artists before they become established," John observed of the painting by a now very renowned artist.

The gallerylike display of art objects (sculpture, paintings, etchings, and drawings) lining both sides of the entryway and dining area flows into the living room. There they mingle with Eskimo sculpture, Oriental objects, and a needlepoint tapestry and pillows. Pamela enjoys needlepointing and several of her pillows are scattered throughout the house. She and John chose to keep most of the floor space free of rugs and the windows unadorned by draperies that would only obscure the view. Instead she uses the tapestries and pillows she makes to contribute warmth and texture to their contemporary setting.

There are also a few antiques, yet even they have an up-to-date flavor. Flanking the beige sectional sofa are two English period chairs, upholstered in crisp white leather so that their traditional lines have been modernized in an exciting way.

All the bedrooms feature built-in drawers, shelves, and closets that add to the clean, spare look of the house. "I love a place that's easy to maintain," Pamela pointed out. "That's also why the baths are all tile and all the floors are tile or marble."

The couple is justifiably proud of the new Japanese-style swimming pool, framed by sculptured rocks, located between the front of the house and the water. "We like it because it doesn't announce the fact that it's a pool—it fits into the landscape so well," said John.

The pool, while typifying the decorating philosophy of the couple, was difficult to accomplish. "We rarely take the easy, worn path. Unique decorating in our home is a priority and we enjoy sharing this experience with our family and friends. For us that's what decorating is all about."

## *The Modernist* Personality Window Treatments

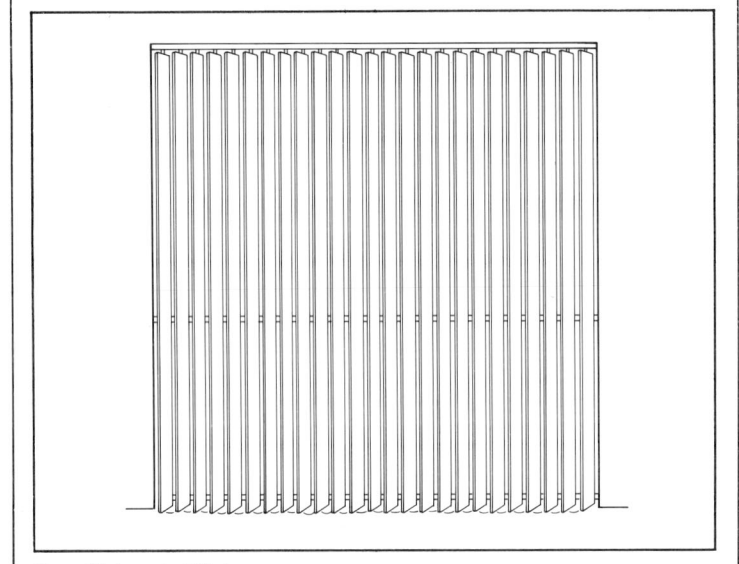

Woven fabric vertical blinds.

Gauze rectangles held back with white architectural hold backs.

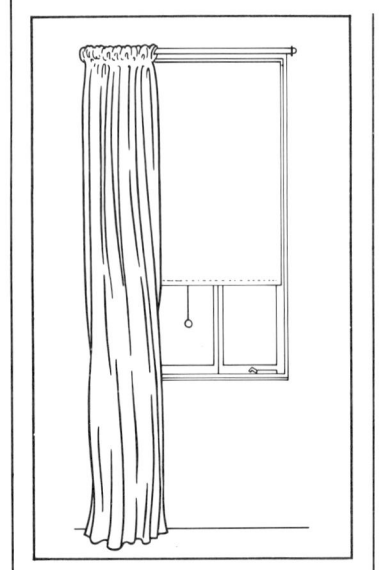

Monochromatic, full-gathered drapery with coordinated canvas shade.

Metal micro-mini blinds.

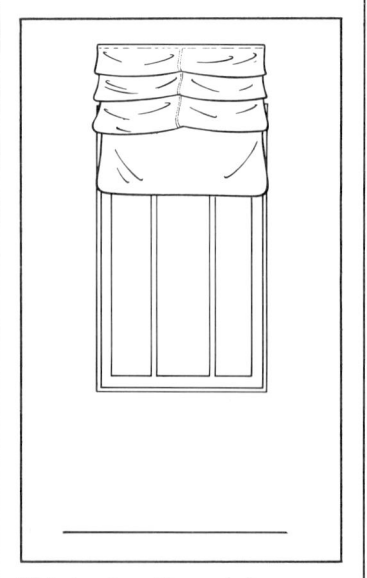

White, translucent Roman shades.

## Major Furnishings

**Name:** Two-door hall chest
**Item no:** 70-420D
**Company:** Mastercraft, Division of Baker Furniture
**Dimensions:** 48"W X 13"D X 30"H
**Materials:** Brass, lacquer
**Price range:** Top of the line

**Name:** Chair
**Designer:** John Mascheroni
**Item no:** 879
**Company:** Swaim
**Dimensions:** 34"W X 34"D X 35"H
**Price range:** Moderate

**Name:** Cocktail table
**Item no:** 3014
**Company:** Casa Bique Ltd.
**Dimensions:** 43-1/2"W X 43-1/2"D X 16"H
**Materials:** Solid cast brass with Italian travertine
**Price range:** Moderate

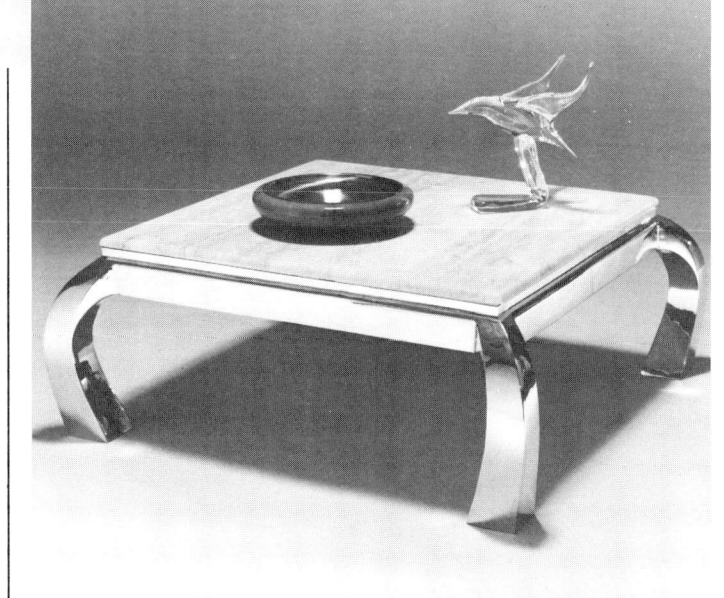

|  | Major Furnishings | Accessories and Lighting |
|---|---|---|
| Budget | under $1,000 | under $100 |
| Moderate | $1,000-$2,500 | $100-$300 |
| Top-of-the-Line | over $2,500 | over $300 |

*Designates mail order

**Name:** Hall console
**Item no:** 70-300
**Company:** Mastercraft, Division of Baker Furniture
**Dimensions:** 68"W X 18"D X 28-1/2"H
**Materials:** Metallic lacquer, brass
**Price range:** Top of the line

**Name:** Queen bed
**Designer:** John Mascheroni
**Item no:** 875
**Company:** Swaim
**Dimensions:** 69"W X 89"D X 28"H
**Price range:** Moderate

**Name:** Façade Collection console
**Designer:** John Saladino
**Item no:** 5565
**Company:** Baker Furniture Company
**Dimensions:** 44"W X 22"D X 28-3/4"H
**Price range:** Top of the line

**Name:** Chair, sofa, loveseat
**Item nos:** 1965, 1967, 1966
**Company:** Thayer Coggin, Inc.
**Dimensions:** Chair: 33"W X 38"D X 35"H; sofa: 84"W X 38"D X 35"H; loveseat: 66"W X 38"D X 35"H
**Price range:** Moderate

**Name:** Sofa from the Drexel Contemporary Classics Collection
**Item no:** 99-1085
**Company:** Drexel Heritage Furnishings
**Dimensions:** 86"W X 86-1/2"D X 32-1/2"H
**Price range:** Moderate

**Name:** Modern wing chair
**Designer:** John Saladino
**Item no:** 334-35
**Company:** Baker Furniture Co.
**Dimensions:** 35"W X 34"D X 40"H
**Price range:** Moderate

**Name:** Castro's "La Chaise"*
**Company:** Castro Convertibles
**Dimensions:** 93"L X 34-1/2"D X 27"H; mattress: 74" X 54" (longline)
**Materials:** Wood frame, polydacron cushions
**Price range:** Moderate

**Name:** Lounge chair
**Item no:** 1011
**Company:** Thayer Coggin, Inc.
**Dimensions:** 33"W X 32"D X 34"H
**Price range:** Budget

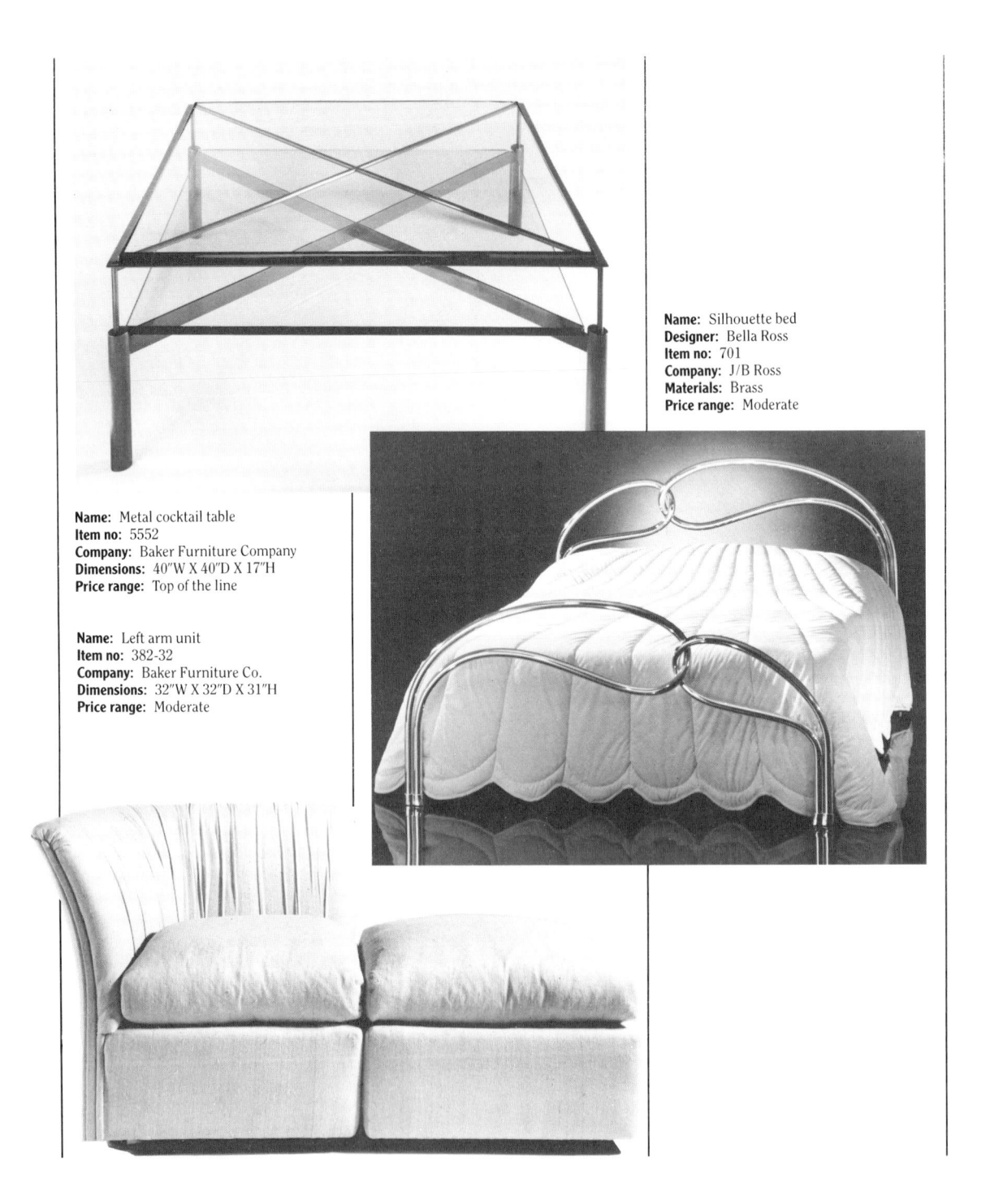

**Name:** Metal cocktail table
**Item no:** 5552
**Company:** Baker Furniture Company
**Dimensions:** 40"W X 40"D X 17"H
**Price range:** Top of the line

**Name:** Left arm unit
**Item no:** 382-32
**Company:** Baker Furniture Co.
**Dimensions:** 32"W X 32"D X 31"H
**Price range:** Moderate

**Name:** Silhouette bed
**Designer:** Bella Ross
**Item no:** 701
**Company:** J/B Ross
**Materials:** Brass
**Price range:** Moderate

**Name:** "Columns Collection" round dining table with Neo-Classic side chairs
**Item nos:** 66650 (table); 4000 (side chairs)
**Company:** Casa Stradivari
**Dimensions:** Table: 60" dia.; 30"H
**Materials:** Table: wood; chairs: maple
**Price range:** Moderate

**Name:** Sofa
**Item no:** 336-86
**Company:** Baker Furniture Co.
**Dimensions:** 86"W X 34"D X 32"H
**Price range:** Top of the line

**Name:** Sectional
**Item no:** 877
**Designer:** John Mascheroni
**Company:** Swaim
**Dimensions:** Sofa: 98"L X 37"D X 30"H
Right arm: 89"L X 37"D X 30"H
**Price range:** Top of the line

**Name:** Mies couch*
**Item no:** 337
**Company:** Palazzetti
**Dimensions:** 38"W X 77"D X 24-1/2"H
**Materials:** Wood, steel legs, leather-covered foam upholstery
**Price range:** Top of the line

191

**Name:** Loveseat
**Item no:** 332-48
**Company:** Baker Furniture Co.
**Dimensions:** 48"W X 35"D X 30"H
**Price range:** Top of the line

**Name:** Flexible lounge chair
**Item no:** 1095
**Company:** Thayer Coggin, Inc.
**Dimensions:** 36"W X 37"D X 42"H
**Materials:** Base in chrome or brass
**Price range:** Moderate

**Name:** Bretz leather armchair
**Company:** Regba-Diran N.Y., Inc.
**Dimensions:** 38"L X 36"D X 28"H
**Materials:** Leather
**Price range:** Moderate

**Name:** Mies arm chair*
**Item no:** 305
**Company:** Palazzetti
**Dimensions:** 22-3/8"W X 33"D X 32"H
**Materials:** Mirror polished and chrome plated steel tube frame; hand woven natural cane
**Price range:** Budget

**Name:** Profile V chair
**Company:** IPF International Inc.
**Dimensions:** 20-1/2"W X 22"D X 34"H
**Materials:** Wood, lacquer, fabric
**Price range:** Budget

**Name:** Tubular Bruno chair*
**Item no:** 355
**Company:** Palazzetti
**Dimensions:** 21-3/4"W X 24"D X 31"H
**Materials:** Mirror polished and chrome plated steel tube frame; leather
**Price range:** Budget

**Name:** Bar unit
**Item no:** 5592
**Company:** Baker Furniture Co.
**Dimensions:** 39"W X 21-7/8"D X 84"H
**Price range:** Top of the line

**Name:** "Columns Collection" round cocktail table
**Item no:** 66340
**Company:** Casa Stradivari
**Dimensions:** 40" dia.; 16-1/2"H
**Materials:** Wood
**Price range:** Budget

193

# Accessories

**Name:** "DO" "RE" "ME" Pedestals
**Item nos:** 1860, 1861, 1862
**Company:** Gampel-Stoll Corp.
**Dimensions:** 16-1/4" X 16-1/4" X 16";
19-3/4" X 19-3/4" X 24"; 19-3/4" X
19-3/4" X 40"
**Materials:** PVC pipe and filled polyester resin
**Price range:** Top of the line


**Name:** Mirror
**Item no:** 5512
**Company:** Baker Furniture Co.
**Dimensions:** 28"W X 49"H
**Price range:** Top of the line

**Name:** Vase
**Item no:** 33-5592
**Company:** Toyo Trading Co.
**Dimensions:** 7"H
**Materials:** Bronze
**Price range:** Moderate

**Name:** Free-form faceted design clock*
**Designer:** G. J. Fedden
**Item no:** G-3
**Company:** Natico Originals, Inc.
**Dimensions:** 11"W X 5"D X 14"H
**Materials:** Plexiglass
**Price range:** Top of the line

**Name:** The Riviera
**Item no:** 612-230
**Company:** Howard Miller Clock Co.
**Dimensions:** 6-3/4"W X 2-3/8"D X 8-1/2"H
**Materials:** Polished brass frame; glass crystal; quartz clock works
**Price range:** Budget

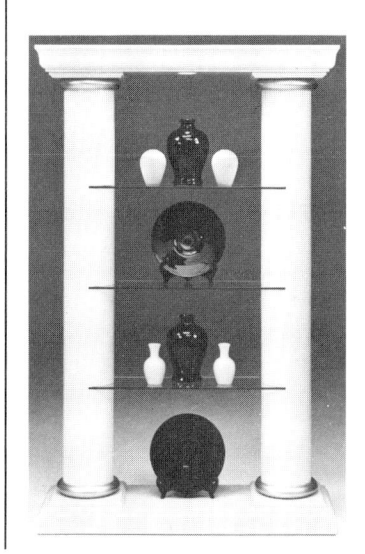

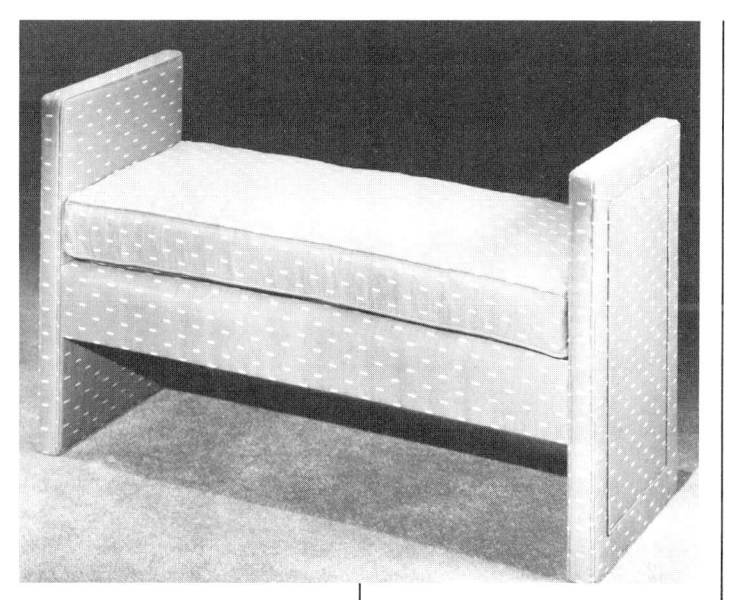

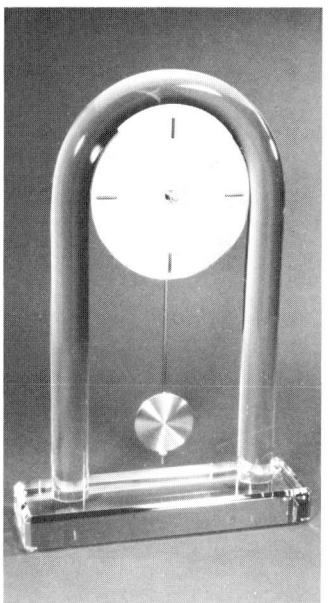

**Name:** "Columns Collection" étagère
**Item no:** 66483
**Company:** Casa Stradivari
**Dimensions:** 53"W X 17"D X 83"H
**Materials:** Wood
**Price range:** Moderate

**Name:** Upholstered bench
**Item no:** 33-926
**Company:** Century Furniture Co.
**Dimensions:** 43"W X 16"D X 25"H
**Materials:** Upholstered frame
**Price range:** Top of the line

**Name:** Arch design clock*
**Designer:** G. J. Fedden
**Item no:** G-2
**Company:** Natico Originals, Inc.
**Dimensions:** 13"W X 4"D X 19"H
**Materials:** Plexiglass
**Price range:** Moderate

195

## Lighting

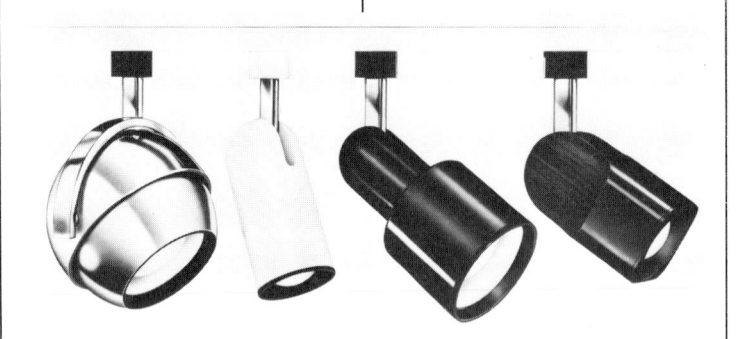

**Name:** Halo Trac Lighting
**Item nos:** L792, L725, L726, L721
**Company:** Halo Lighting, Cooper Industries, Inc.
**Dimensions:** L792: 6-3/8"W X 5-1/4"L X 8-1/2" maximum extension
L725: 2-5/8"W X 5-1/2"L X 7-5/8" maximum extension
L726: 3-3/4"W X 7"L X 9-5/8" maximum extension
L721: 3-3/4"W X 6-3/4"L X 9-3/4" maximum extension
**Materials:** Metal
**Price range:** Budget (all)

**Name:** Olympia table lamp
**Item no:** 107-1
**Company:** Norman Perry
**Dimensions:** 19"H
**Materials:** Solid cast brass
**Price range:** Top of the line


**Name:** Ceiling fixture
**Item no:** 5027
**Company:** George Kovacs, Inc.
**Dimensions:** 6-1/2"H; 23-1/2" dia. cymbol shade
**Materials:** Polished aluminum
**Price range:** Moderate

**Name:** Art Deco Table Torchiere
**Item no:** 1938-1004
**Company:** Paul Hanson Co., Inc.
**Dimensions:** 18"H
**Materials:** Polished brass, white satin glass shade
**Price range:** Moderate

**Name:** Celeste
**Item no:** 101-1
**Company:** Norman Perry
**Dimensions:** 63″ or 75″H
**Materials:** Solid brass base, hand-blown glass globe
**Price range:** Top of the line

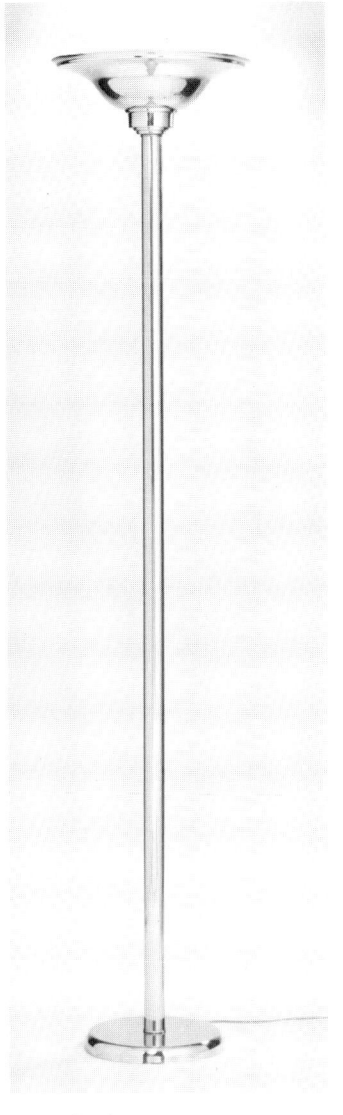

**Name:** Floor lamp
**Item no:** 5025
**Company:** George Kovacs, Inc.
**Dimensions:** 68″H; 14-1/2″ dia. shade
**Materials:** Solid brass
**Price range:** Top of the line

**Name:** Table lamp
**Item nos:** 3205
**Company:** Laurel for Westwood, Westwood Lighting Group, Inc.
**Dimensions:** 28″H
**Materials:** Polished brass finish
**Price range:** Moderate

**Name:** Table lamp
**Item no:** 2463
**Company:** Casual Lamps of California, Inc.
**Dimensions:** 12-1/4″W X 27″H
**Materials:** Ceramic with Lucite base and painted parchment shade
**Price range:** Moderate

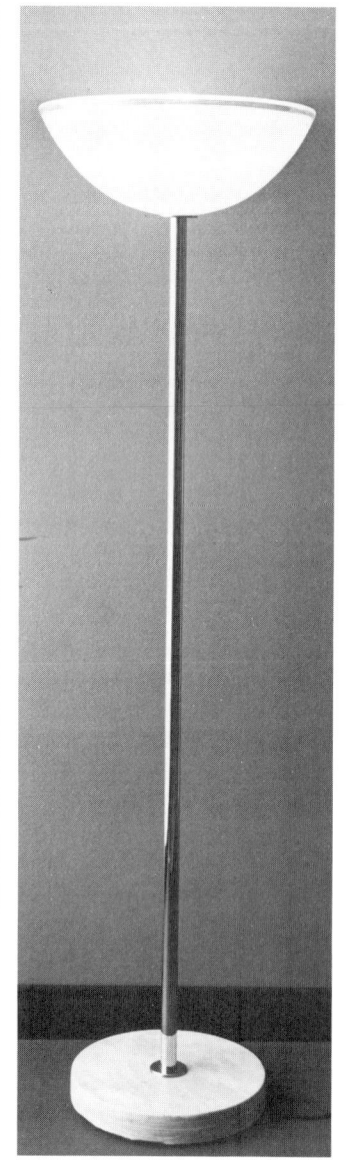

**Name:** Onfale floor lamp
**Company:** Artemide, Inc.
**Dimensions:** 71"H; 19" base
**Materials:** Marble, chrome, handblown glass
**Price range:** Top of the line

**Name:** Column lamp
**Item no:** 6050
**Company:** George Kovacs, Inc.
**Dimensions:** 73"H; 9-1/2" dia. column; base and cap, 14" dia.
**Materials:** White aluminum
**Price range:** Top of the line

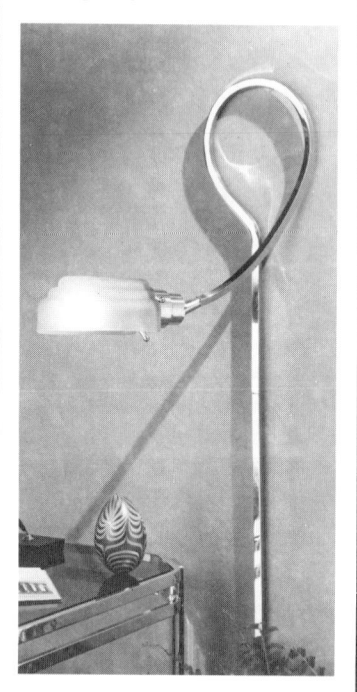

**Name:** Apricot Sconce-Swooping Success
**Item no:** 5051-65049
**Company:** Beth Weissman Co., Inc.
**Dimensions:** 12"W X 14"D X 22"H
**Materials:** Apricot satin-glass and polished brass
**Price range:** Top of the line

198

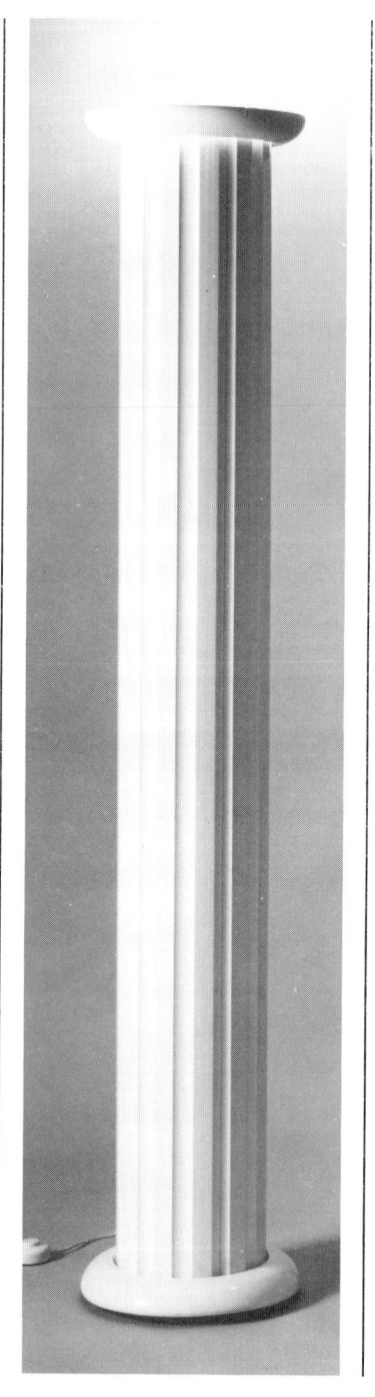

*The Futurist*
**Sourcebook**

## The Futurist Kitchen

## The Futurist

Pictured Opposite: *Suspended factory reflector lamp. Rolling stainless-steel operating table. Metal wall grid. Steel laboratory stools. Commercial soap and paper dispenser. Steel footstool-safety ladder. Wire glass placemats. Commercial dome-top waste receptacle. Black vinyl Dekplate flooring. Restaurant dinnerware.*

Forever seeing new possibilities for altering their lives as well as their spaces, Futurists are attuned to new trends, from the hottest night spot and cuisine to the most avant-garde furniture designs.

In decorating, Futurists make their own rules: durable plastic or canvas outdoor furniture moves inside, a turquoise hand-me-down vinyl sofa receives star billing in the living room, street-found fifties-era dining chairs get new hand-painted fabric chair seats, discarded cardboard tubing is born again as low-cost, unique seating.

Futurists are generally more interested in space planning than decorating in the accepted sense of the word. Some might partition off an unfinished loft by hanging quilted moving pads on a ceiling track (or from the exposed pipes with heavy rings). Those in a tiny studio might relieve the tedium of their boxy one room by painting walls and floor in an original design.

Furniture designs favored by Futurists include high-tech styles originally produced for industrial use, twentieth-century revivals (thirties to sixties), outré Italian Memphis, and furnishings and decorative objects created from discovered finds (e.g., wooden cable spools and skids, commercial building materials, and multicolored telephone wire).

Futurists tend to be as experimental in their color choices as in their furniture. Color schemes range from a palette dominated by white, black, and metal gray (or all-white and all-black) to one in which the neon-bright shades prevail (hot pink, chartreuse, wild canary).

Some Futurists make their personal decorating statements with color as a focal point. Rather than using color as a background for their furnishings, these Futurists might turn their loft into a hot-pink palace or make over an ugly bathroom by painting it a high-gloss black.

Futurists extend their dramatic creativity into all areas of their living space. Futurists who elect for fifties-funk might choose old-fashioned metal venetian blinds to cover their windows; others may opt for a shade made from a painter's drop cloth, or simple mosquito netting for a softer look. The criteria for selecting light fixtures go beyond adequate illumination. One Futurist we know mounted a neon sign from a forgotten diner to serve as light, sculpture, and a conversation piece; another set a floor can under a photographer's silver umbrella mounted on a tripod; a third chose to highlight objects with theatrical spots from a ceiling track.

With spontaneity and flux as hallmarks of the Futurist decorating personality, many in this category share a common philosophy: "No sooner have I finished decorating a space than I get new ideas for changing or starting all over again!"

If you're a Futurist, you're the kind of person who can see value and beauty in objects often overlooked for interior choices. Your friends admire you for your flair and unorthodox approach and ability to put a dash of personal energy into whatever design project you tackle.

The Futurist decorating directory reflects the experimental nature of this far-reaching personality. The Futurist takes risks but the design results invariably pay off. Because there are as many different faces to the Futurist as there are Futurists, we have pictured here furnishings and accessories that cover the spectrum from functional industrial designs to more offbeat styles. Bear in mind also that many Futurists fabricate their own furnishings from castoffs and buy artists' originals—and these cannot be readily purchased at retail.

## Michael Braverman Talks About the Futurist

Cynthia Hill

"I think Futurists like me are drawn to a less involved, minimal look that's in direct contrast to the heavier textures—thick carpeting, hot colors, the more 'decorated' look—so typical of the contemporary rooms in the sixties.

"Futurists are more likely to select pieces on the basis of their individual uniqueness and display them in a way that will show off their specialness to best advantage. They often react and respond in a spontaneous way to something they see in a store or even on the street. For me one of the most appealing aspects of this style is its inherent spontaneity. Furniture and display objects can always be added (either found or built); for example, bases for tables can be fashioned from concrete or wood blocks and topped off with stone or glass. Factory-discarded wooden barrels and a steel rack on wheels are other examples. The rack may become a serviceable, mobile bedroom closet and the barrels (with chair pads added) extra seating in tight quarters, which can then be tucked under a table.

"Futurist-style furnishings, particularly those purchased at institutional supply houses, are well made and a good value. Items like commercial bathroom and kitchen fixtures, industrial floorcoverings, and metal shelving are easy to care for and more durable than those made for residential use. And the clean designs lend themselves to a Futurist setting.

"The industrial carpeting I chose for my studio is virtually maintenance-free and holds up to the heavy traffic it gets (I love to throw huge parties with trays of food everywhere), and yet it affords the ideal frame around my art collection. It doesn't impinge on anything it comes in contact with. The Swiss-cheese chairs in the kitchen are metallic, so I don't have to fuss over any upholstery spills; the institutional green shades at the windows need no laundering, just an occasional damp cloth.

"The floor ledge was one of my happiest inspirations. With it I can easily change my art arrangements (no redesigning wall groupings or filling in old nail holes), and display three-dimensional objects like pottery and sculpture next to two-dimensional artwork. At parties the ledge makes for good seating.

"I think many Futurists are, like myself, either involved directly in the arts or have a strong creative side to them and probably live in metropolitan areas where their interests get frequent stimulation. Whether they prefer paper sculptures, metal mobiles, or bonsai, it's important that these objects have space around them so they can be fully appreciated. And this spare, serviceable look gives just the right background for viewing art collectibles.

"My friends feel at ease when they're here—and that's very important to me. They don't worry about setting down a perspiring glass or putting their feet up on my coffee table (marble won't scratch like wood). It's a comfortable space and a good arena for entertaining—and it's a place where I feel I've made a personal statement about art and interior design without spending a fortune on furniture."

## Profile of a Futurist

**Name:** Michael
**Residence:** one-room apartment
**Setting:** urban
**Occupation:** senior designer, interior design firm
**Favorite furniture styles:** Bauhaus (especially Eileen Gray's textiles), Biedermeier, Mackintosh
**Decorative materials preferred:** stone, granite, marble, industrial glass, leather, suede

**Favorite color schemes:** gray, white, and black; forest green and taupe
**Most creative interior endeavor:** installing a carpeted ledge; making a marble-topped coffee table
**Most treasured objects:** art collection, including ceramics, textiles, paper pieces, wood constructions, painting, and Josef Hoffman reproduction chairs
**Decorating pet peeves:** matching sets of furniture, "in" colors, superslick chrome looks
**Dream house:** a thirties-style clapboard on the ocean
**Favorite at-home entertaining:** large special-occasion parties, catered buffet style
**Pastimes:** theater, driving in the country, going to the ocean
**Ideal getaway:** the beach, St. Bart's (future)
**Philosophy:** "I want to fill my interior with furnishings I love, be it sculpture or chairs that can stand on their own as artwork. It's important to me that when friends open the door they point to something new and be excited by it."

The cornerstone of Michael's decorating style is his desire to introduce and maintain an element of surprise in his living space. He achieves this by juxtaposing shapes, styles, and colors, which belie his small, square, one-room home.

Here, Michael has interspersed several looks, among them high-tech, new wave fifties, Bauhaus, and minimalism. The result is a creative collaboration that's totally unique.

Taking his cues from two reproduction Josef Hoffmann chairs, the originals of which were designed in 1903 for a Swiss sanitarium, Michael decorated his apartment with pieces that are art objects in themselves. "I buy furniture that I'll always cherish—but not to the extent that I'll get uptight if someone rests their leg on a tabletop," Michael said.

Michael used an up-to-date checked fabric on the Hoffmann chairs, an example of his own brand of eclecticism in a studio marked by turn-of-the-century moldings and fireplace. "I guess you'd call it period-modern," he explained.

He chose the gray industrial carpet for the living area because, "it was reasonable, and I knew it would unify the space and hold up to a lot of wear and tear." The gray carpet extends onto a low ledge built along one wall of the room. Building the platform was both a functional and an aesthetic design decision. It affords additional seating when entertaining and also serves as a display area for the artwork Michael continually rotates, depending on the occasion and his whim.

The carpet is also used on the sides of the square coffee

table, which Michael made himself out of chipboard and a slab of black marble. His preference for black industrial materials is further exemplified in his choice of black metal filing cabinets for a sideboard and as an occasional table.

Over the marble coffee table hangs a light fixture of Italian design, a particular favorite of Michael's. Called a "Frisbee light," its outer ring—true to its name—appears to float when illuminated.

The 1950s black-and-white checked vinyl tiles on the kitchen floor seem a natural extension of the living area's checked chair fabric and the gray carpet. Michael treasures this room's graceful French windows, opening outdoors—especially on a sunny spring morning. "I didn't want to block the light, but I did need privacy, so I hung *roll-up* shades. They're actually dark green school shades," Michael noted. To answer the need for security without obscuring the view, he installed chrome towels bars at discreet distances. "The sunlight literally dances on the bars," he smiled.

The kitchen chrome chairs, nicknamed "Swiss-cheese chairs" for obvious reasons, also contribute to the pervasive sparkle in the kitchen, as do the white industrial glass countertops and the black laminate table.

The tiny bath, which is the one open space in the apartment that Michael admitted he "didn't have to change at all," is the perfect testament to his decorating goals. "When people open the door and see the unexpected burst of 1930s-style gleaming turquoise tiles, from floor to ceiling, they are delighted and surprised. And those are the two factors that then make me happy—I know it works!" Michael said.

## *The Futurist* Personality Window Treatments

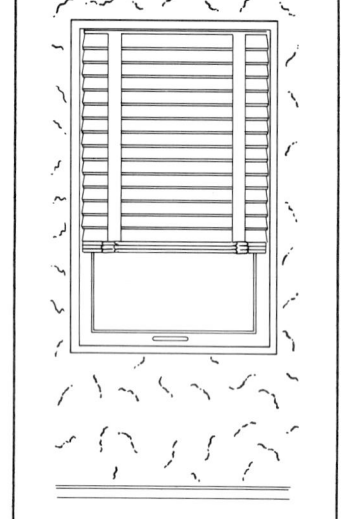

Full, wide metal venetian blinds.

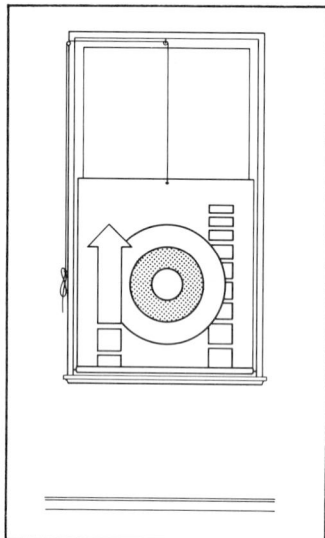

Painted canvas or fabric pull-up shade.

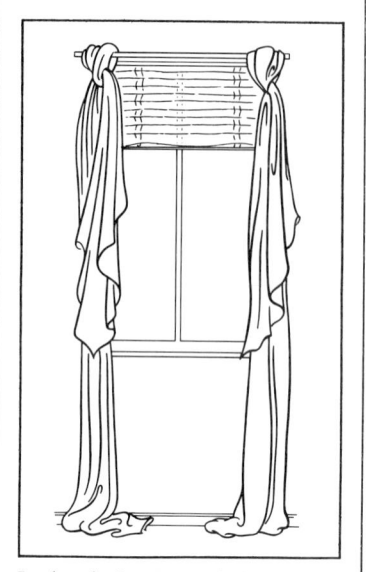

Prepleated vellum Roman shade with knotted cascades of muslin.

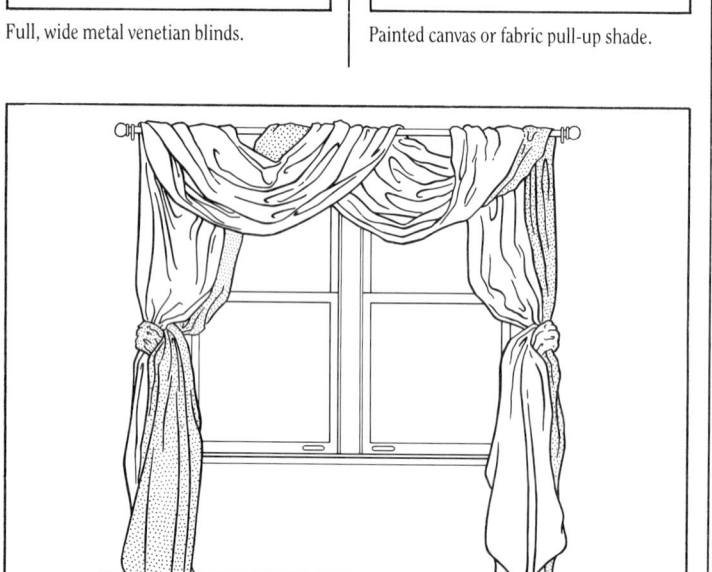

Dyed gauze (or cotton canvas) swag draperies in contrasting colors.

Japanese rice paper shades.

## Major Furnishings

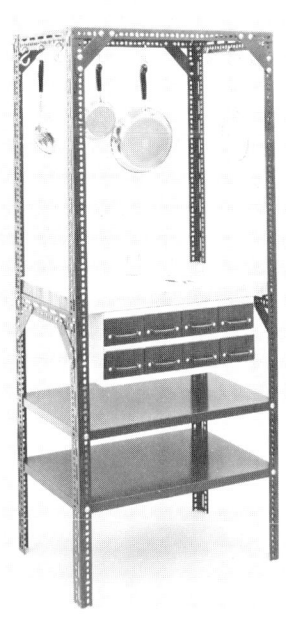

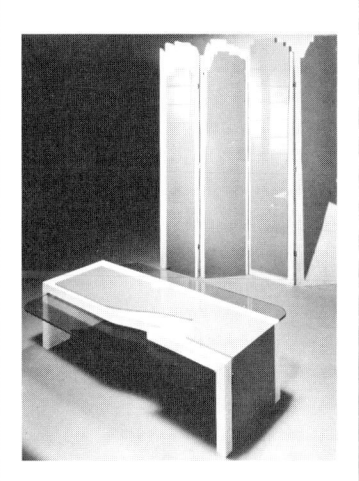

**Name:** Cocktail table and four-panel screen*
**Item nos:** 6601 (table); 6419/1/2/3/4 (screen)
**Company:** Erwin-Lambeth, Inc.
**Dimensions:** Table: 60"W X 20"D X 16"H; screen per panel: 18"W X 84"H
**Materials:** Oak veneer/maple veneer overlay
**Price range:** Table: moderate; screen: top of the line

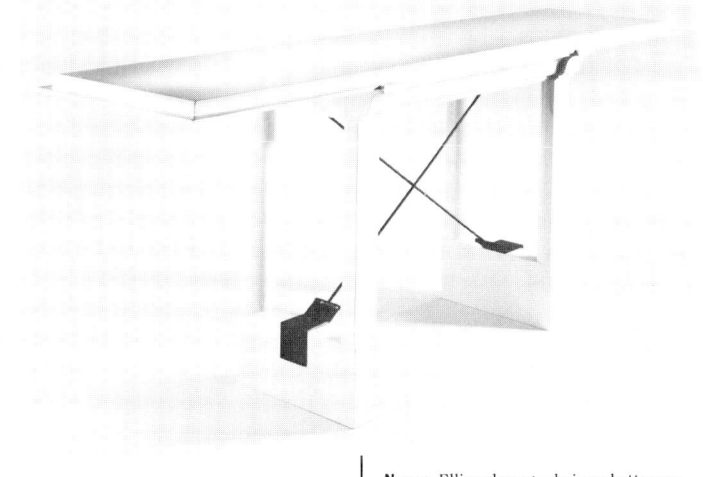

**Name:** Console
**Item no:** 5564
**Company:** Baker Furniture Co.
**Dimensions:** 68"W X 18"D X 27"H
**Materials:** Wood, lacquer
**Price range:** Top of the line

**Name:** Gourmet center *
**Item no:** EQ-24
**Company:** Equipto, Aurora, IL.
**Dimensions:** 30"W X 16"D X 80"H
**Materials:** Steel, 1-3/4" butcherblock
**Price range:** Moderate

**Name:** Ellipse lounge chair and ottoman
**Item nos:** 1501 (chair); 1500 (ottoman)
**Company:** Thayer Coggin, Inc.
**Dimensions:** Chair: 29"W X 39"D X 32"H; ottoman: 29"W X 22"D X 16-1/2"H
**Materials:** Gunmetal billiard cloth (75% wool; 30% nylon)
**Price range:** Moderate (combined price)

|  | Major Furnishings | Accessories and Lighting |
|---|---|---|
| Budget | under $1,000 | under $100 |
| Moderate | $1,000-$2,500 | $100-$300 |
| Top-of-the-Line | over $2,500 | over $300 |

*Designates mail order

**Name:** Etagere *
**Item no:** EQ-16
**Company:** Equipto, Aurora, Ill.
**Dimensions:** 36"W X 18"D X 72"H
**Materials:** Slotted angle frame, glass shelves
**Price range:** Budget

**Name:** Pedestal indoor/outdoor table
**Item no:** 5/4310
**Company:** Kartell USA
**Dimensions:** 31-1/2"W X 31-1/4"D X 28-1/3"H
**Materials:** ABS plastic
**Price range:** Budget

**Name:** Ellipse sofas
**Item nos:** 1515R/1515L
**Company:** Thayer Coggin, Inc.
**Dimensions:** 90"W X 42-1/2"D X 36-1/2"H
**Price range:** Moderate

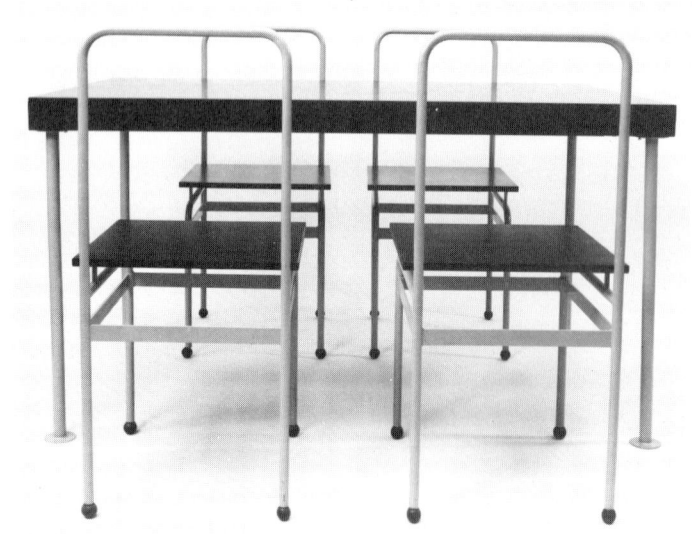

**Name:** Dining table and four chairs
**Designer:** J.J.P. Oud
**Company:** Furniture of the Twentieth Century, Inc.
**Dimensions:** Table: 35"L X 16-3/4"W X 55-1/8"D X 29-5/8"H; Chair: 16-3/4"L X 16-3/4"W X 34-3/4"H
**Materials:** Lacquered steel, matte black finished wood
**Price range:** Top of the line

**Name:** Shirt chest
**Company:** Furniture of the Twentieth Century, Inc.
**Dimensions:** 29-1/2"H X 18-1/2"W X 24"L
**Materials:** Lacquer with nickel-plated details
**Price range:** Budget

**Name:** Cafe chair
**Item no:** 395
**Company:** Amisco Industries
**Dimensions:** 19"W X 20"D X 29"H
**Materials:** Tubular steel with cotton canvas or leather seat
**Price range:** Budget

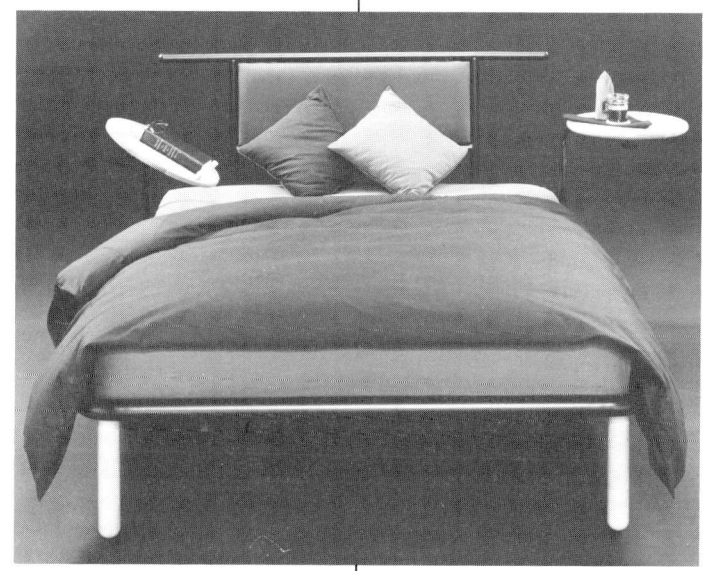

**Name:** Jeeves Bed
**Item no:** 149
**Company:** Amisco Industries
**Dimensions:** 64"W X 84"L X 14"H (queen size)
**Materials:** Tubular steel with choice of cotton canvas or leather headboard
**Price range:** Budget

**Name:** Gambe sofa
**Item no:** GA-59
**Company:** The Sherwood Corp.
**Dimensions:** 59"W X 33"D X 29"H
**Materials:** Foam, steel frame, wood legs
**Price range:** Budget

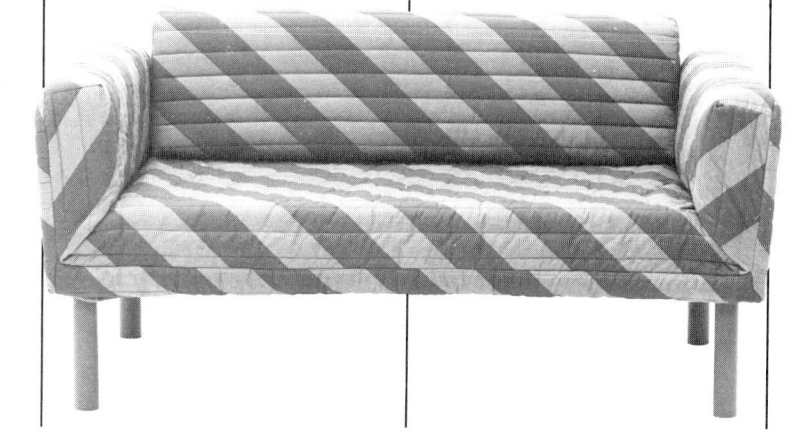

**Name:** Drawer cart*
**Item nos:** EQ-C12
**Company:** Equipto, Aurora, Ill.
**Dimensions:** 30"W X 16"D X 36"H
**Materials:** Steel
**Price range:** Moderate

**Name:** Trolley
**Company:** Kartell USA
**Materials:** ABS plastic, polypropylene
**Price range:** Moderate

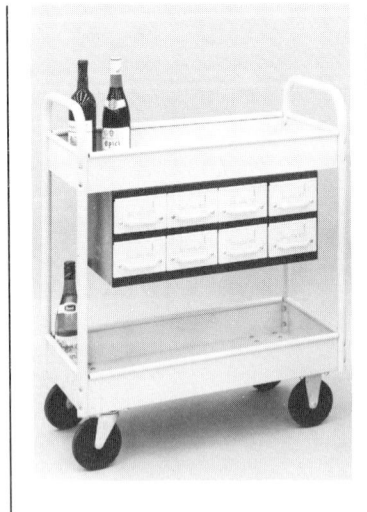

**Name:** Flexible chaise lounge
**Item no:** 1974
**Company:** Thayer Coggin, Inc.
**Dimensions:** 26"W X 66"D X 34"H
**Materials:** Base available in brass or chrome
**Price range:** Budget

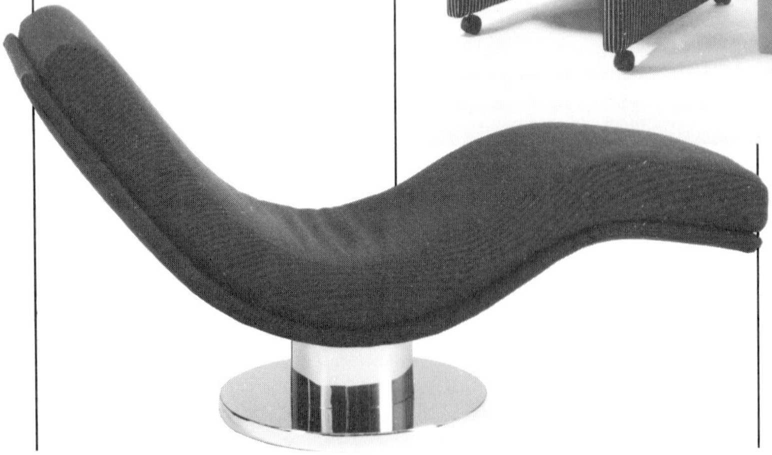

**Name:** Eileen Gray Transat Lounge
**Company:** Furniture of the Twentieth Century, Inc.
**Dimensions:** 31"W X 43"D X 22"H
**Materials:** Black lacquer or clear finish ash; leather or canvas upholstery
**Price range:** Top of the line

**Name:** Geometrics dining chair
**Item nos:** 1034 (arm chair); 1033 (armless chair)
**Company:** Thayer Coggin, Inc.
**Dimensions:** Arm chair: 23-1/2"W X 25"D X 38-1/2"H; Armless chair: 18-1/2"W X 25"D X 38-1/2"H
**Price range:** Budget (both)

**Name:** Prisma sofa
**Item no:** 1574
**Company:** Thayer Coggin, Inc.
**Dimensions:** 81"W X 34"D X 37"H
**Materials:** Wool upholstery
**Price range:** Moderate

**Name:** Pop sofa
**Item no:** POS 80
**Company:** Tiffany & Tiffany
**Dimensions:** 80"W
**Materials:** Hardwood frame
**Price range:** Budget

**Name:** Butterfly chair *
**Item no:** 302
**Company:** Landes
**Dimensions:** 34"W X 35"H
**Materials:** Black wrought iron and canvas
**Price range:** Budget

**Name:** Paimio chair *
**Item no:** 505
**Company:** Palazzetti
**Dimensions:** 23-1/2"W X 31-1/2"D X 25"H
**Materials:** Laminated wood, bent plywood, white or black lacquer finish
**Price range:** Moderate

**Name:** Neo bunching table
**Item no:** 1865
**Company:** Gampel-Stoll Corp.
**Dimensions:** 18"W X 18"D X 18"H
**Materials:** Medium density fiberboard and filled polyester resin
**Price range:** Moderate

**Name:** Sole sofa sleeper
**Company:** Regba-Diran, NY, Inc.
**Dimensions:** 80-1/2"W X 32"D X 26"H
**Materials:** Tubular steel frame, all cotton upholstery
**Price range:** Budget

**Name:** Mallet-Stevens chair
**Company:** Furniture of the Twentieth Century, Inc.
**Dimensions:** 17"W X 16-5/8"D X 32"H
**Materials:** Welded steel
**Price range:** Budget

**Name:** LC Lounge *
**Item no:** 9100
**Company:** Palazzetti
**Dimensions:** 22-3/8"W X 63"D X 28-3/4"H
**Materials:** Leather or "hairyskin"
**Price range:** Moderate

## Accessories

**Name:** Memphasis (Memphis-influenced barware)
**Company:** Georges Briard Inc.
**Price range:** Budget

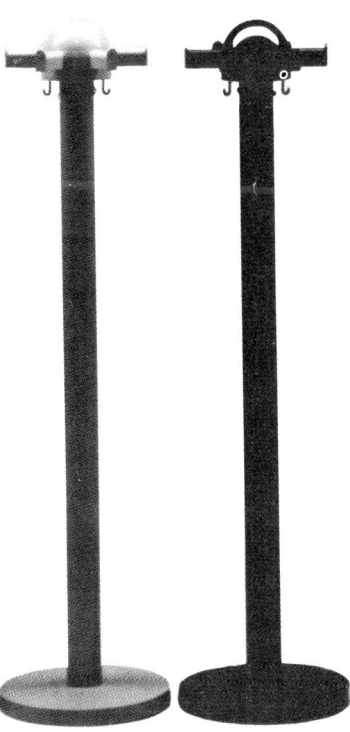

**Name:** Coat rack
**Item no:** 4792
**Company:** Kartell USA
**Dimensions:** 17-1/3"W X 66"H
**Materials:** ABS plastic
**Price range:** Budget

**Name:** Quartz wall clock
**Item no:** 622-290
**Company:** Howard Miller Clock Co.
**Dimensions:** 12-3/4" dia. X 2-1/4"D
**Materials:** Black injected molded plastic case
**Price range:** Budget

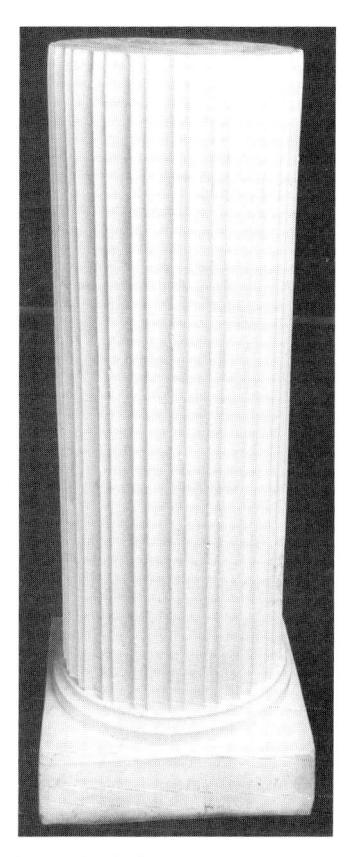

**Name:** Fluted column*
**Item no:** 500B
**Company:** Ballard Designs
**Dimensions:** 29"H X 10" top dia.; base: 12" X 12"
**Materials:** Sandstone, hollow cast
**Price range:** Moderate

213

**Name:** Albero plant stand
**Designer:** Achille Castiglione
**Company:** Furniture of the Twentieth Century, Inc.
**Dimensions:** 21"W at base; 60-1/2"H
**Materials:** Lacquered steel (in a variety of colors)
**Price range:** Moderate

**Name:** Servofumo portable standing ashtray
**Designer:** Achille Castiglione
**Company:** Furniture of the Twentieth Century, Inc.
**Dimensions:** 12" dia.; 40"H
**Materials:** Steel, ABS plastic
**Price range:** Moderate

**Name:** Red elite clock
**Item no:** 67-1053
**Company:** Toyo Trading Company
**Dimensions:** 14-3/4"W X 12-3/4"H
**Price range:** Budget

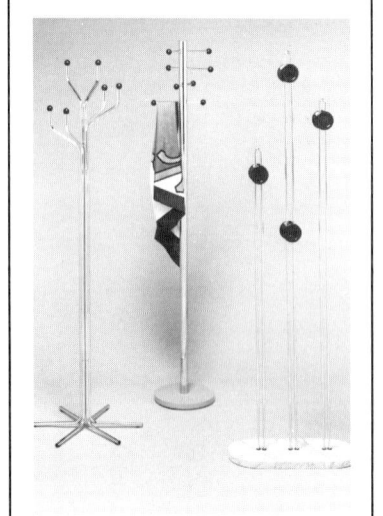

**Name:** Costumers*
**Item nos:** 2090, 2091, 2092 (left to right)
**Company:** Peter Pepper Products, Inc.
**Dimensions:** 2090: 61"H X 21" dia. base; 2091: 67-1/2"H X 11-3/4" dia. base; 2092: 66-1/4"H X 21-1/2"W X 10" dia. base
**Materials:** 2090: polished chrome; 2091: polished chrome with black marble base; 2092: polished chrome with white carrera marble base
**Price range:** 2090 and 2091: moderate; 2092: top of the line

## Lighting

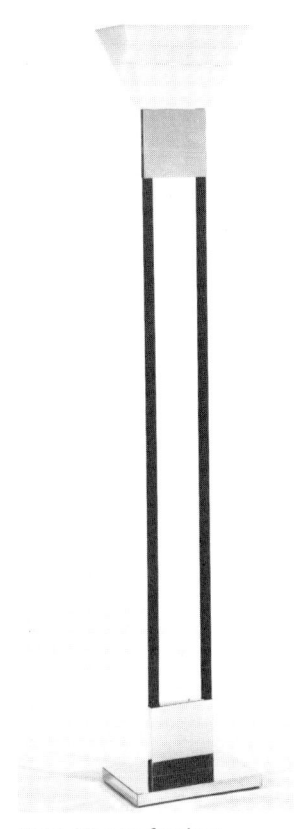

**Name:** 80's retro floor lamp
**Item no:** 3704
**Company:** Alsy
**Dimensions:** 66-1/2"H
**Materials:** Matte black twin square shafts with polished brass mountings; acrylic shade
**Price range:** Moderate

**Name:** Wall-mounted lamp
**Item no:** 6642
**Company:** George Kovacs Inc.
**Dimensions:** 8"W X 5-1/4"D X 12"H; 4-1/2" square back plate
**Materials:** Polished glass, polished chrome or brass, fluorescent bulb
**Price range:** Moderate

**Name:** Dafne table lamps
**Dimensions:** Orni Halloween
**Company:** Artemide, Inc.
**Dimensions:** 14"H X 13"W (shade)
**Materials:** Hand-blown opaline glass, porcelain base (white or glossy gray)
**Price range:** Top of the line

**Name:** Aggregato floor lamp
**Company:** Artemide Inc.
**Dimensions:** 67" maximum height; 15-1/2" base
**Materials:** Anodized aluminum and dark grey lacquered metal; optional cones in metal or opaline plastic
**Price range:** Top of the line

**Name:** Eyeballs (lamps)
**Item nos:** 6700, 6701
**Company:** George Kovacs Inc.
**Dimensions:** 6700: 5″ dia.; 6701: 6″ dia.
**Materials:** Metal
**Price range:** Budget

**Name:** Area 50 floor lamp 160/210
**Company:** Artemide Inc.
**Dimensions:** 63″ or 82″H; 19-1/4″ shade
**Materials:** Metal stem, heat resistant textured synthetic shade
**Price range:** Top of the line

**Name:** Neon sconce
**Item no:** LN-2
**Company:** George Kovacs Inc.
**Dimensions:** 22″W, 3″D
**Materials:** Black painted aluminum triangle
**Price range:** Top of the line

**Name:** Kandido lamp*
**Item no:** NLT 121
**Company:** Nessen Lamps Inc.
**Dimensions:** Adjusts 11″ to 34″H
**Materials:** Metal
**Price range:** Top of the line

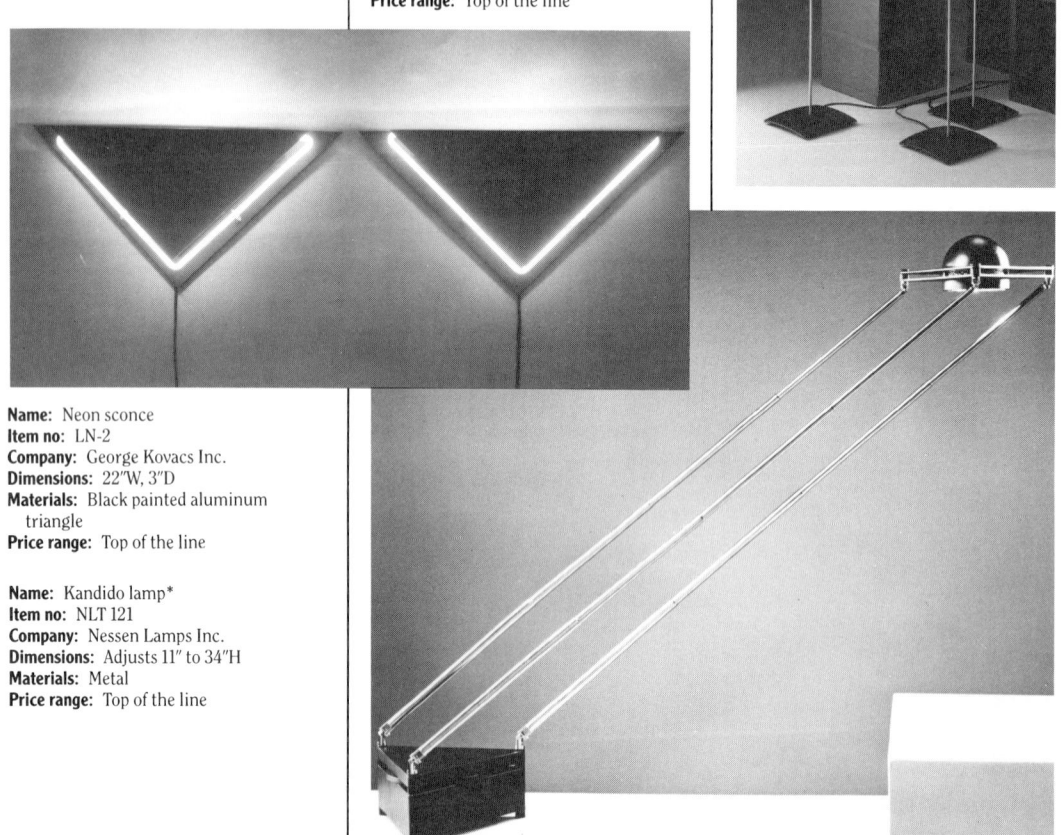

**Name:** "Floating Glass" light fixture
**Item no:** 6525
**Company:** George Kovacs Inc.
**Dimensions:** 20″ dia., 3/8″ glass disk
**Materials:** Polished chrome or brass cap and canopy; polished bull nose glass
**Price range:** Top of the line

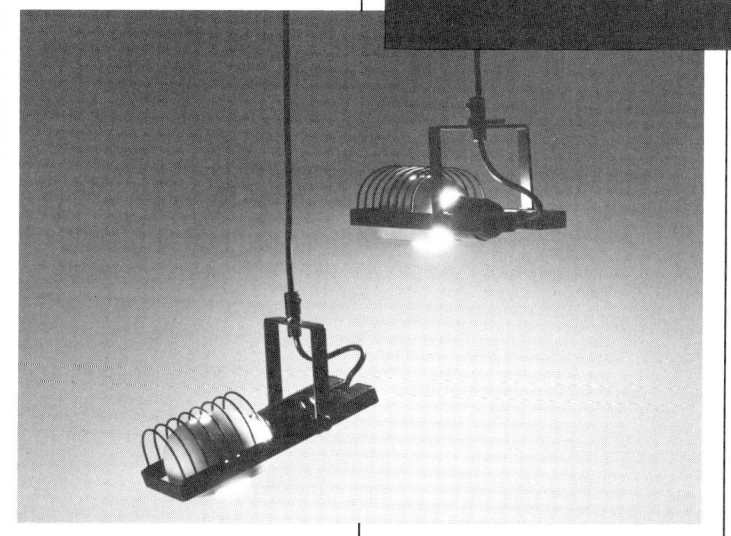

**Name:** Sintesi suspension fixtures
**Company:** Artemide Inc.
**Dimensions:** Maximum length 78-3/4″
**Materials:** Painted metal, anodized aluminum
**Price range:** Moderate

**Name:** Halo traditional lights
**Item nos:** L1528B, L1524B
**Company:** Halo Lighting, Cooper Industries Inc.
**Materials:** Handblown cased-glass shade, metal, brass
**Price range:** Budget

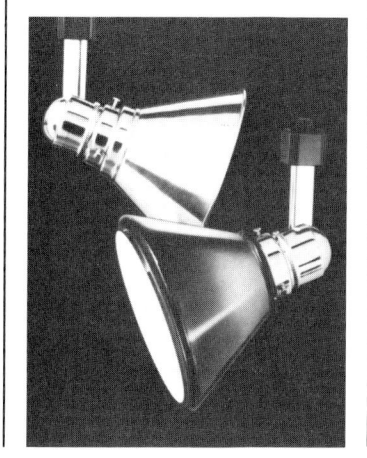

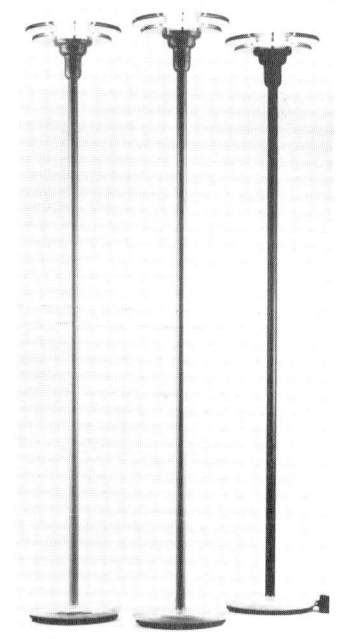

**Name:** Floor lamp
**Item no:** 6310
**Company:** George Kovacs Inc.
**Dimensions:** 70″H; 12″ dia. glass
**Materials:** Marble base, polished bull nose glass, metal stem
**Price range:** Top of the line

217

**Name:** Adonis floor lamp*
**Item no:** NLF 101
**Company:** Nessen Lamps Inc.
**Dimensions:** 74"H
**Materials:** Aluminum, halogen bulb
**Price range:** Top of the line

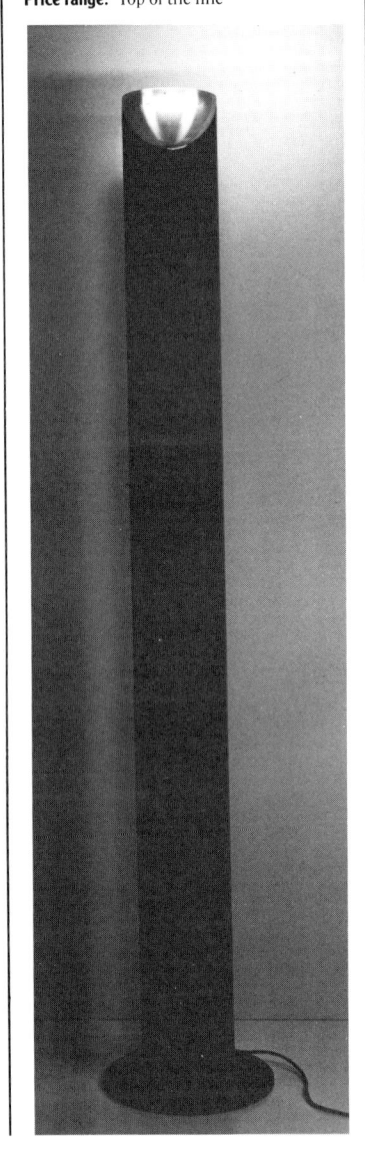

**Name:** Floor lamp
**Item no:** 6140
**Company:** George Kovacs Inc.
**Dimensions:** 41"H with 9" reach
**Materials:** White or black painted metal
**Price range:** Moderate

**Name:** Adjustable pendant fixture
**Item no:** L1534AB
**Company:** Halo Lighting, Cooper Industries Inc.
**Dimensions:** 10"W X 6-1/2"H; cord extends to 85"
**Materials:** Antique brass, etched glass
**Price range:** Moderate

**Name:** Aton modular fluorescent suspension fixture 18/36/58
**Company:** Artemide Inc.
**Dimensions:** 4-1/4"W; choice of lengths: 39-3/4", 63-1/2", 82"
**Materials:** Body in extruded aluminum, lacquered finish; supporting canopies in black molded thermoplastic with steel cable
**Price range:** Top of the line

## Glossary of Decorating Terms

**Adam.** An English neoclassic exterior and interior style developed in the mid-eighteenth century by Robert and James Adam, designer-architect brothers. Furnishings were inspired by Greek and Roman shapes (especially rosettes, medallions, and floral garlands) and often rendered in veneered and painted woods.

*Adam mantelpiece*

**American federal** (1790–1840). Furniture of this period was based on classic revival motifs, with pieces designed mainly in mahogany and often carved with eagles and lyres. The chief exponent of this style was *Duncan Phyfe*.

**Banquette.** A long, upholstered bench, sometimes built in along a wall.

**Bauhaus.** Founded in Germany in 1919, this influential architectural school gave rise to furniture in sculptured tubular steel and laminated woods, such as those designed by Le Corbusier and Marcel Breuer (see below).

*Biedermeier sofa*

**Biedermeier** (1815–1848). A style of German furniture derived from French Empire designs, but lighter and less ostentatious. Like early Victorian furniture in England, Biedermeier pieces were intended for the middle class and the design emphasis is on comfort. The name was taken from a popular newspaper cartoon series that poked fun at the newly emerging middle class.

**Bonbonnière dish.** A small dish used to hold sweets.

**Breuer, or "Cesca," chair.** Tubular steel, wood, and caned armless chair created in 1928 by seminal Bauhaus architect and designer Marcel Breuer (1902–1981). This chair, which represents a turning point in modern furniture design, is widely copied today.

**Cascade.** Draped fabric at ends of valance, usually combined with a swag.

**Chinoiserie.** Furniture or ornaments decorated in the Chinese style. Pieces commonly enhanced by chinoiserie include lacquered chests, screens, and porcelains.

**Chintz.** Lightweight, glazed cotton, with a printed (often floral) design.

**Chippendale.** Thomas Chippendale (1718–1799), a renowned English cabinetmaker and designer who drew from French Louis XV rococo, Chinese, and Gothic design sources, and frequently worked in mahogany. A few of

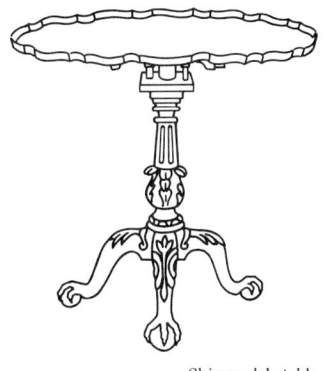

*Chippendale table*

219

Chippendale's trademarks are carved, ball-and-claw feet, armchairs with pierced splat backs, and carved and gilded mirrors.

**Dado.** Lower part of an interior wall that has been treated differently from the upper part, either with paneling or a painted mural (see Classicist prototype dining room, following page 24).

**Damask.** A shiny woven fabric, usually cotton, linen, or silk.

**Dhurrie.** Rugs woven of cotton or wool often with geometric designs, produced in India for more than three thousand years.

**Documentary.** Authentic copy of an antique fabric that is faithful to the period in color and pattern.

**Finial.** Brass or wood decorative end piece on a curtain rod. Finials are commonly shaped like flowers, fruits, knobs, or arrows.

**French Empire** (1804–1815). Popularized by Napoleon I, Empire styles took their design cues from Greek, Roman, Etruscan, and Egyptian sources. Oppressive, grandiose, and uncomfortable, typical pieces (many in red mahogany) included tables with lion-paw feet, beds shaped like boats (especially gondolas), marble-topped pier tables, and porcelain medallions, American cabinetmakers adapted these designs, making French Empire all the rage in the early nineteenth century.

**Gray, Eileen** (1879–1976). Architect, furniture and textile designer, whose avant-garde designs are being reproduced today.

**High Victorian.** Refers to the ornamental revival styles—Gothic, Renaissance, Louis XV rococo—which were popular during the end of the Victorian period (1837–1901), named for the reign of Queen Victoria in England.

**Hitchcock chair.** Early nineteenth-century chair named for Connecticut chair manufacturer Thomas Hitchcock. A design adaptation of the Sheraton period, the chairs were usually painted black and stenciled with floral patterns.

Hitchcock Chair

**Hoffmann chair.** Named for its creator, Josef Hoffmann (1873–1956), a Viennese architect who worked for clarity and order in design, thus paving the way for abstract forms. Chair reproductions are available today.

**Italian style.** Avant-garde furniture designs that are characterized by clean lines and materials such as leather and glass. A recent Italian style called "Memphis" is noted for its playful unconventionality (cabinets with outstretched arms, for example), bright colors, and use of modern industrial elements, such as plastic laminates and metal tubing.

**Jabot.** A shape, e.g., a cone, set between sections of an ornamental valance treatment, such as a *swag* (see below).

**Louis XV rococo revival.** A Victorian revival style that harked back to the reign of King Louis XV (1715–1774) of France. This style is based on fanciful decoration (rock and shell motifs) and intimate scale. Often constructed of fruitwoods, typical pieces include consoles, commodes, pedestal clocks, and bergère armchairs.

**Charles Rennie Mackintosh.** Scottish architect (1862–1928), con-

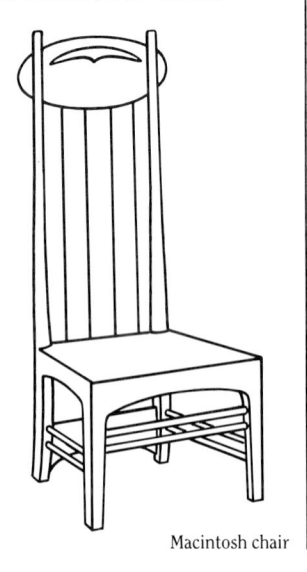

Macintosh chair

220

sidered one of the prime movers of the Art Nouveau movement. His furnishings are characterized by their greatly exaggerated slender verticals and panels decorated with curves and floral motifs.

**Mezzotint.** A type of engraving in which the roughened metal plate is burnished to give a graduating effect between light and dark tones.

**Moiré.** Watermarked silk fabric that has a wavy, watery appearance.

**Mullion.** Thin, vertical strips of wood that are decoratively latticed on exterior surfaces, especially common on English country cottage windows.

Mullion

**New England rushed chair.** American colonial chair, often executed in maple with decorative *turned* legs and back and a rushed woven seat made of fibers from aquatic plants.

**Ottoman.** Upholstered, often overstuffed, bench or footstool.

**Pennsylvania German.** Often mistakenly called "Pennsylvania Dutch." The furniture and decorative arts produced by these craftsmen in the eighteenth and nineteenth centuries included bright colors and motifs such as hearts and tulips. Common pieces are dower (hope) chests, cupboards, and drop-leaf tables with swinging leg brackets known as butterfly tables.

**Duncan Phyfe** (1768–1854). Leading cabinetmaker of the *American federal* period (see above), who, working in New York City, was influenced by the designs of Thomas Sheraton. His later work reflects the spirit of French Empire and Regency styles.

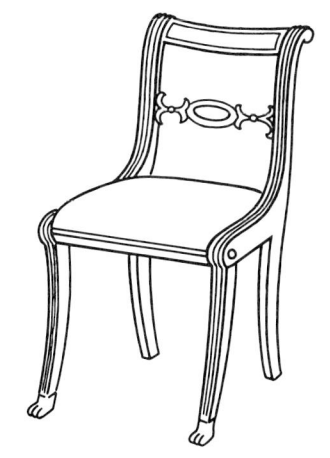

Duncan Phyfe side chair

**Point d'esprit.** Fragile cotton netting with dots.

**Postmodern.** Early 1980s design style rooted in architectural details such as columns (usually fake), arches, pediments, and illusory *trompe l'oeil* (see below) walls and ceilings; often considered a reaction against the minimal look championed in the 1970s.

**Queen Anne.** Queen of England from 1702 to 1714. The important furniture style that bears her name is characterized by a delicate S-shaped scrolled leg (called "cabriole") with "pad" feet. These legs are frequently found on highboys, lowboys, and chairs, often built in walnut, with shell and acanthus (leaf) motifs.

**Récamier.** Backless sofa with a high, curved headrest, popularized by Jacques-Louis David's (1748–1825) portrait of Mme. Récamier, in which she reclined on such a sofa.

**Redware.** Earthenware pottery so called because of its bright red color resulting from a high iron oxide content. First produced in America in the late eighteenth century, redware is still produced today and has a natural, rustic quality.

**Regency.** The period 1811–1820, when English King George IV was Prince of Wales (Regent).

Regency stool

221

Greek, Roman, and Egyptian styles were the chief design sources; caning, chairs with lion-claw feet, and saber-shaped legs were the prevailing decorative elements.

**Renaissance.** Beginning in the fourteenth century in Italy and spanning three centuries, the Renaissance bridged medieval and modern times and was characterized by a revival of classical influence and a flowering of the arts and sciences.

**Sateen.** A smooth, lustrous cotton fabric.

**Shakers** ("Shaking Quakers"). A celibate, ascetic sect founded in England in 1758 and brought to America in 1774. In their communal societies, they produced furnishings and objects that are admired today for their simple beauty, fine craftsmanship, and practicality.

**Sheraton.** A neoclassic style named

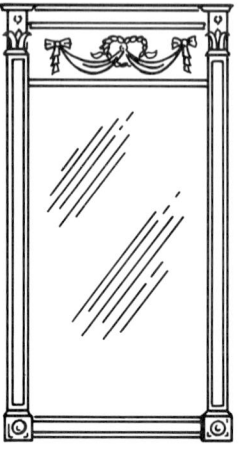

Sheraton mirror

for English furniture and interior designer Thomas Sheraton (ca. 1750–1806), distinguished by straight lines, a lightness and delicacy of form and ornament (notably urns, reeded columns, swags), and a preference for satinwood veneers and inlays.

**Sisal.** A strong, coarse fiber from the leaves of a West Indian plant, used decoratively for durable floor matting.

**Spongeware.** Nineteenth-century earthenware that takes its name from the spongelike design spattered on the background.

**Swag.** A draped valance treatment in which the fabric is decoratively overlapped on a curtain rod. Of classical origin, swags were very popular among such neoclassical designers as Robert and James *Adam* (see above) in England.

**Tieback.** Decorative element in the form of a sash, tasseled cord, or ribbon—or a metal or wood hook, bar, or rosette—used to hold back drapery frabric.

**Trompe l'oeil.** The use of decorative painting to deceive the eye into mistaking the apparent for the real; that is, a scene in perspective painted on a wall or wood painted to imitate marble (*faux marbre*).

**Turning.** The process of shaping wood in a lathe decoratively by rotating it, a common practice on chair legs and stretchers.

**Twill.** Woven cloth with diagonal lines.

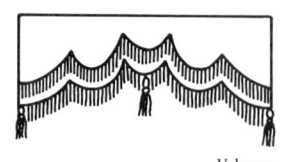

Valance

**Valance.** A top horizontal window treatment used to conceal the rod.

## Personality Montage Product Information

### Naturalist Montage

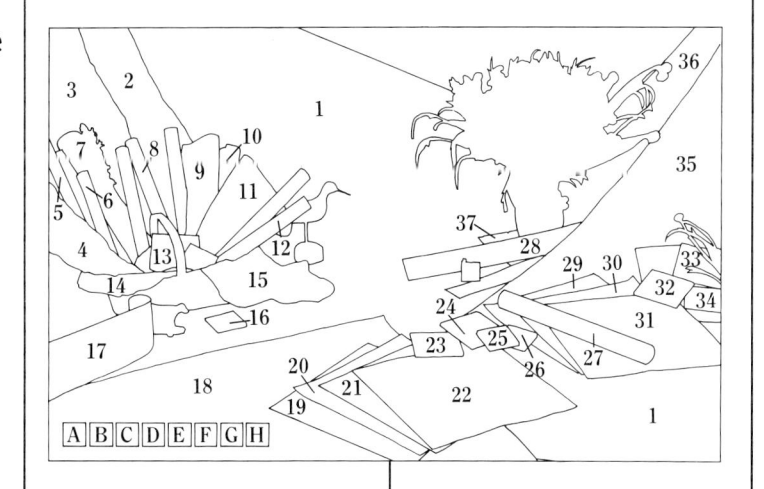

1. Rug, "Heartland Stencil," designed by Jodi Lester, F. Schumacher & Co.
2. Fabric, coordinate to "Heartland Stencil" rug, F. Schumacher & Co.
3. Fabric, "Lancaster Quilt," F. Schumacher & Co.
4. Fabric, "Stitchwort," Laura Ashley (*).
5. Wallpaper, "Country Diamond," Concepts, Waverly.
6. Wallpaper, "Classic Dot," Wall-Tex Sampler III, Wall-Tex.
7. Cotton stencil dhurrie rug, "Schoolhouse," Garden Basket, Waverly.
8. Wallpaper, "Sunshine," Garden Basket, Waverly.
9. Fabric, "Cranston Plaid," Laura, Waverly.
10. Wallpaper, "Colcha Embroidery Stitchwork," The America West™ Collection, The Museum of American Folk Art, Imperial Wallcoverings.
11. Fabric, "Star Quilt," F. Schumacher & Co.
12. Wallpaper, Red Lion Inn, Eisenhart Wallcoverings Company.
13. Glazed ceramic decorative tiles, "Hearts," Terra Designs.
14. Fabric, "Deauville," Pierre Deux.
15. Fabric, "Anjou Stripe," Waverly.
16. Ceramic decorative tile, "Wheat," Terra Designs.
17. Wallpaper border, "Apple Yard," The New American Country, Imperial Wallcoverings.
18. Stenciled floorcloth, "Rabbit Run," Good Stenciling.
19. Wallpaper, "Country Tulips," Concepts, Waverly.
20. Wallpaper, "Micro Geometric Stripe," Laura, Waverly.
21. Wallpaper, "Country Schoolhouse," Laura, Waverly.
22. Wallpaper, "Ticking Stripe," The Red Lion Inn, Waverly.
23. Unglazed terra cotta tile, Gamebird Relief Collection, Terra Designs.
24. Glazed ceramic decorative tile, "Pineapple," Terra Designs.
25. Glazed ceramic decorative tile, "Cow," Terra Designs.
26. Glazed ceramic decorative tile, Country Corner Collection, Terra Designs.
27. Wallpaper, "Newcombe," Lancaster Country Stencils, Eisenhart Wallcoverings.
28. Vinyl tile, "Stripwood," Azrock Floor Products.
29. Fabric, "Newcombe," Lancaster Country Stencils, Eisenhart Wall coverings.
30. Wallpaper, "Hearts and Tulips," Wall-Tex Sampler III, Wall-Tex.
31. Wallpaper, "Little Baskets," The Red Lion Inn, Waverly.
32. Glazed ceramic decorative tile, Country Butter Mold, #15 corner design, Terra Designs.
33. Unglazed terra cotta tiles, Gamebird Relief Collection, Terra Designs.
34. Unglazed terra cotta tile (solid), Terra Designs.
35. Rag rug, Thomas Woodard.
36. See listing for #29.
37. Floor tile, "Saddle Lombardic," Summitville Tiles, Inc.

(*) indicates mail order source

### Colors

| | | | |
|---|---|---|---|
| A. | Nutmeg | E. | Wild Rose |
| B. | Harrow | F. | Store Blue |
| C. | Barn Red | G. | Navy |
| D. | Cinnamon | H. | Bottle Green |

223

# Romanticist Montage

1. Portuguese needlepoint rug KD 3908, designed by Manjit Kamdin, Kamdin Designs.
2. Wallpaper, "Tulips," Color House, Imperial Wallcoverings.
3. Wallpaper, "Sunshine," Garden Basket, Waverly.
4. Wallpaper, "Bows," Wheatlands, Eisenhart Wallcoverings.
5. Fabric, "Sweet Pea," Liberty of London Shops (*).
6. Twisted-cord tieback, "Sapphire," Laura Ashley (*).
7. Glazed decorative ceramic tile, "Cottage Spring," Laura Ashley (*).
8. Glazed decorative ceramic tile, "Peach/Jade/Linen," Country Corner Collection, Terra Designs.
9. Glazed decorative ceramic tile, "37 Pastel/Milk," English Garden Collection, Terra Designs.
10. Glazed decorative ceramic tile, "Conservatory," Laura Ashley (*).
11. Braid, "Plum/Saddle/Cream," Laura Ashley (*).
12. Wallpaper, "Brighton Rock," Laura Ashley (*).
13. Wallpaper, "Lace," Collage, Motif Designs.
14. Wallpaper border, "Royal Bow," Chantilly, F. Schumacher & Co.
15. Carpet, Obligato, Silver Lilac, Einstein Moomjy.
16. Wallpaper, "Tulip," Tricia Guild Soft Furnishings, Imperial Wallcoverings.
17. Wallpaper, "Garden Path," Tricia Guild Soft Furnishings, Imperial Wallcoverings.
18. Carpet, "Le Basque/Mauve," Einstein Moomjy.
19. Capet, "Victor Victorian," Einstein Moomjy.
20. Fabric, "Amberly," In an English Garden Collection, Cohama Riverdale.
21. Fabric, "Kate," Laura Ashley (*).
22. Fabric, "Carnation," Liberty of London Shops(*).
23. Fabric, "Lydall," Liberty of London Shops(*).
24. Fabric, "Fluer-de-Lis," Collage, Motif Designs.
25. Fabric, "Country Roses," Laura Ashley (*).
26. Wallpaper, "Kate," Laura Ashley (*).
27. Wallpaper, "Seashell," Laura, Waverly.
28. Wallpaper, "Seashell Stripe," Laura, Waverly.
29. Braid, William Ginsburg.
30. Wallpaper, "Kipling Floral," Ralph Lauren Home Collection.
31-
33. Carpet, Fashion Show, Cabin Craft Carpets.
34. Fabric, "Doves," Rue de France (*).
35. Vinyl tile, "Heritage Gallery," Fashioncraft, Tarkett.
36. Wallpaper border, "T210 Sapphire/White," Laura Ashley (*).
37. Fabric, "Pucker Chintz," Barclay Traditionals, Eisenhart Wallcoverings.
38. Fabric, "Lydall," Liberty of London Shops (*).
39. Satin ribbon, Cherchez.
40. Fabric, "Lace," Collage, Motif Designs.
41. Fabric, "Petronella," Liberty of London Shops (*).

(*) indicates mail order source

Colors
A. Sheer Pink
B. Tea Rose
C. Plum
D. Celadon
E. Cornsilk
F. Hunter Green
G. Wood Violet
H. Misty Blue
I. Antique White

# Traditionalist Montage

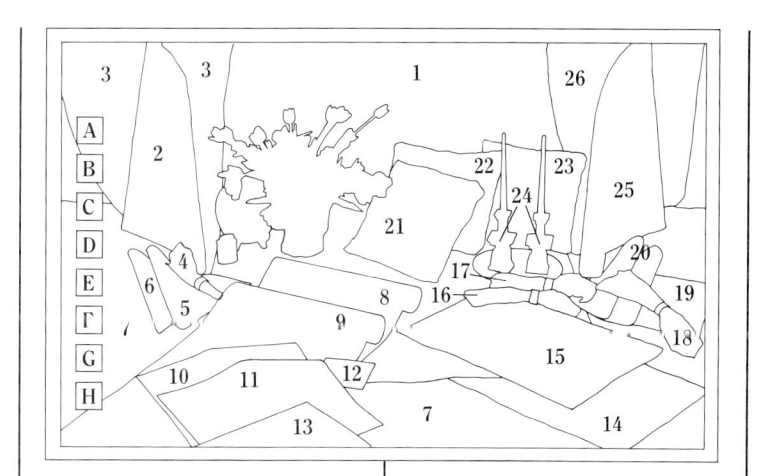

1. Rug, "Delhi" dhurrie, Kamdin Designs.
2. Wallpaper, "Ming Stripe," Jay Yang's House Calls Collection, Carefree Wallcoverings.
3. Fabric, "Early Crocus," Waverly.
4. Fabric "Briarwood," Liberty of London Shops (*).
5. Wallpaper, "Amical," French Collection, Waverly.
6. Wallpaper, "Foulard," Ralph Lauren Home Collection.
7. Needlepoint rug, Kamdin Designs.
8. Wallpaper, "Indian Beadwork Floral," The America West™ Collection, The Museum of American Folk Art, Imperial Wallcoverings.
9. Wallpaper, "Colcha Embroidery Stitchwork," The America West™ Collection, The Museum of American Folk Art, Imperial Wallcoverings.
10. Wallpaper, "Caroline," Pierre Deux.
11. Wallpaper, "Mid-Town," Catalina II Collection, Richard E. Thibaut, Inc.
12. Ceramic decorative tile, "Conservatory," Laura Ashley (*).
13. Ceramic Floor Tile, "Country Gray Summitstone," Summitville Tiles, Inc.
14. Carpeting, "Viridian," La Parade, Masland Carpets.
15. Carpeting, "Woolcraft," Karastan.
16. Fabric, "Ribbon Paisley," Cohama Riverdale.
17. Fabric, "Orientalia," Jay Yang Collection, Fabriyaz.
18. Fabric, "The Cross of St. George," Hallie Greer (*).
19. Ceramic floor tile, "Normandie Bronze," Metropolitan Ceramics.
20. Wallpaper, "Fleur-de-Lis," Collage, Motif Designs.
21. Fabric, "Orientalia," Jay Yang Collection, Fabriyaz.
22. Fabric, "Palmetto," Laura Ashley (*).
23. Fabric, "Kelly," French Country Prints Collection, Imperial Wallcoverings.
24. "Kangxi Candlesticks," for Metropolitan Museum of Art, by Mottahedeh.
25. Wallpaper, "Country Ribbons," Clarence House, Imperial Wallcoverings.
26. Fabric, "Salon," Laura Ashley (*).

(*) indicates mail order source

Colors
A. Cocoa Brown
B. Apricot
C. Terracotta
D. Garnet
E. Jonquil
F. Regimental Blue
G. Seafoam
H. Spruce Green

# Classicist Montage

1. Fabric, "Sun, Moon, and Stars." Brunschwig & Fils, Inc. for Winterthur Reproductions (*).
2. Wallpaper border F274, Burgundy/Navy/Sand. Laura Ashley (*).
3. Wallpaper border, "Tara." Richard E. Thibaut, Inc.
4. Rug, "Tabriz," 738. Karastan.
5. Tassel fringe. Ibiza.
6. Wood flooring. "Haddon Hall," Angelique teak. Hoboken Wood Flooring.
7. Wallpaper, "Kent." Albert Van Luit & Company for Winterthur Reproductions(*).
8. Wallpaper, handprinted Victorian reproduction. Bradbury & Bradbury Wallpapers (*).
9. Wallpaper, "Chimerique." Albert Van Luit & Company for Winterthur Reproductions (*).
10. Wallpaper, "Laurens Street." Scalamandré for Historic Charleston Reproductions(*).
11. Wallpaper, "Fenimore." Albert Van Luit & Company for Winterthur Reproductions (*).
12. Braided cord. Regency Fabrics.
13. Fabric, "Rutland." Stroheim & Romann for Winterthur Reproductions (*).
14. Fabric, "Honeysuckle." Liberty of London Shops (*).
15. Cotton fringe. William Ginsburg.
16. "Turkish Church Rug." Karastan for Colonial Williamsburg (*).
17. Silk tassels. G. Elter.
18. Fabric, "Orientalia," Jay Yang Collection. Fabriyaz.
19. Wallcovering, "Indienne," Clarence House. Imperial Wallcoverings.
20. Fabric, "Toile Cherubin." Pierre Deux.
21. Wallcovering, "La Mandarine," Clarence House. Imperial Wallcoverings.
22. Fabric, "Colette." F. Schumacher & Company.
23. Fabric, "Pin Dot Velvet." F. Schumacher & Company.
24. Fabric, "Williamsburg Apples." F. Schumacher & Company.
25. Chinoiserie Tile. Winterthur Reproductions (*).
26. Japanese bronze vase, c. 1890. The Armory, N.Y.
27. Fabric, "Orne." Stroheim & Romann for Winterthur Reproductions (*).

(*) indicates mail order source

Colors
A. Parchment
B. Viridian Green
C. Copper
D. Burnt Orange
E. Oxblood
F. Delft Blue
G. Regal Blue
H. Marigold

## Individualist Montage

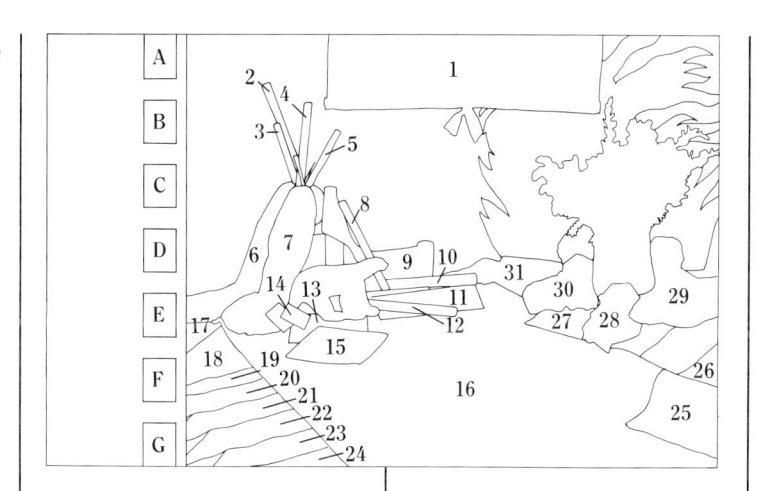

1. Fabric, "Mariola," Chantilly, F. Schumacher & Co.
2. Wallpaper, "Crest," Rose, Motif Designs.
3. Wallpaper, "Cricket Stripe," Ralph Lauren Home Collection.
4. Wallpaper, "Indiana Amish Patchwork," The America West™ Collection, The Museum of American Folk Art, Imperial Wallcoverings.
5. Wallpaper, "Check," Caprice 2, Benchmark Wallcoverings.
6. Fabric, "Shadow Dance," Gear, Cohama Riverdale.
7. Fabric, "Simple Strokes," Options, WHS Lloyd.
8. Wallpaper, "Polka Dot," Options, WHS Lloyd.
9. Wallpaper border, "Indiana Amish Stripe," The America West™ Collection, The Museum of American Folk Art, Imperial Wallcoverings.
10. Wallpaper, "Basket," Rosie, Motif Designs.
11. Wallpaper, "Simple Strokes," WHS Lloyd.
12. Wallpaper, "Pencil Stripe," Options, WHS Lloyd.
13. Vinyl tile, "Toned Gray CT-1020," Azrock Floor Products.
14. Ceramic decorative tile, "Whisper tiles," American Olean Tile Co.
15. Woven floorcovering, "CT160 Maize," Import Specialists (*).
16. Indian wool dhurrie, Meuniers.
17. Wallpaper, "Harmony," Raindrops, Wall-Tex.
18. Fabric, "Cricket Tattersal," Ralph Lauren Home Collection.
19. Fabric, "Checkers," Collage, Motif Designs.
20. Fabric, "Florentina," Laura Ashley (*).
21. Fabric, "American Beauty Rose," Gear, Cohama Riverdale.
22. Fabric, "Ticking," Rosie, Motif Designs.
23. Fabric, "Kandi," Conran's (*).
24. Fabric, "Arrangements, Celebration Collection," Cohama Riverdale.
25. Wool woven rug, "Grid Pattern Warp-Faced," Elizabeth Eakins, Inc.
26. Carpet, Philadelphia Carpets.
27. Woven sisal floorcovering, Conran's (*).
28. Fabric, "Diamonds," Conran's (*).
29. Fabric, "Ophelia," Conran's (*).
30. Fabric, "Emma," Laura Ashley (*).
31. Fabric, "Piusto," Marimekko.

(*) indicates mail order source

Colors
A. Taupe
B. Toast
C. Old Pewter
D. Candy Pink
E. Warm Red
F. Nantucket Blue
G. Navy

227

## Young Professional Montage

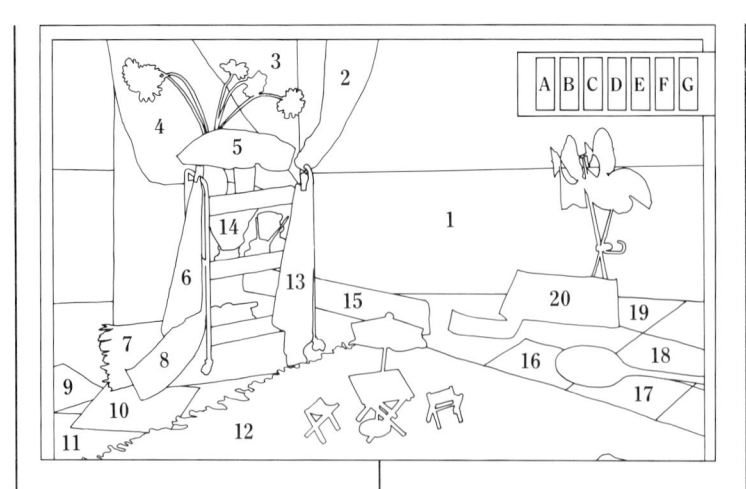

1. Wallpaper, New Country Gear 76111, Imperial Wallcoverings.
2. Fabric, "Checkers," Collage, Motif Designs.
3. Wallcovering, "Fleur-de-Lis," Joyce Howell, Style-Tex.
4. Fabric, "Arithmetic III," Marimekko.
5. Fabric, "Ready or Knot," Collage, Motif Designs.
6. Fabric, "Sailing," Aerobics II, Waverly.
7. Rag rug, "Cherry," Folkheart Rag Rugs (*).
8. Wallpaper border, "Cherry," Fokheart Rag Rugs (*).
9. -
10. Vinyl tile, "Grid," Azrock Tile.
11. Vinyl tile, Accent China Blue 70030, Congoleum.
12. Dhurrie rug, "Chitki," Conran's (*).
13. Fabric, "Itomaki," Fabriyaz.
14. Fabric, "Gear Kids," Gear, Conran's (*).
15. Wallpaper, "Spring Bulbs," Rosie, Motif Designs.
16. -
17. Vinyl tile, "Blue and White Squares," Top Floor Company, Pintchik.
18. Wallpaper, "Café Tile," Rosie, Motif Designs.
19. Wallpaper, "Stitches," Rosie, Motif Designs.
20. Wallpaper border, "Checkers," Collage, Motif Designs.

Colors
A. Sand
B. Daffodil Yellow
C. Gray Flannel
D. Slate Blue
E. Spring Green
F. Poppy Red
G. Midnight Blue

(*) indicates mail order source

## Modernist Montage

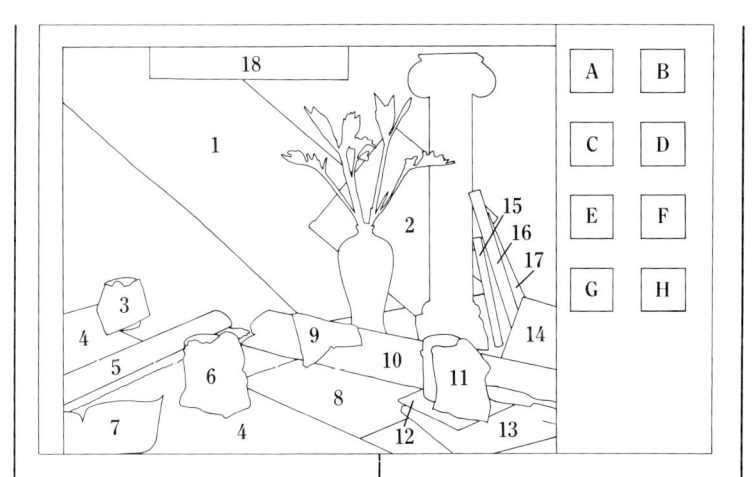

1. Wallpaper, "Illyana," design friends, ltd.
2. Wallpaper, "Cassandra," design friends, ltd.
3. Fabric, "Illyana," design friends, ltd.
4. Wallpaper, "Derby," Clarence House, Imperial Wallcoverings.
5. Dhurrie rug, "Marble Blocks Two," Import Specialists (*).
6. Fabric, "Starfire," Cohama Riverdale.
7. Wallpaper border, "Savoy Border," Chantilly, F. Schumacher & Co.
8. Wallpaper, "Travertine Marble," Chantilly, F. Schumacher & Co.
9. Fabric, "Genji," Fabriyaz.
10. Dhurrie rug, Kamdin Designs.
11. Fabric, "Medley," Cohama Riverdale.
12. Marble flooring, American Olean Tile Co.
13. Ceramic floor tile, "Parchment #316," Summitville Tiles, Inc.
14. Wallpaper, "Diamond Jim," James Harris for design friends, ltd.
15. Wallpaper, "Drift," Neographics, F. Schumacher & Co.
16. Wallpaper, "Pomona," Eclipse, Richard E. Thibaut.
17. Wallpaper, "Spring Stripe," Raindrops, Wall-Tex.
18. Painting, "Big Red," by Don Munson.

(*) indicates mail order source

Colors
A. Champagne
B. Peach
C. Pale Mauve
D. Dove Gray
E. Aquamarine
F. Black
G. Azure
H. Chinese Red

# Futurist Montage

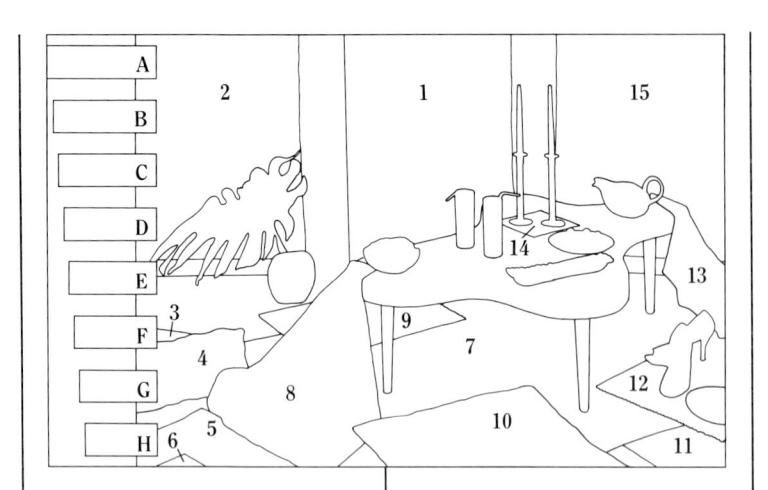

1. Wallpaper panels, "Confetti," Chantilly, F. Schumacher & Co.
2. Wallpaper, "Geo," designfriends, ltd.
3. Carpet, "Clarion/Granite," Karastan.
4. Fabric, "Cat's Cradle," California Drop Cloth (*).
5. Rubber Pirelli tile, "Regular Stud/Yellow," Jason Industrial.
6. Wallpaper, "Mat-Sticks," Caprice 2, Benchmark Wallcoverings.
7. Dhurrie rug, "Leopard One," Import Specialists (*).
8. Fabric, "Waterfall," Rosie, Motif Designs.
9. Rubber flooring, "Black Duckboard," Ad Hoc (*).
10. Fabric, "Soaring," Aerobics, Waverly.
11. Wallpaper, "Skipper," Coming Attractions 4, Benchmark Wallcoverings.
12. Rubber flooring, "Red Duckboard," Ad Hoc (*).
13. Fabric, "Iso Antii," Marimekko.
14. Vinyl tile, "Hi Tech Circles/ Checkerboard," GMT International Collection.
15. Wallpaper, "Streamers," designfriends, ltd.

(*) indicates mail order source

Colors
A. Black
B. Bubblegum Pink
C. Steel Gray
D. Wild Canary
E. Cobalt
F. Fire Engine Red
G. Burnished Gold
H. Jungle Green

## Personality Room Product Information

We are indebted to the following people, who made their products available to us in photographing the personality rooms. Unless noted here, all objects were personal possessions of the owners.

### THE NATURALIST ROOM:

Quilt on love seat, *Made in America*, New York City. Quilt pillows, coverlet pillows, swan decoy, *Museum of American Folk Art Shop*, 125 West Fifty-fifth Street, New York, New York 10019. Pierced-paper lamp shade, *Pineapple Primitives at the Seaport, Inc.*, 19 Fulton Street, New York, New York 10004.

### THE ROMANTICIST ROOM:

"Gazebo" sheets for walls, dust ruffle, curtains; "Gazebo" Priscilla curtains, comforter, and sheets on bed, *Gloria Vanderbilt Creations, Inc.*, through *J. P. Stevens*, 1185 Avenue of the Americas, New York, New York 10036. "Moments Delight" carpet by *Gulistan* for *J. P. Stevens*. Upholstered wing chair, bed bench, sofa, *Clyde Pearson*, a division of *The Lane Co.*, 1420 Progress Street, High Point, North Carolina 27261. Antique desk, cupboard, bamboo tables, Venetian mirror, Chinese drum table, bronze flower lamp, shell floor lamp, accessories in cupboard, *Limited Editions*, 253 East Seventy-second Street, New York, New York 10021. Paintings, vanity accessories, candlesticks, candlestick lamp, *John Roselli*, 255 East Seventy-second Street, New York, New York 10021. Area rug, *Stark Carpet*, 979 Third Avenue, New York, New York 10022. Antique quilts, decorative pillows, throw on chair, *The Gazebo*, 660 Madison Avenue, New York, New York 10021. Flowers and plants, *Zeze*, 398 East Fifty-second Street, New York, New York 10022. Decorative sewing by *George Bari*, 312 West Twentieth Street, New York, New York 10011. Walls upholstered and shirred by *Fleming Hegner Studios*, 6026 Munroe Place, West New York, New Jersey 07093.

**THE TRADITIONALIST ROOM:**

Flowers arranged by *Ann Lurie Berlin*, 350 East Fifty-seventh Street, New York, 10019.

**THE INDIVIDUALIST ROOM:**

"Rosie's Crest" fabric and wallcovering, *Motif Designs*, 15 Beechwood Avenue, New Rochelle, New York 10801. Silver "Bel-Esprit" carpet (51067), in Antron Plus by Dupont, *Philadelphia Carpets*, a division of *Shaw Industries, Inc.*

**THE YOUNG PROFESSIONAL ROOM:**

"Serena" sheets by Bassetti, *Springs Industries*, 104 West Fortieth Street, New York, New York 10018. All furniture, rug, lamp, sconces, *Conran's*, 160 East Fifty-fourth Street, New York, New York 10022. Blinds, *Levolor Lorentzen, Inc.*, 720 Monroe Street, Hoboken, New Jersey 07030. Table setting, *D. F. Sanders & Co.*, 952 Madison Avenue, New York, New York 10021.

## Personality Room Interior Designers

The following are the designers whose room designs appear in the first color insert of *Personality Decorating*. The authors are grateful for their cooperation.

James Bloor Interiors
117 West Fifteenth Street
New York, New York 10011

Michael Braverman Design, Inc.
245 West Fourth Street
New York, New York 10014

Beverly Ellsley Interior Design
87 Redcoat Road
Westport, Connecticut 06880

Stanley Hura Interior Design
14 Sutton Place South
New York, New York 10022

Georgina Fairholme Interior Design
185 East Eighty-fifth Street
New York, New York 10028

Sybil Levin Interior Design
339 East Fifty-seventh Street
New York, New York 10022

Nicholas Pentecost Interior Design
142 East Twenty-seventh Street
New York, New York 10016

Lyn Peterson
Motif Designs
90 Lyncroft Road
New Rochelle, New York 10804

## Buyer's Guide

All companies whose products are pictured in the *Personality Decorating* shopping directories are listed below. The authors are grateful for their cooperation.

*Ad Hoc Softwares
842 Lexington Avenue
New York, New York 10021
(212) 752-5488

Allibert, Inc.
Customer Service
100 Northfield Avenue
Edison, New Jersey 08837
(201) 225-4167

Alsy Corporation
15 East Twenty-sixth Street
New York, New York 10010
(212) 725-1517

American Olean Tile Co.
1000 Cannon Avenue
Lansdale, Pennsylvania 19446
(215) 855-1111

Amerock Corporation
4000 Auburn Street, P.O. Box 7018
Rockford, Illinois 61125-7018

Amisco Industries
C.P. 250
L'Islet, Quebec
Canada GOR 2CO
(418) 247-5025

*Amish Country Collection
R.D. #5, Sunset Valley Road
New Castle, Pennsylvania 16105
(412) 656-1755
Catalogue: $5.00

Ethan Allen, Inc.
Ethan Allen Drive
Danbury, Connecticut 06811
(201) 743-8000
Catalogue: Free

*Arise Futon Mattress Co. Inc.
65 Terrytown Road
White Plains, New York 10607
(914) 946-8740
Catalogue: $2.00

Artemide, Inc.
150 E. Fifty-eighth St.
New York, New York 10155

(212) 980-0710
Catalogue: Free

*Laura Ashley
714 Madison Avenue
New York, New York 10021
And 50 other locations
(800) 367-2000
Catalogue: $5.00
Laura Ashley
Dept. 874-H, 70 Marcus Drive
Melville, New York 11747

Azrock Floor Products
Consumer Service Department
P.O. Box 34030
San Antonio, Texas 78265

Baker Furniture Company
1661 Monroe N.W.
Grand Rapids, Michigan 49505
(616) 361-7321
Note: See Historic Charleston Reproductions listing to mail order Historic Charles pieces by Baker. Item numbers will vary.

*Ballard Designs
P.O. Box 12255
Atlanta, Georgia 30355
(404) 351-5099
Catalogue: $1.00

*Bartley Collection, Ltd.
121 Schelter Rd.
Prairie View, Illinois 60069
Catalogue: $1.00

Beaumont Glass
Box 803
Morgantown, West Virginia 26505
(304) 292-9401
Catalogue: $5.00

Benchmark Wallcoverings
Corporate Place 128, Building 3, Suite 25
Wakefield, Massachusetts 01880
(617) 246-5130

*Richard Bissell Fine Woodworking
R.D. #2 Signal Pine Road

*Indicates company sells items through mail order*

Putney, Vermont 05346
(802) 387-4416
Catalogue: Free

*Bradbury & Bradbury Wallpapers
P.O. Box 155-D
Benicia, California 94510
(707) 746-1900
Catalogue: $3,00

Georges Briard Inc.
225 Fifth Avenue
New York, New York 10010
(212) 689-0385

*California Drop Cloth, Inc.
712 Grandview Street
Los Angeles, California 90057
(213) 389-2988
Note: Minimum fabric order 10 yards.

Cabin Crafts Carpets
Dalton, Georgia 30720
(800) 241-4062

Carefree Wallcoverings
23645 Mercantile Road
Cleveland, Ohio 44122
(216) 464-3700

Casa Bique, Ltd.
P.O. Box 788
Thomasville, North Carolina 27360
(919) 475-9136
Catalogue: $5.00

Casa Stradivari
200 Lexington Avenue
New York, New York 10016
(212) 684-5990

*Castro Convertibles
1990 Jericho Turnpike
New Hyde Park, New York 11040
(516) 488-3000
Catalogue: $2.00

Casual Lamps of California, Inc.
P.O. Box 2168
Gardena, California 90247
(800) 824-8228 nationwide;
(800) 874-1445 California

Century Furniture Company
Marketing & Advertising Depts.
P.O. Box 608
Hickory, North Carolina 28603
Set of brochures: $5.00

Chapman Lamps
21 E. Twenty-sixth St.
New York, New York 10016

Cherchez Antiques & Potpourri
864 Lexington Ave.
New York, New York 10021
(212) 737-8215

Cohama Riverdale
200 Madison Avenue
New York, New York 10016
(212) 561-8500

*Cohasset Colonials
555JX Ship Street
Cohasset, Massachusetts 02025
(617) 383-0110
Catalogue: $1.00

*Colonial Williamsburg
Box CH
Williamsburg, Virginia 23187
(800) 441-9240; (804) 229-1000 in Virginia
Catalogue: Free

Color House Wallcoverings
23645 Mercantile Road
Cleveland, Ohio 44122
(216) 464-3700

Congoleum
(800) 447-2882 for dealer referral.

*Conran's
Mail Order Dept. 4000
145 Huguenot Street
New Rochelle, New York 10801
(914) 632-0515
Store only items at:
Citicorp
160 E. Fifty-fourth Street
New York, New York 10022
(212) 371-2225
Catalogue: $2.00

Council Craftsmen, Inc.
P.O. Box 398
Denton, North Carolina 27239
Catalogue: $3.00

designfriends, ltd.
19 West Twenty-first St.
New York, New York 10010
(212) 677-4868

*Pierre Deux Catalogue
350 Bleecker Street
New York, New York 10014
(212) 243-7740

*Pierre Deux
870 Madison Avenue
New York, New York 10021
(212) 570-9343

Drexel Heritage Furnishings, Inc.
Drexel, North Carolina 28619
(800) 447-4700; in Alaska and
Hawaii (800) 447-0890

Elizabeth Eakins, Inc.
1053 Lexington Ave.
New York, New York 10021
(212) 628-1950

Einstein Moomjy
150 East Fifty-eighth Street
New York, New York 10155
(212) 758-0900
And other locations

Eisenhart Wallcoverings Company
Pine Street
Hanover, Pennsylvania 17331
(717) 632-5918

G. Elter
740 Madison Avenue
New York, New York 10021
(212) RE4-4680

*Equipto, Division of Aurora Equipment Co.
225 S. Highland Avenue
Aurora, Illinois 60507
Catalogue: $1.00

*Erwin-Lambeth, Inc.
201 E. Holly Hill Road
Thomasville, North Carolina 27360
(919) 472-2700
Catalogue: $2.00

Fabriyaz
41 Madison Avenue
New York, New York 10010
(212) 686-3311

*Faith Mountain Country Fare
Main Street, P.O. Box 199
Sperryville, Virginia 22740
(800) 822-7238
Catalogue: $2.00

Fashon Wallcoverings
401 Hackensack Avenue
Hackensack, New Jersey 07601
(201) 489-0100

Nora Fenton
107 Trumbull Street
Elizabeth, New Jersey 07206
(201) 351-5460

Ficks Reed Company
4900 Charlemar Drive
Cincinnati, Ohio 45208
(513) 561-2100

*Folkheart Rag Rugs
18 Main Street
Bristol, Vermont
(802) 453-4101
Catalogue: $1.00 plus self-addressed stamped envelope

Friedman Brothers Decorative Arts
9015 N.W. 105 Way
Medley, Florida 33178
(305) 887-3170
Note: See *Historic Charleston Reproductions* listing to mail order Historic Charleston mirrors by Friedman Brothers. Item numbers will vary.

Furniture of the Twentieth Century, Inc.
227 West Seventeenth St.
New York, New York 10011
(212) 929-6023

Gampel-Stoll Corp.
376 President Street
Brooklyn, New York 11231

Gear
19 West Thirty-fourth St.
New York, New York 10001
(212) 736-8499

William Ginsburg
242 West Thirty-eighth Street
New York, New York 10018
(212) 244-4539

GMT International Collection
1225 Oak Point Avenue
Bronx, New York 10474
(212) 991-8500

*Good Stenciling
Box 387
Dublin, New Hampshire 03444
(603) 880-3480
Catalogue: $2.00

Morris Greenspan Lamps
P.O. Box 078678
West Palm Beach, Florida 33407
(800) 252-LAMP

Habersham Plantation Corporation
P.O. Box 1209
Toccoa, Georgia 30577
(404) 886-1476
Catalogue: $12.50

*Hallie Greer
Cushing Corners Road, P.O. Box 165
Freedom, New Hampshire 03836
(603) 539-6007
Catalogue: $2.00

Halo Lighting
Cooper Industries
400 Busse Road
Elk Grove Village, Illinois 60007
(312) 956-8400

*Hancock Shaker Village Community
  Industries
Hancock Shaker Village, P.O. Box 898
Pittsfield, Massachusetts 01202
(413) 442-8381
Catalogue: $1.00

Paul Hanson Company, Inc.
610 Commercial Avenue
Carlstadt, New Jersey 07072
(201) 933-4873
Catalogue: $5.00

Harden Furniture, Inc.
McConnellsville, New York 13401
(315) 245-1000

Henredon Furniture Industries, Inc.
P.O. Box 70
Morganton, North Carolina 28655
(704) 437-5261
Villandry Catalogue: $3.00
Folio 16 Catalogue: $3.00
Avington Park Catalogue: $2.00

Hickory Chair Company
P.O. Box 2147
Hickory, North Carolina 28603
(704) 328-1801
Catalogues:
James River Occasional & Upholstery $5.00
James River Dining Room & Bedroom $5.00
American Digest Collection $3.00

Hickory Manufacturing Company
P.O. Box 998
Hickory, North Carolina 28601
Catalogue: $3.00

Hoboken Wood Flooring
969 Third Ave.
New York, New York 10022
(212) 759-5917

*Martha M. House
1022 South Decatur Street
Montgomery, Alabama 36104
(205) 264-3558
Catalogue: $2.00

Imperial Wallcoverings
23645 Mercantile Road
Cleveland, Ohio 44122
(216) 464-3700

Ibiza
42 University Place
New York, New York 10003
(212) 533-4614

*Import Specialists
82 Wall Street
New York, New York 10005
(800) 334-4044;
in New York City (212) 709-9633

IPF International, Inc.
11-13 Maryland Ave.
P.O. Box 905
Paterson, New Jersey 07503

*William H. James/Stephen A. Adams
  Furnituremakers
Mill Hill Road, Box 130
Denmark, Maine 04022
(207) 452-2444
Catalogue: $2.00

Jason Industrial
340 Kaplan Drive
Fairfield, New Jersey 07006
(800) 447-1982 Sweets Buyline

Kamdin Designs
791 Lexington Avenue
New York, New York 10021
(212) 371-8833

Karastan
919 Third Avenue
New York, New York 10022
(212) 980-3434

Kartell USA
P.O. Box 1000
Easley, South Carolina 29641
(800) 845-2517

Kaylyn, Inc.
P.O. Box 2366
High Point, North Carolina 27261
(919) 884-2244

Kindel Furniture Company
Grand Rapids, Michigan 49507
Note: See *Winterthur Museum and Gardens*
listing to mail order Winterthur
Reproduction pieces by Kindel.
Item numbers will vary.

*Landes Manufacturing Co.
P.O. Box 2197
Gardena, California 90247
(213) 327-1777
Mail Order through:
Chan, Etc.
P.O. Box 48
Redondo Beach, California 90277
Catalogue: $5.00

237

The Lane Col, Inc.
Box 151
Altavista, Virginia 24517
(800) 447-2882
Catalogue: $3.00

Ralph Lauren Home Collection
Motif Designs
20 Jones Street
New Rochelle, New York 10801

*Liberty of London Shops
229 East Sixtieth Street
New York, New York 10022
(212) 888-1057

Lightolier
346 Claremont Avenue
Jersey City, New Jersey 07305

W.H.S. Lloyd
2113 Forty-ninth Street
North Bergen, New Jersey 07040

*Magnolia Hall
726 Andover
Atlanta, Georgia 30327
(404) 237-9725

Marimekko, Inc.
One Dock Street
Stamford, Connecticut 06902
(203) 325-9380

Masland Carpets
50 Spring Road, Box 40
Carlisle, Pennsylvania 17013

Metropolitan Ceramics
P.O. Box 9240
Canton, Ohio 44711
(216) 484-4876

Meuniers
140 Montague Street
Brooklyn Heights, New York 11201
(718) 855-7835

Milbrook Wallcoverings
23645 Mercantile Road
Cleveland, Ohio 44122
(216) 464-3700

Howard Miller Clock Company
860 East Main Street
Zeeland, Missouri 49464
(616) 772-9131
Catalogue: $2.50

*Gates Moore Early American Designs
 of Lighting Fixtures
River Road, Silvermine
Norwalk, Connecticut 06850

(203) 847-3231
Catalogue: $2.00

Motif Designs
20 Jones Street
New Rochelle, New York 10801

Mottahedeh
225 Fifth Avenue
New York, New York 10010
(212) 685-3050
Note: See *Historic Charleston Reproduction, Winterthur Museum and Gardens,* or *Colonial Williamsburg* listings to mail order reproduction pieces made for them by Mottahedeh. Item number will vary.

Natico Originals, Inc.,
 The National Import Co.
225 Fifth Avenue
New York, New York 10010
(212) 685-5307
Mail order through:
Asentar Enterprises, Ltd.
P.O. Box 125
Plainview, New York 11803
Catalogue: Free

*Natural Design
P.O. Box 60134
Chicago, Illinois 60660
(800) 323-5996
Catalogue: $2.50

*The Natural Light
P.O. Box 216
Grove, Oklahoma 74344
(800) 331-3898
Catalogue: $2.00

*Neat and Tidy, Inc.
27 Pine Brook Road
South Spring Valley, New York 10977
Catalogue: $2.00

*Nessen Lamps, Inc.
621 East 216th Street
Bronx, New York 10467
(212) 231-0221
Mail order through:
Hammacher-Schlemmer
(312) 664-7745
Catalogue: Free

New Horizons
116 West Washington Street
Jefferson, Wisconsin 53549

Nichols & Stone
232 Sherman Street
Gardner, Massachusetts 01440
(617) 632-2770

O'Asian Designs, Inc.
1100 West Walnut Street
Compton, California 90220
(213) 604-8594

Old Deerfield Fabrics, Inc.
134 Sand Park Road
Cedar Grove, New Jersey 07009
(201) 239-6600

Palacek
P.O. Box 225 Station A
Richmond, California 94808
(415) 236-7730; (800) 227-2538 in
continental United States except CA
Catalogue: Free

*Palazzetti, Inc.
215 Lexington Avenue
New York, New York 10016
(212) 684-1199
Catalogue: Free

The Pearson Company, Division of Lane
Box 827
High Point, North Carolina 27260
(800) 447-2882

Pennsylvania Firebacks, Inc.
1011 East Washington lane
Philadelphia, Pennsylvania 19138
Catalogue: $2.00 (refunded with first order)

Pennsylvania House
137 North Tenth Street, Box 472
Lewisburg, Pennsylvania 17837
Attn: Keith Erdman
(800) 782-9663 nationwide;
(800) 782-2273 in Pennsylvania

Norman Perry
501 West Green Drive
High Point, North Carolina 27260
(919) 889-1555

Perfection Furniture Co., Inc.
P.O. Box 400
Claremont, North Carolina 28610
(800) 438-7659 for local dealer referral

*Peter Pepper Products, Inc.
17929 South Susana Road, P.O. Box 4758
Compton, California 90224
(213) 979-0815
Catalogue: $25.00

Philadelphia Carpet Co.
441 Lexington Avenue
New York, New York 10017
(212) 557-2424

Pintchik
278 Third Avenue
New York, New York 10010
(212) 982-6600

*Pot•pour•ri
Department PD
204 Worcester Street
Wellesley, Massachusetts 02181
(800) 225-4127
Catalogue: Free

Progress Lighting
Erie Avenue and G Street
Philadelphia, Pennsylvania 19134

Regba Diran N.Y., Inc.
105 Madison Avenue
New York, New York 10010
(212) 683-2350

Regent Fabrics
122 East Fifty-ninth Street
New York, New York 10022
(212) 355-2039

*Renovator's Supply
Renovator's Old Mill
Millers Falls, Massachusetts 01349
(413) 355-2039

Riverside Furniture Corporation
P.O. Box 1427, 4100 South Sixth Street
Forth Smith, Arkansas 72902

*Charles P. Rogers Brass Beds
899 First Avenue
New York, New York 10022
(800) 272-7726;
in New York City (212) 935-6900
Catalogue: $3.00 subscription

J/B Ross
409 Joyce Kilmer Avenue
New Brunswick, New Jersey 08901
(800) 932-0620
Catalogue: Free

*Rue de France
Department PD
78 Thames Street
New Port, Rhode Island 02840
(401) 846-2084
Catalogue: $1.00

Scandinavian Design/Scandinavian Gallery
603 Worcester Road
Natik, Massachusetts 01760
(617) 655-2830

Schott Furniture
R.G. Schnoor Inc.
225 Fifth Avenue
Suite 223
New York, New York 10010

F. Schumacher and Company
919 Third Avenue
New York, New York 10022
(212) 644-5914

*The Seraph
P.O. Box 500
Sturbridge, Massachusetts 01566
(617) 347-2241
Catalogue: Free

*Shaker Workshops
P.O. Box 1028
Concord, Massachusetts 01742
Catalogue: $1.00

The Sherwood Corp.
P.O. Box 519
Spring City, Tennessee 37381
(615) 365-5433

Simms and Thayer
P.O. Box 35 PD
North Marshfield, Massachusetts 02059
(617) 585-8606
Catalogue: $3.00

S.P. Skinner, Inc.
P.O. Box 5
Naugatauck Park,
Naugatauck, Connecticut 06770

Sligh Furniture Company
1201 Industrial Avenue
Holland, Michigan 49423
(616) 392-7101
Catalogue: $5.00

Southwood Reproductions
P.O. Box 2245
Hickory, North Carolina 28601

The Stiffel Company
700 North Kingsbury Street
Chicago, Illinois 60610

*Sturbridge Yankee Workshop
Blueberry Road
Portland, Maine 04104
(800) 343-1144
Catalogue: $2.00

Style-Tex Wallcoverings
Corporate Place 128, Building 3, Suite 25
Wakefield, Massachusetts 01880
(617) 246-5130

Summitville Tiles, Inc.
Summitville, Ohio 43962
(216) 223-1511

*The Sunflower Shoppe
1409 Front Street
Binghampton, New York 13901

(607) 723-5990
Illustrated brochure subscription $1.00
(refundable with first order)

Swaim
P.O. Box 4147
High Point, North Carolina 27263

Tarkett, Inc.
800 Lanidex Plaza
Parsippany, New Jersey 07054
(800) FOR-TARKETT

Terra Designs
4 John Street
Morristown, New Jersey 07960
(201) 539-2999

Thayer-Coggin, Inc.
P.O. Box 5867
427 South Road
High Point, North Carolina 27262
Attn: Dot Coggin
(919) 889-1700

Richard E. Thibaut, Inc.
706 South Twenty-first Street
Irvington, New Jersey 07111
(201) 399-7888

Seth Thomas
General Time Corp.
520 Guthridge Court
Norcross, Georgia 30092

Thomas Industries
Residential Lighting Division
207 East Broadway
Louisville, Kentucky 40202
(502) 582-3771
Catalogue: Free

Thomasville Furniture Industries, Inc.
Dept PPD
PLO. Box 339
Thomasville, North Carolina 27360
(800) 225-0265 nationwide; (800) 672-4224
in North Carolina
"Mini-Catalogue": Free;
Full-size Catalogue: $3.50

Tiffany & Tiffany
323 Spruce Street
Philadelphia, Pennsylvania 19106
(215) 629-0184

Toyo Trading Co.
13000 South Spring Street
Los Angeles, California 90061
(800) 843-9193 nationwide;
(800) 843-9194 in CA

240

Typhoon International
121 Nine Street
San Francisco, California 94103

*Jeanne Van Etten
2354 Main Street, Route 6A
Brewster, Massachusetts 02631
(617) 896-6614
Catalogue: Free

Vanguard Lighting
6900 Alameda Street
Huntington Park, California 90255

*Victorian Lighting Company
P.O. Box 579
Minneapolis, Minnesota 55440
(612) 338-3636
Catalogue: $4.00

Virginia Metalcrafters
1010 East Main Street, P.O. Box 1068
Waynesboro, Virginia 22980
(703) 949-8205
Note: See *Colonial Williamsburg* listing to mail order Colonial Williamsburg pieces made by Virginia Metalcrafters. Item numbers will vary.

Wall-Tex
Columbus Coated Fabrics
1280 North Grant Avenue
Columbus, Ohio 43216
(614) 225-6167

Waverly Fabrics
919 Third Avenue
New York, New York 10022
(212) 644-5914

Weiman
P.O. Box 626
Bassett, Virginia 24055
(703) 629-7511

Beth Weissman Co.
260 Smith Street
Farmingdale, New York 11735
(516) 694-7950
Catalogue: $5.00

Westwood Lighting Group, Inc.
177 Genesee Avenue
Paterson, New Jersey 07503
(201) 684-8484

*Eldred Wheeler Handcrafters of Fine Eighteenth-Century American Furniture
60 Sharp Street
Hingham, Massachusetts 02043
(617) 337-5311
Catalogue: $2.00

John Widdicomb Company
601 Fifth Street N.W.
Grand Rapids, Michigan 49504
(616) 459-7173

*Lt. Moses Willard, Inc.
7805 Railroad Avenue
Cincinnati, Ohio 45243
(513) 561-3942
Catalogue: $2.00

*Winterthur Museum and Gardens
Direct Mail
Winterthur, Delaware 19735
Catalogues:
Winterthur Reproductions $10.00.
Winterthur Gift Catalogue and Gift and Garden Sampler $2.00.

Thomas K. Woodard
835 Madison Avenue
New York, New York 10021
(212) 988-2906
Catalogue: $5.00

Workbench
470 Park Avenue South
New York, New York 10016
(212) 532-5700
Catalogue: $2.00

# Index

## A

Accessories
   Classicist, 40, 137–38
   Futurist, 41, 213–14
   Individualist, 41, 156
   Modernist, 194–95
   Naturalist, 40, 76–78
   Romanticist, 40, 95–96
   Traditionalist, 40, 11–17
   Young Professional, 41, 173–74
American style, 4
Antiques, classical style, 5
Architectural details, color selection and, 36
Art, space and use of, 55–56
Art Deco, 6
Ashley, Laura, 4

## B

Barker Bros., 31
Bloor, James, 7, 31
Braverman, Michael, 7
Buatta, Mario, 37

## C

Classicist, 5
   accessories for, 40, 137–38
   color schemes for, 40
   furnishings for, 40, 129–36
   lighting for, 44, 139–40
   Period quiz and, 27
   profile of, 123–27
   sourcebooks for, 121–40
   window treatments for, 48, 128
Collectibles, space and use of, 55–56
Color, 34–41
   Classicist, 40
   collecting samples of, 37–38
   cool tones, 38
   fads and, 35–36
   Futurist, 41
   Individualist, 41
   Modernist, 41
   modifying space with, 50–51
   Naturalist, 40
   paint chips, use of, 37, 39
   relationship to personality, 34
   Romanticist, 40
   room dimensions and, 38–39
   selection of, 35–38
   sunlight and, 38
   Traditionalist, 40
   Young Professional, 41
Combining styles, 20–22
Conran's, 31
Contemporary quiz, 19, 28–32
   analysis of, 30–32
Crate & Barrel, 31

## D

Decorating styles
   Classicist, 5
   Futurist, 7
   Individualist, 6
   Modernist, 6–7
   Naturalist, 4
   Romanticist, 4–5
   Traditionalist, 5
   Young Professional, 6
   *See also* individual styles.
deWolfe, Elsie, 20

## E

Ellsley, Beverley, 7, 26

## F

Fairholme, Georgina, 7, 26
Fifties decor, 32
Fishburn, Angela, 47
French style, 4
Furnishings
   Classicist, 40, 129–36
   Futurist, 207–12
   Individualist, 41, 148–55
   Modernist, 187–93
   Naturalist, 40, 68–75
   Romanticist, 40, 89–94
   Traditionalist, 109–14
   Young Professional, 41, 166–71
   space and use of, 52–53
Futurist, 7
   accessories for, 41, 213–14
   color schemes for, 41
   Contemporary quiz and, 19, 32
   furnishings for, 41, 207–12
   lighting for, 45, 215–18
   profile of, 201–5
   sourcebooks for, 199–210
   window treatments for, 49, 206

## G

General quiz, 16–22
   analysis of, 18–22

## H

Hura, Stanley, 7

## I

Individualist, 6
   accessories for, 41, 156
   color schemes for, 41
   Contemporary quiz and, 19–20, 32
   furnishings for, 41, 148–55
   lighting for, 45, 157–58
   Period quiz for, 20, 28
   profile of, 143–46
   sourcebooks for, 141–58
   window treatments for, 49, 147

## J
Jackson, Virginia, 34
Japanese style, 4

## K
Kron, Joan, 34

## L
Lamps
   Lighting tips, 42–43
   personal style and choice of, 44–45
Levels, use of, 54
Levin, Sybil, 7, 31
Lighting, 42–45
   Classicist, 44, 139–40
   depth/dimension, creating of, 55
   Futurist, 45, 215–18
   Individualist, 45, 157–58
   Modernist, 45, 196–98
   Naturalist, 44, 79–80
   Romanticist, 44, 97–100
   tips for, 42–43
   Traditionalist, 44, 118–20
   Young Professional, 45, 175-77

## M
Mirrors, use of, 54
Modernist, 6–7
   accessories for, 41, 194–95
   color schemes for, 41
   Contemporary quiz, 19, 31–32
   furnishings for, 41, 187–93
   lighting for, 45, 186, 196–98
   profile of, 181–85
   sourcebooks for, 179–98
   window treatments for, 49, 186

## N
Naturalist, 4
   accessories for, 40, 76–78
   color schemes for, 40
   furnishing for, 40, 68–75
   lighting for, 44, 79–80
   Period quiz and, 26, 27
   profile of, 63–67
   sourcebooks for, 61–80
   window treatments for, 48, 68

## P
Painting
   buying paint, 39
   color, 35–39
   paint chips, use of, 37, 39
Patterns, space and use of, 51–52
Pentecost, Nicholas, 27
Period quiz, 22–28
   analysis of, 25–28

Personality, relationship to color preference, 34
Personality decorating
   color, 34–41
   combination of styles, 20–22
   lightinbg, 42–45
   Personality Decorating Quiz, 16–32
   personal style and, 2–3
   window treatments, 46–49
Personality Decorating Quiz, 11, 16–32
   approach to, 14–15
   contemporary quiz, 28–32
   general quiz, 16–32
   period quiz, 22–28
   sourcebooks for, 12–13, 58-218
   space, 50–57
Peterson, Lyn, 7

## R
Romanticist, 4–5
   accessories for, 40, 95–96
   color schemes for, 40
   furnishing for, 40, 89–94
   lighting for, 44, 97–100
   Period quiz and, 26–27
   profile of, 83–87
   sourcebooks for, 81–100
   window treatments for, 48, 88

## S
Scandinavian style, 4
Schreiber, Joanne, 47
Size of rooms,
   use of color, 38–39
   *See also* Space.
Sourcebooks, 12–13, 58-218
   Classicist, 121–40
   Futurist, 199–218
   Individualist, 141–58
   Modernist, 179–98
   Naturalist, 61–80
   Romanticist, 81–100
   Traditionalist, 101–20
   use of, 58–60
   Young Professional, 159–78
Space, 50–57
   art/collectibles and, 55–56
   use of color, 38–39
   depth/dimension, creation of, 53–54
   furniture arrangement and, 52–53
   furniture choice and, 52–53
   lighting and, 55
   modifying with color, 50–51
   patterns and, 51–52
   textures and, 51–52

## T
Textures, space and use of, 51–52
Traditionalist, 5
   accessories for, 40, 115–17
   color schemes for, 40

furnishings for, 40, 109–14
lighting for, 44, 118–20
Period quiz and, 25–26
profile of, 103–7
sourcebooks for, 101–20
window treatments for, 48, 100

# W

Wallcoverings, space and texture of, 51–52
Walz, Kevin, 21, 38
Window treatments, 46–49
    Classicist, 48, 128
    Futurist, 49, 206
    guidelines for, 46–47
    Individualist, 49, 147
    maintenance of, 47
    Modernist, 49, 186
    Naturalist, 48, 68
    Romanticist, 48, 88
    Traditionalist, 48, 100
    Young Professional, 49, 165
Workbench, 31

# Y

Young Professional, 6
    accessories for, 41, 173–74
    color schemes for, 41
    Contemporary quiz, 19, 31
    furnishings for, 41, 166–71
    lighting for, 45, 175–77
    profile of, 161–64
    sourcebooks for, 159–78
    window treatments for, 49, 165